Dr. Salk looked up from his papers as the first guard walked through the door with his hands clasped on top of his head. "What—?" Salk started to ask as the other two guards followed, their eyes straight ahead. But Kirk came in behind them, his gun pointed at their backs, looked over at the doctor, and in a polite, businesslike way, said, "Just keep on doing what you're doing, Doctor."

Kirk instructed the guards to kneel on the floor, keeping their hands on their heads. He removed their guns.

Terrified, Salk's mind raced. What should he do when the shots began to ring out? What had Kirk done with Mary Evans?

Then Mary walked in. Kirk crossed to his young lawyer. "You watch that man over there," he said, indicating the doctor. He placed a gun in Mary's hand.

It was the last day of March 1983, one day before April Fools' Day.

AGAINST THE LAW

AGAINST THE LAW

Sandy Johnson

BANTAM BOOKS
TORONTO • NEW YORK • LONDON • SYDNEY • AUCKLAND

AGAINST THE LAW
A Bantam Book / August 1986

Cover photo of Tim Kirk by Mike DuBose.
Cover photo of Mary Evans by Joe Stewardsen.

ISBN 0-553-26054-5

Published simultaneously in the United States and Canada

Bantam Books are published by Bantam Books, Inc. Its trademark,
consisting of the words "Bantam Books" and the portrayal of a
rooster, is Registered in U.S. Patent and Trademark Office and in
other countries. Marca Registrada. Bantam Books, Inc., 666 Fifth
Avenue, New York, New York 10103.

To my Father

Acknowledgments

I wish to thank the people at the *Knoxville Journal* who more than helped me; they made me feel I was one of their own: editor Ron MacMahon; reporter Roger King; ace court reporter Leslie Henderson and her husband, pipe-smoking pundit Barry Henderson, editorial page editor; columnist Jim Dykes and the lovely Peg; city editor Tom Chester; and features editor Anne Klebenow. And special thanks to Skip O'Rourke and Joe Stewardson for the photographs.

At the *Knoxville News-Sentinel* I have Mike Silence to thank for his help; and at the *Oak Ridger*, Robin Head Intemann and Ruth Eliason, both of whom generously contributed their photographs. I would also like to thank free-lance photographer Mike DuBose for his photographs.

In Nashville I was passed along to the hotshots at *The Tennessean*, to prize-winners Larry Daughtrey and James Pratt, whose unfailing patience saw me through the second leg of the book.

My gratitude to those members of the legal community who guided me through the maze of courtroom procedure: Professor Neil Cohen, Judge Buddy Scott, Charles Fels, Judy McCarthy, Jerry Becker, Zane Daniel and Steve Oberman, Dennis Francis, Joy Heath, Sharon Selby, Randy Reagan, district attorney generals Paul Phillips and James Ramsey; and to the lawyers who steered me around the potholes and pitfalls inherent in writing nonfiction, John Wagster and Marlene Moses.

I am also indebted to former FBI agent Michelle Evans; William Y. Daran, Special Agent in Charge; TBI agent Bill McBee; Warden Mike Dunn at the Tennessee State Prison and his secretary, Mary Dennis, who were so cooperative; Morgan County judge Lee Asbury; and Winzell Shockley, Anderson County court reporter.

My thanks to the friends who helped with housing: in Knoxville, Annie McCarthy of the fabulous Annie's Restaurant, Warren Perry, Steve Smith, Darlene Dagnan of Darlene's Interiors, and architect Donna Kendrick; those indomitable Nashville women, Ann Street, Huldah Sharp, Karin Coble, Teenie Buchtel, and Rose Eskind. I hold all of them responsible for my love affair with Tennessee.

My research assistant, Gay Henry, began her tireless ferreting out of sources and information long distance and still remains ready at the other end of the telephone. I am eternally in her debt.

For editorial advice I thank John Stoll Sanders; and for advice of all sorts, my loving gratitude to Alix Sharp.

I want to thank my enduring editor and friend, Jeanne Bernkopf, and my incredibly supportive agent, Al Zuckerman.

The universe is a void
in which there is a dreamhole
The dream disappears the hole closes. . . .

ALLEN GINSBERG

Chapter One

In Knoxville, Tennessee, southern graciousness has an edge to it, hard and ragged like the mountaintops. The men and women are sons and daughters of dirt farmers and wear pinstripe polyester; they are not plantation people in white linen. They don't drawl in the singsong southern way; they chew on their words the way their grandfathers chewed on tobacco—slowly and steadily—and what comes out is a one-note nasal twang. Those who seek an education go to the University of Tennessee, one of Knoxville's two main industries. The other is the Tennessee Valley Authority, a sprawling bureaucracy that covers seven states and is headquartered in Knoxville.

The four square blocks of downtown Knoxville reflect the contradictions of a city caught between the industrial North and the Deep South. The streets still bear patches of cobblestone, and the buildings are a mixture of nineteenth-century colonial, 1920s rococo, and Manhattan-style glass towers.

Right at the point where three major interstates converge to feed into the city, a huge billboard looms some fifty feet above the traffic. The message, in bold white lettering set against a garish blue background, calls out the warning, "Jesus Is Lord Over This City."

1

The blue-collar café downtown is Joanne and Earl's Farragut Diner. Here Joanne takes a hamburger patty, slaps on it a square of processed cheese, gives it a turn or two on the grill, and adds a leaf of lettuce, a slice of tomato, a couple of slivers of pickles, and onion (on request), somehow making magic of it all. The beer is served in the bottle. The diner is a small place with six or seven booths upholstered in cracked leatherette and a jukebox that plays only country-and-western songs. The city at heart is a hillbilly picking on a guitar. At the far end of the diner is a bandstand of sorts: a microphone, a set of speakers, and a couple of stools set on a small platform. On most days you'll find Shorty and Hat Shorty here. Just plain Shorty doesn't wear a hat.

The white-collar café is around the corner. It's called the Bistro and is considered risqué by some because of the gilt-framed Rubenesque nude above the bar. The tables are marble-topped, and the doors, crown molding, and ceiling are of oak, all salvaged from nineteenth-century buildings in the old part of town that were torn down to make way for progress. On most days there you'll find journalists, bankers, and lawyers having spinach-and-mushroom quiche for lunch with the obligatory glass of white wine.

The Bistro, like Knoxville itself, is overrun with lawyers. Knoxville churns out lawyers at the University of Tennessee Law School; students from around the country graduate, find an apartment (housing is relatively cheap), join a law firm, and stay.

In a city of fewer than 200,000, there are 680 practicing lawyers. Seventy-seven of them are women.

On March 31, 1983, several women attorneys and two women judges were gathered at lunch at the Bistro. Their conversation centered on the formation of an organization for female attorneys. They decided they would pattern it after LAW, the Lawyers Association for Women in Nashville. They planned to meet once a month.

At precisely the same moment a twenty-six-year-old attorney was speeding along the interstate to keep a one o'clock appointment in Oak Ridge, some thirty miles west of Knoxville. Mary Evans had recently left the thriving Knoxville firm of Tipton and Bell, where she'd worked as an associate, and had accepted a job with the public defender's office in London, Kentucky. She was still, however, representing William Timothy Kirk, an inmate at Brushy Mountain State Prison, who was charged with the murder of two fellow inmates.

Now thirty-six, Kirk had spent most of his adult life in prisons—for burglary, a string of auto thefts, and two convictions for armed robbery. His last conviction had landed him a sixty-five-year sentence. He'd been sent to Brushy Mountain in 1980 for repeated escape attempts from the main prison in Nashville. Two months later he found himself caught in a power struggle when a group of black inmates waged a war against the white prison population. The war ended in a shoot-out on February 8, 1982. Kirk was the accused triggerman.

The following August, the firm of Tipton and Bell had been appointed by the court to represent Kirk. Mary Evans, fourteen months out of law school, was assigned to the case. It was her first major criminal case, and for the next eight months she worked full-time, tirelessly, on it. Today's would be her final appointment. Kirk's trial was scheduled to begin in a week. Mary had arranged to have her client evaluated by Oak Ridge psychologist Gary Salk to see if Kirk might qualify for an insanity or diminished-capacity defense.

But instead of a briefcase, she had with her, in the back of her red Toyota Celica, a large brown paper shopping bag. It contained four rolls of plastic shipping tape three inches wide, a pair of scissors, a man's tan Calvin Klein sweater, a pair of men's Levi's, size thirty-four—

and, as she would later confess to authorities, a .25 caliber gun.

She reached forward to push in the cigarette lighter. Her dark blond hair, shoulder-length, fell across her cheek as she bent to find her cigarettes in her shoulder bag. Mary's was a pretty face, though not in any conventional sense. The forehead was almost too broad, the cheekbones flared, bold, and there was a certain hardness to the well-sculptured chin and jaw. The way she outlined her green eyes in dark pencil made them look as if they were continually aflash with anger. Often they were. Unlike her colleagues she preferred to dress casually—as she had today—in a longish denim skirt and a plaid cotton shirt and boots.

A daughter of the privileged upper middle class, Mary was a champion of the rights of the indigent; as a criminal lawyer she was adamantly opposed to Tennessee's newly reinstated death penalty. She was known as a loner. In restaurants, Mary would have lunch by herself at a table by the window. Her colleagues might nod and wave a greeting, but few felt free to join her. Mary might look up from her salad, her eyes cold, and stop the unsuspecting intruder with a withering glance.

She had the same sort of chilling effect when she entered a room full of people. The chemistry changed. The conversation faltered, becoming a little less animated.

Mary had been raised in a strict Bible Belt family. Her father, B. H. ("Bob") Pentecost, was vice-president of the University of Tennessee School of Agriculture. He was also a lawyer, and Mary had chosen her career to please him. Tall and proud, his face chiseled in granite, Bob Pentecost was a deacon at the Mount Olive Baptist Church and the fierce yet loving ruler of his household.

By the time Mary got to college, she'd stopped attending church and had become quick-tongued and sarcastic. Wearing the armor she had constructed, she marched autonomous and alone until her sophomore year. Then the little girl in her who longed to be taken care of began to war against the unyielding façade. The conflict sent her careening into marriage. Tom Evans, Jr., was the son of a wealthy executive, and the marriage earned Mary the approval of both her parents—for the three and a half years it lasted.

The sign marked "Oak Ridge" fairly shouted at her. It loomed into view so suddenly that Mary had to slow her car to let the behemoth truck barreling down on her right pass before she could swing over to make the exit. She glanced at her watch; she was on schedule. She turned the car onto the exit ramp and got her breath back.

Unlike Knoxville, Oak Ridge is a new town, a true baby-boomer town. Built during World War II for the Manhattan Project, the houses, under their striped awnings and added-on rooms, still retain their basic barrack-style design. Many of Oak Ridge's citizens claim descent from the city's founding fathers, the atomic scientists who worked on the top-secret weapon that forced an end to the Second World War.

Thirty-nine-year-old Gary Salk and his wife, Martha, both practicing Quakers, had moved to Oak Ridge from Pennsylvania in 1975. Martha, a botanical ecologist, had been offered a job in the Oak Ridge National Laboratories, and Gary thought it a logical place to set up his practice. As a rule highly trained, well-educated professionals don't hesitate to seek counseling when they feel they need it.

Tall—six feet, four inches—bearded, almost biblical-looking, Gary recently had become a member of the Prison Aid Society of Tennessee, an organization that offered free counseling services to inmates. He was strongly opposed to the death penalty and found penal institutions, especially in this part of the world, brutal places. Brushy Mountain was one of the worst. Gary had gone there on more than one occasion, most recently at the request of an attorney who needed an evaluation done on an inmate charged with stabbing a fellow inmate.

Today at one o'clock Gary was scheduled to do another such evaluation, but to his profound relief, he would do it in his office. He had gone home for lunch, and was telling Martha ("Marty") about the young woman attorney who'd come to his office the week before to set up the appointment. Most attorneys, he explained, did that with a telephone call, so he was impressed that she had taken the time to come meet him face to face. Still, he mused, she was strange.

"Strange how?" Marty asked. She sat three-year-old Ted in his highchair and put the peanut butter sandwiches she'd just made on the table. Five-year-old Carl was in kindergarten.

"For one thing, she wore an awful lot of eye makeup. And she had those really long fingernails that were painted bright red."

Marty grimaced. He was sounding like a Quaker. "Is she attractive?"

"I didn't find her attractive, no. She was cold. I felt she was trying to be intimidating. The friendlier I tried to be to her, the more aloof she was to me." He thought a minute as he munched his sandwich. "And she has this thing she does with her head—keeps it tilted up in a way so she has to cast her eyes down to look at you." He shrugged. "I don't know. Maybe she's just trying to be lawyerlike."

As Marty poured their iced tea he told her about the handcuffs. The lawyer had explained that the prisoner's hands would be manacled to a belly chain. She had asked if he wouldn't want them removed.

"I told her I thought it would be useful to have his hands free since some of the tests require manipulating pieces."

"There'll be guards there with him, won't there?" Marty asked, as she tried to get Ted to finish his lunch.

"I think she said two or three. She checked all the entrances and exits, because she said the guards would want to know everything—for security reasons—and that once they make up their minds, that's it."

"What's that supposed to mean?" Marty asked.

"I don't know." He finished his tea, then reached down to lift Ted out of his highchair. He hugged him and handed him to his mother. "If I'm not back by five . . ." he quipped, as he got ready to leave.

Marty stood on tiptoes to kiss him. "Yeah, I know."

Gary Salk pulled into his usual space in the parking area. His office was on the ground floor of a two-story building that housed two other sets of offices. He got out of his car, locked it, and saw a van. It was white, institutional-looking; the official state seal was emblazoned on the door. A uniformed guard sat behind the wheel. As Salk walked past the van, he noticed the heavy steel meshing behind the driver's seat. It reminded him of a dogcatcher's car. He caught a glimpse of bright orange in the back seat. It was almost one o'clock; he quickened his step.

Just inside the door, standing in the hallway, was the woman attorney. She was talking to one of the three uniformed guards who had brought Kirk. Salk greeted them, apologized for keeping them waiting, and led them into his office. His mind was occupied with the selection of tests best suited for purposes of a defense.

The attorney interrupted his thoughts, speaking brusquely. "I told the guards you'd need the handcuffs and chains removed." Her voice was deep, slightly husky; her speech was rapid. "I put in a formal request—in your name."

He looked at her, not quite understanding. "To whom?"

Instantly her manner became confrontational. "To the prison administration, of course. Didn't you say you'd need all the restraints removed for the testing?"

"Yes—I did."

The guard frowned. "Leg irons too?"

Salk's eyes moved to the .38 the guard wore prominently at his hip. During one of Salk's counseling visits to the prison, he'd seen a man in leg irons. The man was made to wear a weighted boot that dragged and clunked with each step, and Salk had had to turn away. To look into the face of a man whose last shred of dignity has been stripped from him—for whatever reason—diminished them both, he felt.

"Yes, leg irons too," Salk answered.

The woman managed a small smile then. Salk guessed her smiles were given sparingly. As a reward, perhaps. She pressed on. "I'd like to be present during the testing," she said.

"No, that won't be possible." He searched his memory for her name. "No, Miss Evans."

"Doctor," the guard asked, "d'you mind if I look the rooms over? We need to make sure there's nothin' could be used as a weapon. Standard security measure."

"Go right ahead." Salk watched as the man made a thorough search of both his office and the empty receptionist's office. A pair of heavy metal braces used to support bookshelves was propped up against the bookcase; a pair of large scissors lay on his desk; a hammer that Salk used to tack things to the wall was sitting on top of the filing cabinet.

"Let's get 'em out of sight. If he can't see 'em we don't have to worry about 'em."

Salk pointed to the filing cabinet. "How about putting them inside one of those drawers?"

William "Tim" Kirk sat waiting in the back of the van. The long, copper-colored hair and shaggy beard all but hid his handsome, cleanly defined features, but his clear brown eyes missed nothing.

For most of the trip, he'd been silent. Now he leaned

forward to look out the window. "I know that's a Cadillac," he said, gesturing with his head, "but I've been in prison so long"—he looked over at a little red car—"what kind of car is that?"

Officer L. C. Jones, sitting beside him, answered. "That's a Toyota, I think."

Officer Jerry Higgs, in the driver's seat, turned. "Yep. Toyota Celica, that's what that is."

Kirk nodded. His eyes drifted down to the .38 at L.C.'s waist. He remembered a day a couple of months ago out in the yard. Kirk had been lifting weights. L.C. walked past holding a pair of handcuffs, which he showed to Kirk. They were the kind used in maximum-security federal penitentiaries. The lock was set inside a heavy black steel box so that even if the prisoner wearing them had the key, it would be impossible for him to maneuver it into the lock. The box also added another four or five pounds to the weight of the handcuffs.

"Hey Tim," he'd said. "You seen these yet? We're getting ready to start usin' 'em. You think you c'n get ahold of one of these kind of keys?"

And Kirk had answered him evenly, "I don't know. I'll have to shop around. Maybe I can come up with one; who knows?" But he had looked him dead in the eye and thought, Son of a bitch. One of these days, you smartass, we'll just see.

Kirk saw the door to the office open; James Copeland, a guard, came walking out. Kirk, his jaw set tightly, allowed the men to help get him down out of the van and lead him into the office. Higgs was to stay behind and keep an eye on the entrance.

Salk's head turned at the clatter and clanging of the chains. He stared open-mouthed at the man in the orange Day-Glo jumpsuit, who was chained like some wild animal. He shook his head in disgust and went back into his office leaving the men to remove the restraints.

"Doctor?" Mary was at the door. "I need a word with my client—we'll just use the other office for a minute."

He heard the door to the receptionist's office close behind lawyer and client.

Salk had just sat down at his desk when Kirk came in and took the chair opposite him. A window to the right of the desk overlooked the parking area. Kirk moved his chair a few inches to the left and swiveled slightly, glancing up at the window.

Good, clean features, intelligent face, Salk noted. But mainly it was the eyes that startled him. Nut brown, piercing, unblinking. This man thinks what he thinks behind those eyes and nobody gets anything from him he doesn't want to give.

Kirk moved the chair again, so that now he was facing the window. "You'll have to excuse my nervousness. I've never been to a psychologist before."

Salk looked at him, surprised. He hadn't detected the slightest bit of nervousness in Kirk; the man was as cool as a cucumber. He just didn't seem to want to sit with his back to the window. Maybe prisoners don't like to sit with their backs to anything.

Salk passed him the first batch of questions. "What I want you to do," Salk said, "is to complete the sentences. Use the word or words that come immediately to mind. Begin."

Kirk read the first:

I like _____. His answer was "freedom." To the second, *The happiest time* _____, Kirk wrote, "is when I'm with someone I care for."

His eyes flew to the window.

The next question was: *The thing I do best* _____, "make dreams reality," he answered.

What angers me _____ "someone trying to get over on me."

My mother _____, deeply love her."

In school _____, "bored."

Some day _____, "I want to be a free man again."

I need _____, "someone I can trust with my love."

I hate _____, "phoney people."

When I'm angry _____, "I try to maintain unless I have no choice."

Ten years from now I would like to _____, "be free."

Ten years from now I will probably _____, "be in prison."

Rules are _____, "for weak people."

Some days later Salk would study the next answer, wondering whether or not Kirk had slipped when he omitted the "out" in "without":

My biggest fear _____, "is life with freedom."

About an hour had passed. Kirk said he thought he'd like to use the bathroom—and to have a cigarette out in the hall.

A few minutes later Salk heard them all talking. Curious, he went and stood in the doorway. The guards were exchanging complaints about how it was to work for the state. Some worked for as little as $945 a month, well below the national average of $1,158.

Both Kirk and Mary were listening sympathetically. She told the guards of her plans to move to London, Kentucky, where she had taken a job with the public defender's office that paid only fourteen thousand a year.

"I hear it's a right pretty place, London, Kentucky," one of the guards said.

She nodded. A smile started to flash across her face, then vanished.

Officer Copeland took his wallet out of his pocket to show them the income tax refund check he'd just received for twelve hundred dollars. "*This* is what I'll be livin' off of."

Kirk shook his head in dismay as he and Salk went back into the office to continue the testing.

Forty-five minutes later Kirk said he needed to consult with his attorney about some of the questions on that particular page. Once again they used the empty receptionist's office. When he came back he seemed distracted. It seemed as though he was scribbling answers to the remaining questions hurriedly, with one eye glued to the window.

Men are _____, "men."
Women are _____, "women."
Sex is _____, "wonderful."
Death is _____, "dying."

Salk turned to the window to see what it was Kirk kept looking at out there. The van was parked where it had been earlier, but the driver, Salk noticed, was gone. He'd probably come in to use the bathroom, he figured.

Kirk handed the papers across the desk. Salk took them and said Kirk could go wait out in the hall while he scored the tests.

Mary walked out the front door as soon as Kirk came out of the office, leaving the three guards alone with him. Kirk leaned his shoulder against the wall and turned a quarter of a turn away from them. His right hand was deep inside the pocket of his jumpsuit, clutching a .25 revolver. Out of the corner of his eye he saw L.C.'s hand resting on the butt of his gun. Remembering that day in the yard, Kirk thought, Well now, you got your hand on yours, I got my hand on mine. It's time to find out who you are, you son of a bitch.

He waited a beat, feeling the moment, then in one smooth motion brought the gun from his pocket to position, arms outstretched, and took aim at all three. "All right now, understand this. I don't want to hurt anybody." His voice was quiet and deliberate. "But you know what my situation is, and that I'll do whatever I have to do." His eyes swept over the men, stopping at L.C., whose hand had just dropped away from his gun. Kirk smiled to himself and thought, Now we know who's who, don't we?

The men's faces had gone white. L.C. spoke. "What d'ya want us to do, Tim?"

"Be real, real calm. Put your hands on top of your heads, and march your asses into that office."

Salk looked up from his papers. The first guard to walk through the door was the driver, whom he hadn't really seen before. The man had a scar that curved upward from the corner of his mouth, which, from where Salk was sitting, made him look as though he was smiling. And with his hands clasped on top of his head, Salk thought for a minute this was some sort of macabre joke.

He stared as the other two followed, their eyes straight ahead. "What—?" Salk started to ask.

But Kirk, his gun pointed at their backs, looked over at the doctor and in a polite, businesslike way said, "Just keep right on doing what you're doing, Doctor."

Then Kirk instructed the guards to kneel on the floor, keeping their hands on their heads. He removed their guns. Instinctively, it seemed, the three men kept up a steady stream of reassuring remarks, always calling Kirk by name.

Terrified, Salk's mind raced. What should he do when the shots began to ring out? Throw himself to the floor? Try to hide his six-foot frame behind the desk? What had Kirk done with Mary Evans?

Just then Mary came in. She was holding a brown paper shopping bag. "Got the tape?" Kirk asked her.

Salk was stunned. She was in on it with him. They'd planned this all along, right from that first visit to the office a week before, when she made the point about the handcuffs. Angered now, almost to the point of forgetting his fear, he watched the way the two of them carried it out. Kirk was no longer the prisoner; he was in charge, a man with a gun in his hand.

Mary's movements were brisk but unhurried. She

took a large pair of scissors out of the bag and snipped the cord of the telephone on Salk's desk. She looked at him. "Do you have a radio?"

"Yes," he answered. "There's one in the receptionist's office."

There was a second phone on that desk; she cut that wire too, and then turned the radio on loud, to a rock-and-roll station. When she came back she handed Kirk one of the rolls of Tucktape she'd brought. It was three-inch-wide fiberglass filament tape, the kind used for packing.

"You watch that man over there," he said, putting the gun in her hand and indicating the doctor, who was still seated at his desk.

The guards were lying noses to the floor, their hands behind their backs. Kirk proceeded to bind them. He rolled up their sleeves and wound the tape several times around and between their wrists.

Jerry Higgs winced.

"That too tight, Jerry?" Kirk asked.

"Well, I got that bursitis in my shoulder, Tim."

"I'll loosen it a little. That better?"

"Yeah. Thanks, Tim."

Mary kept the gun trained on Salk, her cold, expressionless eyes only half seeing him. She tapped her foot impatiently.

Kirk repeated the process, going from one to the next. He rolled up their pant legs and told them to cross their ankles. He turned to Mary. "Do you want to give me a hand with this?"

"No," she said, "I think you better do it."

To Salk, Kirk said, "Okay, it's your turn." Kirk came around the desk and very carefully, the way an optometrist would, removed Salk's glasses by the stems. "Lie down on the floor with your hands behind your back, please."

Salk felt his legs tremble as he got up from his desk. He wondered if his knees would buckle and give way. He tried to swallow, but his mouth was dry. Thoughts of Marty and the kids flashed in his mind; he wished Carl hadn't been at nursery school when he was home at lunchtime. He'd have liked to have seen him too. He guessed they wouldn't be very proud of their father, lying here face down on the floor, letting these people treat him like an object. No heroics, though; they'd kill him without a thought if he tried anything. Of the two, it was the woman he feared most. Somehow he believed she could stamp him out as easily as she would a bothersome bug.

"Doctor Salk, do you have any appointments this afternoon?" Kirk asked politely.

"No," he answered dully.

"What time do the people in the other offices leave?"

"Four-thirty. Some stay later."

The tape hurt. His hands were already growing numb.

Kirk was questioning the guards about any communications devices they had.

"Just the radio in the van, Tim," one of them answered.

"Any of you got any medical condition—heart trouble or anything?"

"I've got a little high blood pressure, Tim," Copeland answered.

"Well, try to relax; take it easy. You think you can stand it for a half hour?"

"Yeah, Tim, I think I can."

Mary came over and began putting strips of tape on their mouths.

"No, not that way," Kirk said. And he wrapped the tape twice all the way around their heads.

"Where're the clothes?" he asked.

"Out in the receptionist's room."

He was in the middle of removing his underwear when Mary walked in. Puzzled, she asked, "What're you doing that for?"

A grin spread over his face. "Because, honey, I never wear 'em."

One of the guards tried to lift his head when Kirk came back. But Kirk quickly warned them all not to try to do that. He didn't want them to see what he was wearing. He went over to where Salk was lying and removed the wallet from his hip pocket. He opened it and found twenty-five dollars and all the doctor's IDs. "I'm going to take the doctor's money," he said. "He can afford it more than you guys can. I'll leave you your refund check, Copeland."

He took one last look at the men. Higgs's nose was running. Kirk knelt beside him, took a handkerchief out of the man's pocket, and wiped his nose.

"I'll call someone in half an hour to let them know you're here."

It was now four o'clock. Mary rushed out to the parking area and drove her car around to the entrance of the building. Kirk came out a moment later, glanced quickly to his right and to his left, walked to the van, reached inside, and yanked the microphone from the radio. Then he got into the Toyota. It was the last day of March 1983, one day before April Fools' Day.

Mary drove the car onto the heavily trafficked main thoroughfare. Tim Kirk was at her side. They both stared straight ahead for several minutes, saying nothing. Then when their car was merely one of countless in the flow, when they began to realize who they were and where they were going, they turned and looked at each other. Mary reached for Tim's hand, and they grinned.

Chapter Two

At 5:49 P.M. an Oak Ridge police dispatcher received a call on the emergency line from James Copeland, a guard at Brushy Mountain Prison. He reported that prisoner William T. Kirk had escaped custody and that he had his young female attorney, Mary Evans, with him.

Twenty-nine-year-old police officer Jon Shipley was on patrol when the call came over his car radio. Thinking the escape had just happened, he turned on his siren and lights and sped, fighting his way through peak rush-hour traffic to the office of psychologist Dr. Gary Salk. He was certain they had a hostage situation on their hands. Shipley's supervisor had pulled in ahead of him in his car; behind was a backup car. Only two years before, Shipley had been shot by an escaped felon, a man he'd put in jail. Now he had wasted no time getting a backup.

Shipley found the guards and the doctor still trying to peel the plastic shipping tape from their hands and ankles. It had taken almost an hour and a half before Officer Copeland had managed to stand, get his hands free, and hop his way into the hallway and to the telephone in the next office.

The guards were badly shaken, but their nervousness had another side to it. Shipley recognized the syndrome.

17

It was the same as when a cop is involved in a shooting; the question that invariably accompanied the report was, "Did *I* do anything wrong?"

Shipley figured the guards might not have stuck strictly to procedure; if they had, Kirk wouldn't have been able to get all three of them inside the building at one time.

The guards had their theories as to why the lawyer had played a role in the escape. One was that Kirk had probably threatened her or members of her family if she didn't help him.

L.C.'s was, "The man's a dangerous murderer. They was gettin' ready to send him to the chair next week when he goes to trial."

Salk, who was in a state of near shock, strongly disagreed. "She was as cold as ice standing there, tapping her foot. I'm not sure I wouldn't rather have Kirk pointing a gun at me than Mary."

Shipley would have to go back to interview Salk two or three times to get the whole story. It would take that long before the doctor would remember all the details. When he did, his conclusion was, "I think she was in love with the guy."

Shipley took down their statements and returned to headquarters, where he broadcast descriptions of Kirk and Evans and issued statewide teletypes.

The heavy rush-hour traffic in Knoxville doesn't begin to lighten until six-thirty. There are only three main arteries leading from the city out to the suburbs; cars crawl homeward bumper to bumper.

Attorney Jim Bell always waited till after rush hour to leave his office. It was just after six when the call came from the Oak Ridge police. His secretary hadn't left either; she buzzed him on the intercom. "I think you better take this one," she said, having just heard the news on the radio.

Jon Shipley announced himself. He said he was calling to inform Bell that his client, William Timothy Kirk, had just escaped custody, and that Mary Evans was with him. He added that Ms. Evans, to whom Bell had assigned the Kirk case, was a suspected accomplice.

"That's impossible," Bell said flat out. "You're mistaken. First of all, Mary Evans is in Nashville."

Shipley assured Bell that both the psychologist and the three guards had positively identified Mary. Stunned, Bell called Mary's boyfriend, attorney John Lockridge. Lockridge, he learned, was in New York, but his office could reach his partner, Jerry Becker. Bell left an urgent message for Becker to meet him at the Oak Ridge police station.

The Pentecosts lived on a seventy-six-acre farm in South Knoxville, an easy commute to Bob Pentecost's office on the UT campus. It was six-fifteen and the family was just sitting down to supper when the phone rang. Sergeant Gary T. Ogle of the Oak Ridge Police Department was calling to inform Mr. Pentecost that his daughter's client, William T. Kirk, had escaped custody—and that Mary had left with him. There was a long silence before Bob Pentecost hung up the phone and rushed to the police station.

The protestations of the loyal, protective father with his deeply rooted Christian principles and his abiding love for his daughter were heartbreaking even to law enforcement authorities whose hearts were least fragile. His argument for Mary's innocence raged on long after the police were certain Mary was guilty of aiding and abetting a criminal. Bob Pentecost was certain his daughter had been the victim of a kidnapping—and that they'd better use every last resource available to find her.

By the time Bell got to the police station, investigators were trying to locate Mary's roommate, Janet Vest. Bell had known that Kirk was scheduled for psychological examination, but he believed that Mary was at the main prison in Nashville with Bob Ritchie and Janet interviewing witnesses. Ritchie, who had been Bell's law partner, had a mobile phone in his Mercedes; at nine-thirty that night, Bell reached Ritchie who was halfway between Nashville and Knoxville.

"Good grief!" Janet said when she heard the story. "She's lost it for real this time."

At a little after eleven Bob Ritchie and Janet Vest arrived at the police station. Officer Shipley, uncertain of Janet's involvement, handed her a rights form and also a waiver of rights to sign. Ritchie, halfway across the room talking to one of the other officers, strode over to Shipley and grabbed the papers.

"Is Ms. Vest being charged with something?" he asked angrily.

"No," Shipley said, "but due to the limited knowledge we have of the matter, it's my opinion that the rights form is appropriate."

"We're not signing anything," he said, throwing the papers to the floor. "You may question Ms. Vest—in my presence."

Janet explained that she had awakened that morning at five-thirty to find Mary in her bedroom very upset. But Mary refused to talk and rejected offers of help. Mary, Janet said, was in the process of making a move to London, Kentucky, where she had accepted a job in the public defender's office.

At two-thirty the following morning, Janet consented to a search of their apartment. A caravan led by Bob Ritchie pulled into the parking area of the complex: two Mercedes, a Fiat, and three state cars. Jim Bell was in the second Mercedes. Attorney Jerry Becker, Lockridge's partner, was in the Fiat. Ross Haynes and Rick Morrell of the Tennessee Bureau of Investigation and Officer Jon Shipley followed in their cars.

Janet showed the group through the apartment, pointing out personal belongings of Mary's that were missing.

Among them were her jewelry, makeup, and address book; in the bathroom her toothpaste and toothbrush were gone, along with the birth-control pills she always kept next to her water glass on the sink.

Jim Bell noticed a file folder on the dining-room table that he recognized as belonging to Mary. In it was a power-of-attorney document, drawn up by Mary and signed by Kirk. Bell said he had no knowledge of such a document, that he had not authorized it, and that it was not drawn up by his office. It read: "I, William Timothy Kirk, do hereby make, constitute and appoint Mary P. Evans attorney for me and in name, place and stead for the following purposes: endorsing and delivering for deposit or collection all negotiable instruments made payable to me at any bank." It was notarized and dated February 25, 1983. Also in the file was a blank power-of-attorney form from the offices of Lockridge and Becker.

A handwritten note from Ron Moorman, brother of Brushy Mountain inmate Ricky Moorman:

Mary Evans,
This is money from Rick Moorman. He asked me to send it to you. Please let Rick know as soon as possible that you have received this money so that he can get back to me. Thank you very much,

Ron Moorman

A receipt, dated March 3, 1983, for five hundred dollars indicated that the money order had been cleared through a bank in Denver, where Ron Moorman lived. And there was a Federal Express envelope that the money order had come in. All these items were taken by Bob Ritchie.

The caravan, minus Janet, who had been told to stand by the phone in case Mary called, went on to Lockridge's A-frame, where he'd moved after his divorce. The police and TBI agents were aware that Mary had a key to her boyfriend's house.

Becker led the way. In total darkness they felt their way up the stairs. Shipley and the two TBI agents had their guns drawn as Becker discovered that the sliding glass door was partly open. A space heater in the middle of the floor had been left on; open cans of food were on the kitchen counter. It dawned on Becker that if Mary and Tim were in there, there could be a shoot-out. Concerned as he was for Mary's safety, he was frightened for himself and the other lawyers. None of them had any business there. "Let's get out of here," he said. Just then the officers burst into the house to find it empty.

Bulletins interrupted radio and television programs and rocked the community. Both the Knoxville newspapers, the *Journal* and the *News-Sentinel*, had offices in the same building. They scattered reporters in every direction, each trying to outscoop the other. They went knocking at the doors of everyone who ever knew—or might have known— Mary Evans.

At the bars around town where two-for-ones were being served during Happy Hour, business boomed. On Thursdays the Bistro served three-for-ones, or, as James Pratt, business reporter for *The Tennessean*, figured it, twenty-seven-for-nines. On this Thursday the crowd was rowdy; the news was greeted with mixed and somewhat unpredictable reactions. "How in the hell—?" . . . "She's got to be nuts." . . . "Who is she?" . . . "Mary Evans, John Lockridge's girlfriend, works for Jim Bell."

Blond, blue-eyed Leslie Henderson, plucky court reporter for the *Knoxville Journal*, shook her head. "God *damn*, that's one hell of a story."

Columnist Jim Dykes, a Tennessee version of New York's Jimmy Breslin, lifted his bourbon in a salute: "Another bad girl gone good."

A male attorney said he intended to offer Lockridge

his services, should he decide to sue Tim Kirk for alienation of affection. Another quipped that if Mary Evans got Tim Kirk to a motel and he couldn't perform, she should move to have the escape annulled.

Over at Joanne and Earl's the blue-collar crowd watched the news on the TV over the bar. "She's a hero, that's what she is. They was goin' to fry that boy for killin' some mean nigras that needed killin' anyway. She was right to bust him out."

The next afternoon, Friday, April 1, at five-thirty-five, Mary's red Toyota was found parked on Shagbark Road in the Scenic Woods subdivision located off the Norris Freeway on the Knox County side of the Anderson County line. The car was searched and the items found were taken as evidence: a plastic University of Tennessee cup, a paper bag containing a wrapping for a roll of plastic Tucktape and a receipt dated March 31, a pack of GPC cigarettes, a road map of Kentucky, a bank book belonging to Mary Evans showing a balance of $600, and a brown paper bag containing one pair of men's briefs, one pair of men's socks, a set of jumper cables, and a map of Atlanta. In the ashtray was a check torn into pieces, made out to "cash" in the amount of $102, and signed by Mary Evans. Neighbors in the area remembered seeing the red car parked there at about five-thirty the evening before.

Banner headlines blazed across the front pages of the local newspapers, and the story was picked up by wire services and carried in papers and magazines around the world. Every day new angles were pursued. Friends and family, business associates, former classmates, teachers, college professors, anyone who'd ever met Mary, and people who'd only heard of her were hounded for interviews.

Leslie Henderson and Roger King of the *Knoxville Journal* wrote a profile of Mary Evans, a composite of the many interviews. The portrait that emerged was of a "cold, aloof, intelligent and possibly troubled woman; one whom few people knew well and even fewer understand." The story quoted a man who knew Mary well but who insisted on anonymity: "She's a tough cookie. I'm not at all surprised that she wasn't unnerved during the actual escape." He also said Mary had undergone psychiatric treatment in the past and had difficulty relating to people. "She is a woman with a strong temper."

Attorney Jim Bell, never one to shun publicity, announced to the press that Mary had spent "hundreds of hours on the case and may have gradually become psychologically hypnotized by Kirk. She may be suffering from what is known as the Stockholm Syndrome," he explained. "That's when a person is controlled psychologically and under the power of another person. This has been written about in scientific magazines and studies by the FBI."

Dr. Salk thought this was utter nonsense. "It's hard for a man in prison to brainwash his lawyer. I think you have to consider the male-female aspect of this thing."

Imogene King, a Knoxville lawyer and former classmate of Mary's, said, "Mary is not the kind of person who, if she was going to fall in love, would have to find a convict. I cannot imagine her doing this of her own free will." She was convinced that Kirk had applied some sort of coercion.

Debbie Stevens, who worked as an associate to John Appman, appointed to represent Kirk's codefendant, Earl Neeley, was angered by it all. "Oh boy, there go women attorneys right down the drain."

"That's right," echoed another female colleague. "It's back to the coffee machines for us. They'll never trust us now."

Mary's father, refusing to comment, repeated to each caller, "We are only concerned for her safety. She is in our prayers." His fear was that all the publicity about Mary would make her a liability to Kirk and that he would harm her.

TBI agent Ross Haynes agreed to postpone release of Mary's photograph.

Day after day the papers portrayed Kirk as a vicious killer, a con man who knew how to sweet-talk a lady. And Mary was a Patty Hearst, a rebel in search of a cause.

On the second day the pair was sighted at a gas station ten miles south of Knoxville on Highway 411 at two in the morning. They were seen in Chattanooga at 4:00 A.M. Another sighting put them on Highway 411 heading north toward Knoxville at seven-ten in the morning. At the same time they were reported seen in Athens, Georgia.

Chapter Three

The Pentecost family is rooted deep in the heart of the Bible Belt, in Wheatley County, some five hundred miles west of Knoxville. (Tennessee stretches across five hundred miles, covers two times zones, and is "kissed"—as Tennesseans are fond of saying—by five states.)

Palmersville, in Wheatley County, is the home of House Speaker Ned Ray McWherter, a contemporary and distant relative of Bob Pentecost. "On a Saturday afternoon the population of Palmersville is eighty; weekdays it's sixty," the Speaker drawls in deep tones that resonate with the sound of the heartland. About the Pentecosts he says, "The entire family is a pillar of the church. Cayce Pentecost, Senior, Bob's second cousin, was a judge, county executive, a Baptist minister who's preached more funerals than any minister you can name."

Mary had begun to show signs of rebellion by the time she was sixteen. Until then, each and every Sunday she'd sit with her parents listening to the warnings and admonitions of the preacher at Mount Olive Baptist Church. The Reverend Lewis Gourley is a deeply conservative Southern Baptist.

"Don't let the devil hold you back! Bow your head! Has your soul been washed in the Blood of the Lamb?

Deep in your heart, beyond a shadow of a doubt, do you know that you're a Christian? Have you been saved by the Grace of God? Hell is the place where sinners go and hell is full of fire!"

Mary would shrink back into the pew when he would look right at her, as if he were talking to her. Finally she would refuse to go to church again.

The Reverend Mr. Gourley had known Mary from the age of ten but had got to know her best as a teenager. Before the Pentecosts had moved onto their farm, Mary had wanted her own horse, but there was no place to keep one. Finally her father suggested she ask the preacher if he'd allow her to stable a horse at his place. Gourley lived on an eleven-acre farm. He agreed, and Mary was given a saddle horse, which she stabled with the one the preacher owned. "But when she came out to ride, she'd always want to ride alone," Gourley recalled.

"I would have to lead her into conversations. She was a person who stayed to herself. When I tried to move closer to her, she'd move away.

"Mary would lose her temper easily. I think her temperament—she was a whole lot like I am—choleric. She was choleric and prone to tell you what she was thinking. She was a champion of minority groups. . . . we would get into conversations about that. That girl knew how to hold her own in a debate. When rock music began and dress started to change, I told her I took a dim view of that. Mary told me she didn't. She didn't see a thing wrong with dressing in blue jeans; it was more comfortable.

"She was afraid of not living up to her father's expectations. She used to get into angry conversations with him. Mary was real smart. But I also know she had mixed emotions about things. She could switch moods on you real quickly. Mary was opinionated, and she didn't mind telling you what those opinions were."

Ten years later, when Mary became headline news, the Reverend Mr. Gourley would say, sadly, "I always felt she was a sweet child, but for no real reason she could swing around and hurt you with her tongue. I always knew Mary had troubles within herself. . . . I was sorry I wasn't able to help her." His voice dropped. "And I was so sorry she got her life so twisted."

Southern Baptist dogma forbids dancing, smoking, cursing, and drinking. Sixteen-year-old Mary took up each of these "sins" in turn and added a few of her own, including smoking marijuana and flirting with strange men in bars. She and a friend, Cheryl Smith, would get into Cheryl's yellow Triumph Spitfire and drive to Atlanta or Nashville. Cheryl worked for the Hyatt Hotel chain, which as a benefit gave employees two free nights a month at other Hyatts in other cities. They'd go into the hotel bar, light cigarettes, and order exotic drinks with foreign-sounding names. Then, lifting their drinks to their lips, the girls would glance sideways at the men at the next table. The object of the game was to get the men to pay for their drinks and then run out on them before the men had a chance to ask for anything in return.

The Bible Belt is rich ground for adolescents sowing seeds of rebellion. When the evangelist Billy Adams came to Knoxville crusading against devil worship, drugs, and illicit sex, the *Knoxville Journal* ran the story:

> Speaking at the South Knoxville Church of God, the fiery preacher cried out for the destruction of "Satanic" record albums and tapes. "The heavy beating of the drums and brass distorts the pituitary and causes it to spurt too many chemicals into the brain, wiping out the person's moral inhibitions. A girl can be turned on by the music and realize her own sexuality." His sermon was followed by several minutes of prayer and record-smashing.

Evangelist Billy Adams was the former leader of a fifties band, "Billy Adams and the Rocketeers," and was best known for his 1959 recording of "The Return of the All-American Boy," written to commemorate Elvis Presley's return from the army.

At Doyle High School, Mary Pentecost was perceived as shy and reticent, overly serious. Her hair was drab then, worn plainly, middle-parted, and hanging loose to just below her shoulders. Without makeup her eyes were small and unexpressive, giving more emphasis to her strong jaw.

Even then her friends were few and seemed to fall into two contrasting categories: the very top of the socio-economic ladder and the bottom. The in-between majority alternately thought Mary a snob or a slummer.

She had come to prefer the company of the rougher, redneck crowd from Vestal. Vestal is the blue-collar neighborhood on the wrong side of South Knoxville. It is recognizable by the abandoned cars that adorn the lawns. These lawn ornaments often are propped up on cement blocks, as though someone had intended to work on them and had had a change of mind. Weeds grow up around them.

There are respectable conservative blue-collar neighborhoods in South Knoxville, as well as the more affluent section where the Pentecosts' seventy-six-acre farm lies, but Vestal is considered "no-collar." It is a place nice girls are cautioned never to drive through alone at night.

Vestal boys drive around in pickup trucks with over-sized wheels, a six-pack of Bud in front and a shotgun in the gun rack behind. Before gas got to be so expensive they drove around blasting their music and tossing beer cans at road signs. When they couldn't afford the price of gas, they would congregate in parking areas behind Seven-Elevens and leave the tape decks running.

It was there Mary learned to talk in the slangy, tough way that is still her style.

About the time the Vestal boys were teaching her how to curse and swagger, Mary joined a religious club called the Crusaders. It was a nondenominational church group for high-school-age girls led by a University of Tennessee student, Linda Evans.

On New Year's Eve in 1972, Linda gave a party in her apartment on campus and invited several club members. Among them was Mary Pentecost, who met Linda's handsome younger brother, Tom, there. Tom Evans, Jr., was a wholesome all-American boy with the kind of face you'd expect to see on a poster ad for fresh dairy products: straight, hemp-colored hair, blue eyes, strong athletic build.

He flashed a genuine, boyish smile as he remembered their first meeting at that party.

"She says I tried to pick her up. Her date got mad, and they got into a big fight. He wanted to leave, but Mary didn't want to.

"The next time we met, she picked me up," he said with a grin. "It was over a year later, during fall registration at a coffee shop on campus. Mary was registering for her freshman year [at law school]; I was just starting my junior year [of college]. She came over to where I was sitting and reminded me of the New Year's Eve party. I could tell she was nervous. She didn't date a whole lot. She said she never did this sort of thing"—he winked— "sounded like a real line to me.

"Mary was a lot like my sister Linda. Serious and introspective. She took things to heart. She was different from the girls I'd grown up with—little, sweet airhead types. Mary always tried to get beneath the surface of things. She was so smart and independent, always had these the-truth-hurts kinds of comments. For a while I thought it was great."

Tom, indecisive about his future—and even his choice of a major—kept taking semesters off to work at one job or another while Mary raced through college and law school at breakneck speed. So even though Tom was two and a half years older than Mary, he lagged far behind her in school.

Their relationship ultimately led to a winter's eve at the Pentecost home where, after a family supper, Tom asked Mr. Pentecost if they might have a private talk.

They went downstairs to the family room. Tom was extremely fond of Mary's father; over the two years that he and Mary had been dating, he'd grown quite close to Mr. Pentecost. They were similar in many ways. Both were outdoor men; they liked to take long walks in the woods and go dove hunting sometimes.

"Mr. Pentecost was the kind of man who put people at ease. He could sit on a back porch with a country guy and shoot the breeze. He liked to remind people that he was just a poor farm boy himself." Still, Tom was nervous. "I wanted to ask him for her hand. I didn't think it was right to just carry off their daughter. I promised him I'd do my best—and treat her right. We both got kind of emotional. He was real supportive and said he thought I'd do a great job and that he was glad to have me in the family. Even though it was a formality in a way, it brought us closer together. When we shook hands we both had tears in our eyes.

"Mary and her mother were waiting upstairs. It was fun; we were all real happy."

They were married in the spring. The wedding, presided over by the Reverend Mr. Gourley, was held at the same Mount Olive Baptist Church where Bob Pentecost was deacon and Mary had been baptized. In what Tom felt was a preceremony pep talk held in Gourley's office, the preacher came on strong. "Remember," he said, "the man is the soul of the family, the decision maker. A husband has to be prepared to put his foot down at times."

It was a traditional white-lace church wedding with

all the frill and trimmings, flowers and ribbons, bridesmaids and ushers, and solemn, sacred vows.

Mary was in her second year of law school then. For the first year and a half they lived in a small apartment near campus, but they both missed the outdoors. There was a small farmhouse on the Pentecost land; Mr. Pentecost offered it to the young newlyweds rent-free except for utilities. Mary would have her horse—actually, there were two horses on the farm, so she and Tom could both ride. There were the dogs and the river they liked to walk along. It would be ideal.

From the time she started college, Mary had always talked about going to law school. Coincidentally, her father had got his law degree from the University of Tennessee Law School as Mary was starting her freshman year. One of his criminal law clinic instructors was Bob Ritchie, one of Knoxville's young, upcoming criminal defense attorneys. In less than a decade Bob Pentecost would retain his former teacher to defend his adored daughter. But while he was studying to pass the bar, it was his fondest dream that he and Mary, his firstborn, would set up a law practice together.

Mary and Tom furnished the little farmhouse with a water bed and wicker furniture and made it their off-campus home. For a while, they were happy.

But as Mary approached her last year of law school, the pressures began to mount. At twenty-four she was beginning to lose some of her illusions about the judicial system as she saw that it could be manipulated by those who knew how—or had the money to hire someone who did. And the work was grueling.

She and Tom were standing talking one night at the top of the McClung Tower, the tallest building on campus. They looked out at the view of the whole campus, the Clinch River, and in the distance, the dark rolling hills that were the foothills of the Smokies. They had often talked about Canada, about how they'd love to go up there someday and find their dream cabin.

That night Mary turned to Tom suddenly and said, "Why don't we just take off? Go to Canada."

"Yeah," he said. "Wouldn't that be great?"

"Let's do it," she said, and suddenly Tom realized she meant it.

"You've gone through all this. At least get your degree and then we can do something like that."

Mary wasn't ready to give up that easily. She pressed on.

"We could just go up there and live, that's all. We could make a go of it."

"But I don't even have my degree yet," he argued. "What would I do?"

"We'll get jobs and *live*. We'll find a neat little place and live. That's enough, isn't it?"

Mary was depressed for days after that, and she was disappointed that Tom wasn't game just to pick up and go. She believed they could have been happy in Canada. She became more and more withdrawn. They began to argue over little things, everything.

"A lot of it was my fault. In the beginning I used to admire the way she spoke out about things she cared about. But it was starting to get under my skin, the extreme way she'd react to even the smallest things. It really became tough—in normal, social situations, she'd be real nitpicky and impatient.

"And I didn't really have any big ambition; I wasn't making a great living. I wasn't even sure what I wanted to do. I was in my senior year of college, and I was still switching my major. We started getting mean to each other; there just wasn't any more fun.

"Except for the night I found the cat. I was at some guy's house in Fort Sanders, on campus. There was a party going on. I found this poor little white cat—it looked like an albino—it was running around, soot all over it. Her little bones were showing, she was so skinny. Nobody knew whose it was. Someone said they thought it might belong to the guy next door; he'd been out of town for a while. So I gave him five bucks to give to the guy when he got back and took the cat home. Mary loved it. She named her Lily. Lily used to follow us everywhere, when we'd go walking out in the woods. She's still out there, running wild and hunting. She keeps the barn clean."

In law school Mary was considered something of an anomaly, even to one of her professors, Neil Cohen, who, when he noticed her standing outside of his classroom, wondered if she'd wandered in by mistake. "She just didn't *look* like a law student."

Ellen Hobbs, a classmate, now a successful attorney in Nashville, remembered seeing her in the halls "with a hard and bitter look on her face, impatiently tapping her foot, waiting for class to begin. She was an attractive woman mostly because she was so different. That eyeliner—I guess that was her trademark—and those big gold hoop earrings she always wore. Sort of a holdover from the sixties. Everyone else was wearing neat little pretty clip-ons, but Mary dressed the part of a free spirit. She was never without a cigarette. She was forceful, never smiled, and didn't give people a feeling of being real comfortable around her. Even if you didn't know her, you knew who she was. She had a presence—a sinister kind of presence.

"Her father was so well known on campus for being a fine man, charitable, highly principled. It made it all so much more inexplicable when it happened. I was living in Houston, Texas, when I heard the news. Of course I was surprised that anyone—any lawyer especially—would do what she did, but I thought to myself, if I were to choose who in the class would do something that wild, it would be Mary. I could see her standing there tapping her foot. . . ."

* * *

In her last year of law school, Mary participated in the University of Tennessee's legal clinic, a program licensed by the Supreme Court of Tennessee that provides students with actual court experience. Under supervision of instructors, students represent indigent clients. They prepare cases for trial, interview witnesses, and present motions to the court. The clinic is housed in a separate part of the law school building and resembles the offices of a law firm.

Another Nashville attorney, Joy Heath, was in the legal clinic with Mary Evans. It was during their last quarter in law school. The clinic was limited to ten or twelve students, with two instructors. Guest speakers were invited to address the clinic; Bob Ritchie was one of the better-known lawyers who spoke that quarter.

Joy and Mary made a date one afternoon to drive down to the Knoxville jail. They were to meet with the clients they'd been appointed to represent in preliminary hearings.

"I waited for Mary to show up. I might have been a little early, but I waited and waited. When she got there, I smelled alcohol on her breath. She said she'd been having a few drinks with her friend, a married man.

"We went to the jail where we each interviewed our clients separately, in small cubicles. Student and defendant were separated by a glass partition. When I finished I went out to the car. More than half an hour went by before Mary came out. She seemed like she was turned on, said that her client had made a pass at her and the other prisoners wanted to know how come he got such a good-looking lawyer.

"I thought, Why does that excite you? Those people in that jail are lowlifes. But Mary was odd anyway. She was so pale; she looked like a corpse sometimes. And those raccoon eyes—with all that dark eyeliner. She always smoked and had a horrible hacking smoker's cough.

"She seemed mean; she had a big chip on her shoulder. In today's terms, she wore punk stuff. Most law students wore suits, but Mary always wore long skirts and boots. The one time I can remember seeing her in a suit I was shocked."

Tom remembers that it was while she was in her last year of law school that Mary got a job clerking for John Lockridge. "She talked about what a ladies' man he was. She said he had a reputation around town for playing around on his wife. I guess he and I were opposites. He was more a man of the world. He had status and connections, a big practice," Tom said.

Soon it became clear to them both that although opposites may attract for a while, for the long term it's wearying. "I was stimulated by the arguments at first; after a while I was worn down by them. We bickered all the time. There just wasn't anything to be happy about anymore. One day one of us said, 'Maybe we *should* get a divorce.' We both knew it was coming, and we felt relieved."

The marriage was ended without bitterness. The few possessions they'd accumulated were divided down the middle. Tom drove off in his Pontiac, Mary in her Toyota. On September 16, 1980, the Chancery Court of Knox County granted Mary Pentecost Evans an absolute divorce on the grounds of irreconcilable differences. The papers were delivered to her attorney, Sarah Sheppeard of the firm of Lockridge and Becker.

After the divorce, Mary began to date John Lockridge. Lockridge, a man with studied good looks and carefully cultivated charm, was nearly the age of Mary's father—and married.

Mary told Cheryl Smith, her close friend, "Well, I met this guy. My mom and dad would just croak if they knew. He's married and he's trying to keep in good with his wife. I feel so differently about him. I would even have his baby."

In August 1980 they took their first trip together, to Washington, D.C., where they stayed at the chic Madison Hotel; at Christmastime they went to Coral Gables; in March to Palm Beach.

"Mary always talked about flying away with him to the beach for the weekend," Cheryl said. "He'd be real spur-of-the-moment; she never knew what he was going to do next. Mary had never been anywhere before. She said she loved him, felt something for him she'd never felt for anyone before. He would give her things. She was dripping in gold."

In September 1980, Lockridge left his wife, Anne, a sleek, elegant southern beauty; in March 1981, they were divorced.

Mary graduated from law school in June 1981. The following January, Lockridge called his friend Jim Bell, a partner in the firm of Tipton and Bell, and asked him to interview Mary for a job as an associate.

At thirty-four Jim Bell was a "good ol' boy" made good. He and Joe Tipton had had their own practice since June 1981. Before that they had been in partnership with Bob Ritchie. In 1983 their caseload averaged close to two hundred a week.

The offices of Tipton and Bell were on the fifteenth floor of the handsome old Hamilton Building downtown. From his window Bell could look out onto the empty site of the 1982 World's Fair and at the sunsphere, its symbol. Built as a tribute to banker Jake Butcher, chief financier and architect of the fair, the sunsphere stands almost a hundred feet tall, gleams bright gold, and bears a striking resemblance to a gigantic golf ball on a tee. Knoxville bankers chipped in and had a five-thousand-dollar carillon installed inside it. It rings out the hour with a hillbilly tune. This gift, a trinket of sorts, was given to Jake just before he caused the collapse of fourteen banks.

*   *   *

Mary proved to be a thorough researcher and an excellent investigator. "She had a way of going down and talking to the cop on the street who normally wouldn't give a lawyer the time of day," Bell said. "Same with witnesses. People opened up with her."

Not so her coworkers. They found her cynical and sarcastic. The women in the office said Mary would come in, close her door, and rarely deign to talk to them.

Melinda Meter, who was clerking for Tipton and Bell, remembers once when Mary surprised them. "She same into the library where the clerks were doing research, terribly excited. She said that she and John Lockridge were moving in together, that it had been a hard-won battle to get him to leave his wife. That was back in August 1982, but then a few days later Mary was depressed because he hadn't called."

One year later Jim Bell would call Mary into his office and hand her a slim file marked "William Timothy Kirk." He was assigning her her first major criminal case, for first-degree murder—for which her client, if found guilty, would be sentenced to die in the electric chair.

Chapter Four

Tim Kirk had come into adolescence on the streets of Chicago. His family had moved there from their eighty-acre wheat farm just outside of Sikeston, Missouri, in 1951, when farming could no longer support them. Tim was almost five then.

For young Tim it must have seemed as though the world had sprung to life overnight. Only a day ago the world, as far as Tim's eye could see, was made of tall, lion-colored grass, green shade trees, and the house he lived in. All the rest was sky. In this new city world there was little room for sky; everywhere he looked he saw stone and steel, speeding automobiles, and people.

His father had taken a job as foreman on the assembly line at Continental Can Company. His mother, Florence, a former schoolteacher, was a widow with four children when she married William A. Kirk, a man three years her junior who was divorced with one son of his own. After they married, Florence stopped teaching and stayed home with the children; William wouldn't have it any other way. Instead, in order to support his new large family, he took a second job. He'd come home from Continental Can at four o'clock in the afternoon for an early supper; then at eight he'd leave to work at the Admiral TV factory inspecting television sets and not return until midnight—or later. On the nights he had off, the family would gather with friends after dinner and play cards. Tim's oldest half brother, Irv, who no longer lived at home, raced stock cars. William would pile the family into his car and take them to the track to watch his son race.

Tim's five half brothers and sisters doted on their baby brother. "He was very special," Shirley remembered. "An adorable little pup always busting with energy." Shirley was the youngest of his siblings, the one closest to him in age; the oldest was grown and already married.

After they moved from the farm in Missouri, home was a two-bedroom apartment on the second floor of a brick building. Shirley, at age fifteen, was given the second bedroom; Tim slept on a fold-out couch in the living room. He didn't mind that; what he did mind was having to spend so much time indoors waiting for his mother to finish the housework. There was a park across the street with a playground and a water fountain. Daily his confidence grew, like that of a young pup creeping farther and farther from his mother's side to lay claim to his new territory.

"She'd always have to come looking for me, and I'd be hiding in the bushes somewhere, not wanting to come home. She'd have to drag me by the back of my pants."

One afternoon when his mother had come after him, six-year-old Tim managed to slip away just as they reached the front door and run back across the street to the park. He had hoisted himself up to the water fountain when he heard the shouts. He turned to see a man and two women sitting on a park bench not twenty feet away, their faces purplish and contorted with rage. They were exchanging furious shouts in a strange language. A split second later, the man had jumped to his feet and was brandishing a gun. Tim stood frozen as the man fired the gun directly into both the women's startled faces. Blood was everywhere; pieces of flesh exploded in the air. The man turned so that it seemed to Tim that he must be looking right at him, and with eyes full of utter, naked horror, the man raised the gun to his own head and fired again.

Then the sounds of sirens, people running in all directions, brakes screeching in the street, shouts. Tim went and got on the swings, where from a place high in the air, he could watch the curious scene below.

They were all talking about it that night at home and for several days after, but Tim was strangely silent; he never told them that "the awful terrible thing" had happened before his very eyes.

Within days Tim was witness to another spectacle. A boy who lived a few doors down from him was crossing the street, heading in Tim's direction, when a car appeared out of nowhere. Tim stood wide-eyed as the car bore down on the boy. The impact of metal against flesh made a sound no louder than a dull thud. Tim went to have a closer look. The boy lay motionless. A crowd formed; a policeman took charge. He asked if anyone knew the boy or had any idea where he lived. Tim stood silent. To him the boy looked dead; he was sure he was dead. Tim refused to speak up.

As it happened, the boy, although knocked unconscious, had been only slightly hurt. Tim never could explain his silence. "It wasn't that I was scared, it was just something . . . I felt like I had to keep to myself. Back then they didn't show violence on TV the way they do now. Nowadays kids grow up with death and violence. They see it every night on the news; it doesn't have all that much meaning to them."

He remembered his first fights and the fleeting glimpse he had of his own violence. He was about seven the first time, and he was playing with some older, bigger kids. One minute they were just horsing around, and the next, two of them had him pinned to the ground. Someone was pounding his nose with his fist. He felt blood spurt out. He closed his eyes; the pain of it set off fireworks in his head. Suddenly he remembered the man in the park and thought how he'd like to be able to make faces explode.

The next time he let his temper run full out, and again he had a sense of its fearsome power. "I was in the street having a snowball fight with some kids when I saw my sister coming home from work. The day before she'd had a mole removed from her back, and I remember her saying it was sore. When the kids saw her going up the steps to the house, they started throwing snowballs at her. One of them hit her in the back. It must've really hurt, because she cried out. I got so mad I started grabbing sharp pieces of ice and shoving them inside the snowballs. Then at close range I aimed them right at some kid's eye. And I didn't want to stop. I kept picking up more pieces of ice, making snowballs out of them, and just throwing them one after the other."

It took his mother and his sister to finally get him to stop. There was no way, it seemed, to contain such energy. His mother used to say Tim was a human furnace, that you could warm your hands by him. She'd have to chase after him to put his coat and hat on. "But even if you could catch him and get him to hold still a minute, it wouldn't do any good—he'd only take them off in an hour anyway," his mother used to complain to Shirley.

That same energy made school an impossible chore for Tim and a living hell for his teachers. Forced to sit still at his desk, he'd stare out the window, feet swinging, scraping noisily against the floor, his mind working furiously to devise some way to get him out of that classroom. And the poor overwrought teacher would write a note complaining of Tim's disruptive behavior, a note which Tim would promptly tear up on the way home. Years later he wondered how he ever learned to read and write.

It was when the teacher finally called the Kirks at home to find out why they hadn't responded to her pleas for help that Tim began to master the art of con. A con didn't lie. He didn't have to. He could use sincerity and honesty in place of the lie and still lead you where he wanted you to be. Tim's parents were simple, old-fashioned, hardworking folk, easy to convince with a cute, guileless smile and a direct gaze.

Soon Tim began to cut class, was drawn instead to the neighborhood drugstore where a group of teenaged boys hung out. Tim was impatient to put his childhood behind him and join their ranks.

It was 1957, the year the Beat Generation was born. Jack Kerouac's *On the Road* and Allen Ginsberg's "Howl" were underground best-sellers. The guys in front of the drugstore weren't staying home or going to school; they were hanging out, their motorcycles alongside the curb. The bikes glittered in the sunlight to Tim's young eyes. When a cop would come along and tell the boys to beat it, they'd look him dead in the eye and demand to know what law they were breaking. In the end they'd have to move, but it was clear to Tim which of them had got the last word.

The same group sometimes hung out in a fenced-in yard down the street from Tim, where one of them lived. Tim would go and stand at the gate and watch them. One day one of them called to him and told him he could come on in. That made Tim feel good. He was handed a prescription and told to take it into the drugstore, hand it to the man behind the counter wearing the white coat, and "be real respectful, just say it's for your mother." As a reward he was given one of the pills. "Here, kid," he remembers someone saying, "take one of these; you'll feel like you own the fuckin' world."

On the streets, Tim Kirk proved to be an A student. He learned to write a prescription, forge a signature, even talk the pharmacist into giving him a refill: "I was riding my bike home, and the bottle fell out of my pocket. All the pills spilled out on the street, and my mom really needs them." He learned which color pill got you high, which color mellowed you out, which killed the pain, calmed the fear, made you forget. Pick a color, change the reality. After a while they stopped calling him "kid" and started calling him "man."

Tim didn't come of age; he broke into manhood, unleashing his volcanic energies in garages and back porches and alleyways where sex had to be stolen. In neighborhoods like Tim's that were ethnic and largely Catholic, it was less dangerous to be caught stealing a man's property than to be discovered in an embrace with his daughter. Looking back, he would pinpoint that time when, still preadolescent, he was first made to feel like a criminal. "I guess you could say I was oversexed. Every time I got caught fooling with some little girl down the street my dad would take me out back and try to drive the devil out of me."

Finally his parents, at the end of their tether, run ragged by a son they loved and couldn't control, scraped together the money to enroll him in the Junior Military Academy in South Chicago.

It was a dismal-looking place, a single, old brick building with nothing but a cement blacktop area out back for a playground.

"I hated it. Grown men walking around wearing uniforms, calling themselves 'Captain' and 'Colonel,' making us salute. They knew all about discipline. They'd line us up in the gym, the whole 'battalion' they called us, and made us bend over and grab our ankles. Then some six-foot-four son-of-a-bitch captain would take a great big cherrywood paddle and whip our asses.

"They could do anything they wanted to us, and we were too small to do anything about it. I used to think if I was as big as he was maybe I could turn it around and make him scream a little."

Cadets were given weekend furloughs provided they hadn't got any demerits during the week. Tim's weekends were few; when he got one, his parents would come to pick him up. They were impressed with his manners.

"He'd come home just like a little soldier," his father remembered. "He'd go places with Shirley and he'd always be opening doors for her."

In the middle of the second semester, Tim climbed over the wall and ran home.

"I took him back to the academy," his father said. "But the colonel told me it was no use. He couldn't handle him anymore. He said maybe I could try another academy and recommended one down in Tennessee, but I let Tim talk me out of it. I think the trouble was, he got in with another kid—one of those bad boys—and he got messed up taking dope or something.

"The next summer we sent him to a boys' camp in southern Illinois, in Metropolis. It was a place you couldn't run off from. There was the river, and the whole camp was surrounded by woods." Tim was thirteen and just back from a year and a half in the military academy.

The stint in the academy had put an end to whatever illusions he had about the way things were. "I looked at things different when I was back around my folks. They didn't know what went on in that place, and I couldn't tell them. I guess I figured nobody wants to hear about it. You can't go through life being a crybaby. Just got to take your medicine. I had to exist without their help. Nobody was going to help me but me. I guess maybe then I decided I wasn't going to take any shit from anybody anymore."

Some months earlier when he'd been home on a weekend, some of the neighborhood kids had put his initials on his arm with india ink. On the night he got back from the academy, they all went down to State and Congress to get tattooed. Tim got a four-dollar rose put on his arm.

That rose tattoo would be the first of many; the last, emblazoned on his left forearm, would be a robed and sceptered Grim Reaper.

His parents had enrolled him in Kelwyn Park High School, but Tim had little time for classes. He needed money now. For the last year and a half he'd been walking around in a gray uniform with a black stripe down the leg, looking like a tin soldier. Now he wanted tan suede jackets and navy blue double-knit suits.

Tim took a dollar-thirty-five-an-hour job in a bakery pouring doughnut batter into a funnel. He reported for the first day's work at seven o'clock on a Saturday morning. At twelve-thirty he went to lunch and never came back. "It was the dumbest, most boring five and a half hours of my life. I couldn't believe people were willing to spend their lives like that.

"I decided then that I'd do what I felt like doing and whatever happened, happened. If it turned out good, okay; if it turned out bad, okay. But I'd do whatever I had to do. . . . I just made a big mistake, you know, when I picked up the gun and started with armed robbery . . . and decided to be a burglar . . . then wound up with the amounts of time I did.

"I should have stuck with low-profile types of crime."

Tim was fourteen when pretty little Junine Foy caught his eye at a party. He went by her house every day to court her. As a suitor he was inspired. He would bring with him a bottle of champagne and two champagne glasses.

"He was more mature than the other boys," said Junine. "Tim was always his own man; he didn't depend on anybody."

Her mother, Harriet, was equally impressed. "He was a little fox, every hair in place, real cute, slim. And he had a charm that just wouldn't quit."

Tim and Junine began to go steady then. "There was nothing else I could have done but fall in love with him. I got obsessed with him," she said.

He told her of his dreams for the good life, a life of champagne and sports cars and fine clothes. And then suddenly, almost before she realized what was happening, she was going with him on his sprees, along with some of her relatives.

"Tim and I were pretty wild. We were robbing liquor stores, grocery stores. Little stuff. My cousin. . . . was in on it. My uncle, he was a lonely man; he got into it because I guess he wanted to impress my cousin. . . . We were just riding around in the car and we ended up . . . robbing a store.

"Well, there was a gun. I was scared that time. I didn't want to do it but I just didn't have enough guts to say no. To this day I don't know why I didn't just say no."

"I was fifteen the first time someone put a gun in my hand," Tim said. "They sent me into an all-night convenience store and told me what to do. I was a little scared, but I was excited too. Well, it all went the way they said it would, and all of a sudden we had some money.

"It really seemed like we had it made, except that the next time we went out, I had a little surprise that—well, I didn't expect. It was a deli–liquor store. The owners, a man and a woman, were behind the counter. I pointed the gun at them—just like I was supposed to—and said, 'Give me the money out of the cash register.' The woman got real mad. 'No,' she said, 'you can't have it. We're not going to give you our money—now get out of here!' Well, I guess somebody forgot to tell me what to do if they say no, so I just turned around and left."

There was the night they'd been taking drugs, uppers and downers together to balance the high, and they broke into a drugstore to steal the drugs out of the window.

The next day Tim told Junine he was ready to break in again and get some more. They argued over it. Furious, Tim told her he was finished with her, that it was all over between them.

Devastated and half out of her mind on the drugs she'd already taken, Junine swallowed a dozen or more pills.

Tim came back to where he'd left her and found her stumbling around in a daze. Without knowing exactly how many pills she'd taken, he walked her around in the air to wake her up. Then he took her into a pizza parlor to get her something to eat. It was directly across the street from the drugstore. She seemed all right then; he told her to wait there. He crossed the street to the drugstore. This time the police were waiting. Tim was arrested on charges of breaking and entering, possession of illegal drugs, and robbery.

Junine had started to fall asleep at the table. She made her way to the ladies' room and put some cold water on her face. As she reached the sink, she slumped to the floor and passed out.

Tim told the arresting officers that he'd left his girlfriend back there in the pizza parlor and was worried about her. He told them she'd taken a lot of drugs and asked them to send someone in there to find her.

Junine was found unconscious on the floor of the ladies' room. They rushed her to Belmont Hospital where she was pronounced dead on arrival. Miraculously, they were able to revive her.

"I remember waking up in the hospital. The only thing I could think about was wanting to see him. I found out they'd locked him up for breaking into the drugstore. The police probably hoped I'd die so they could get him on a tougher charge."

As each turned sixteen, they dropped out of high school. Junine's parents blamed Tim.

"My dad never liked him. He didn't trust him. My ma is like me. She wants to believe the best in everybody. It takes us a long time to see the bad in people. If you look, you can always see something good.

"One day Tim came over to the house, and he and my dad got into an argument over my income tax refund check. I was supposed to give it to my dad, but Tim was acting real cocky, and he started telling me I didn't owe my dad anything and that he wanted the check. There was a terrible fight, and my dad threatened to have him arrested for disorderly conduct.

"Well, I told my dad if they had Tim arrested, then they'd have to have me arrested too. They did. I spent four days in jail."

Tim and Junine's engagement became official when he gave her a forty-dollar engagement ring. Part of their courtship took place during her visits to him at a camp for juveniles who'd been in trouble. Tim's parents would take her with them on weekends. The young lovers could stroll along the banks of the river holding hands and making plans for their future. He would change, he told her. He'd get a job, and then they'd find an apartment and get married.

He made good on his promise. He took a job at a silver-plating shop, and soon, when they'd both turned eighteen, they got married. In Illinois a girl could marry without written permission from her parents, but a boy had to be nineteen. Tim Xeroxed his father's birth certificate, blocking out the birth date and the middle initial (Tim was William T. Kirk; his father, William A.), and filled it in to meet the legal age requirements.

With the seven-dollar wedding rings Tim had bought at a pawnshop, they drove to Wheaton, Illinois, where a justice of the peace married them. They spent their wedding night in a motel room.

Junine kept her job as a welder at the Leslie Welding Company in Franklin Park, where her mother also worked. The newlyweds rented an apartment at the King Arthur Apartments in North Lake. Tim quit his job soon after, but Junine kept hers until their first son was born. Every Saturday Tim's father would come with a bag of groceries.

"Tim never bought one single bottle of baby food," Junine said.

She remembers the first time he frightened her with his temper. She was down to her last cigarette and he wanted it. "He wasn't working and I was. I told him no, I worked for this cigarette. He could go get a job and work for his own damn cigarettes. I don't know what got into me. I was just being hard-headed. He threw me down on the bed and threatened to cut my throat—for a cigarette.

"He didn't have a job but he had a silver Corvette, so I knew he must be doing something crooked. Once I woke up in the middle of the night and found him rolling tires into the apartment. I knew he didn't buy them; nobody buys sixty tires. I got mad at him because they were making marks on the wall. The next day my mother and I stopped at a gas station near the apartment. There was something wrong with the car, and Tim came and met us there. The gas station attendant was talking about a break-in the night before. Tires had been stolen, he said. Tim started talking and wound up saying something about the break-in! That's one thing about Tim; he never could keep his mouth shut. If he did something he had to brag about it. I always thought a good crook didn't talk about the things he did. . . .

"One day I came home and he had all these guns. He wanted me to read off the serial numbers so he could make a list. I told him I wasn't going to touch them. I wasn't going to put my fingerprints on a gun that would turn up being used to murder someone."

By then Tim had teamed up with Red Nix, a professional car thief. Tim had noticed him one night at a bar and asked the bartender to introduce them. Red was part of a ring that transported stolen cars across the state line to Missouri.

Seven years later Red Nix would be shot and killed by his common-law wife, Dale Graves. Dale would be sentenced to life in the Tennessee State Prison for Women. In 1984, Dale's old friend Tim Kirk would write, beseeching her to keep an eye out for a new inmate who'd just been sent to the prison, Mary Evans. Dale, who'd already served fourteen years and had a certain old-timer status, arranged to have Mary room with her.

Tim's record of arrests started piling up, two and three a month. His prison sentences were growing lengthier. In September 1968, he was sent to the Missouri State Penitentiary for a year.

Junine still stuck it out with him, visiting him in prison whenever she could, missing him, and listening to the songs that made her lovesick heart ache.

"I was brought up to believe that when you fall in love, it's forever. Right or wrong, you stick with him. I just lived for the day when he'd get out. No matter what, we'd always get back together. It didn't matter to me what he did. I kind of got obsessed with him. Nothing mattered but him. And whenever he'd come out of reform school or jail, he'd always talk about how he would change. And for a while it seemed he might. But then he'd start staying out again, and I knew he was out robbing or doing something crooked.

"He'd come home, take a shower, and then he'd leave and stay gone. I was so mad I used to think about killing him. I was all alone, by myself so much of the time. At night I'd put a gun above the bed, in a bookcase over the bed—we had a lot of guns in the house. Sometimes he'd come home drunk. I asked him if he was hanging out with other women. He always said he wasn't. I didn't believe him though."

Junine and Tim moved from their apartment in Chicago to the Kirk family farm in Sikeston, Missouri, where Tim had been born. He had just been released from the state penitentiary in Missouri and told Junine, who was pregnant with their third son, that he intended to change.

The family had offered the house to them rent-free, provided Tim helped out on the farm.

"I was having migraines, and I had this terrible rash from nerves," Junine said. "My lips and eyes were swollen up with hives. I looked terrible. I had such headaches I couldn't even change diapers. Tim used to get real mad and yell at me if I used Pampers. He made me use regular diapers. His sister, Shirley, used to come over and help me. One day I had this terrible migraine and I walked right into a wall with a pot of hot coffee in my hand. Shirley came to take me to the doctor, and I got a prescription I had to have filled. When Tim got home, I asked him to get it filled for me. He said he had something to do first, and he left. The funny thing is, he doesn't think he ever did anything wrong.

"It was three months after the baby was born that I called my parents and went back to Chicago."

Harriett Foy recalled her daughter's call. "Junine telephoned home. 'Please come get me!' The girl was hysterical. He had been terrorizing her for three days. He had her ready to kill herself and her kids. He'd finally left her alone when she called. We put on our clothes and got in the car and drove to Missouri.

"Tim was there when we arrived. So were his parents. He was sulking. Nothing was said. It was a very odd scene. Everybody was unhappy. Tim was stunned that his wife would actually leave him. Very quietly we went about our business, removing everything from the house the kids and our Junine needed. The Kirks were there to see that there was no trouble. As far as I was concerned that was the end of our life with Tim Kirk."

Junine went to live with her parents in Palatine, Illinois. He went to the house to see her once.

"Tim came to Palatine to see the kids—this was before he got in trouble in Memphis—and all he talked about was drugs and stuff," Junine recalled. "I got mad at him. He hit me, but I had tried to hit him first. I tried to hit him in the head with a bottle. I wanted to kill him. . . . he hit me again. I had to go to the doctor, because I had torn ligaments in my neck." The incident happened outside her parents' house while they were inside; she told them she had hurt her neck when a lawn chair collapsed.

"Later he told me he did it deliberately. He wanted me to get mad enough at him so that I'd never want to come back to him.

"I don't think Tim ever had a problem with drugs. Tim just wants to do what he wants to do. He doesn't want to do anything the normal man's way. He once said, 'When I die, I want to go out in blazing bullets like Al Capone.' The last time he got caught, I thought they'd never take him alive.

"He saw himself as a professional crook. How could he be, though? A professional crook doesn't get caught. He was a con man. It's easier for him to be in prison than be out and face responsibility. I think he was born for that life. He couldn't survive out here.

"I talked to him after he got caught. I told him I wished he could have stayed free. He said he thought he could go straight. But being crooked is all he knows. He doesn't know about anything else.

"After Tim and that girl, Mary Evans, were caught, he wanted me to send the kids down there to see him. He said Mary would pick them up at the airport and bring them to the prison. I asked him, 'Are you crazy? No way. She's unstable,' I said. 'Here she is, an educated woman, and she just ups and runs off with you. She threw it all away.' He said, 'Well, you know what it's like to be in love.' I told him, 'I do, but I was only sixteen then.' He got nasty and said, 'If that's the way you feel about it.' . . . I admit, I got hot on the phone.

"He did say he had thought about coming to see me, but he knew the police would be watching the apartment and they were: the FBI was here. They asked me to call them if Tim showed up.

"I said to him, 'You had nothing to lose. That girl had everything to lose. She had an education that she threw away. Everything.' I was in love and stupid, and sixteen.

She was in love and stupid—and had an education! He was only using her. It could have been anybody. . . . he would have used anybody.

"I did hope he could have stayed out, though. But I only knew him one way. I won't give up on him."

Chapter Five

On June 23, 1977, the grand jury of the state of Tennessee, Shelby County, said that William Timothy Kirk and Robert Phillips and Gladys Gibson, before the finding of this indictment,

> did unlawfully, feloniously, violently and forcibly by use of a deadly weapon to wit: a pistol, make an assault on the persons of Howard and Anabel Lincoln and putting them in great danger and bodily fear of his/her life, and did then and there unlawfully and feloniously and with force and violence aforesaid, steal, take and carry away: one watch of the value of $2,000, one ring of the value of $2,600, race track tickets of the value of $1,500, and the sum of $6.00, good and lawful money of the United States, three rings of the value of $4,040, one bracelet of the value of $1,400, and one automobile of the value of $18,000, all of the value of $29,546, the proper goods and chattels of Howard and Anabel Lincoln with the intent feloniously to convert the same to their own use and to deprive the true owner thereof, against the peace and dignity of the State of Tennessee.

*   *   *

On September 14, 1978, a jury found the defendants guilty of robbery with a deadly weapon as charged and fixed punishments at confinement in the state penitentiary for sixty-five years. Kirk's sentence stipulated "that the date of his imprisonment commence from the time of his reception by said keeper, that he be rendered infamous, and that he pay the costs of this prosecution."

Tim Kirk was twenty-one; he would be eligible for parole on March 3, 2008, when he would be sixty-one years old. In the next four years another forty years would be added to his sentence, giving him a possible parole date of 2048, at which time he would be one hundred and one years old.

A sixty-five-year prison sentence is like hearing that the sore or the lump or the hacking cough is cancer. The patient runs from doctor to doctor, the convict files appeals; the patient loses hope and seeks alternative cures, the convict begins to plan his escape.

The main prison in Nashville is a gruesome, castlelike cement structure. Painted a pale yellow that takes on a pinkish hue in the late afternoon light, it rises up from a long, sloping lawn like an apparition in a child's nightmare, with turrets, towers, and spires against a vast, empty sky.

In Tennessee, public sentiment re convicts is of the lock-'em-up, stack-'em-up, and throw-away-the-key variety. In a lawsuit that inmates brought to challenge conditions in the prison's death row, the defense countered that "damned bleeding heart liberals" wanted to turn death row into "some kind of Hilton highway to heaven with clean spacious accommodations that are warm in the winter and cool in the summer."

But a probe by the Tennessee Bureau of Investigation disclosed massive negligence, incompetence, and corruption by prison employees. The report said guards and staff regularly sell guns, run drugs, and have sex with inmates.

Each year the number of deaths caused by inmate

stabbings increase. In a joint letter to state and federal officials and to members of the media, two long-term inmates wrote: "The conditions behind the walls here at Nashville are more repressive than ever. Racism is at its highest under the present administration and a racial explosion is imminent if immediate action isn't taken to redress these conditions."

At twenty-one, Tim Kirk was processed, assigned a number, and turned out into a prison population of more than eight thousand. As time went on, he came to be regarded as a man who could not be threatened or intimidated. Fellow inmate Eddie McMillan said, years later, "Tim Kirk is a solid guy, a guy who could take the fall without involving anyone else when something heavy comes down."

Nor was Kirk the kind of guy who would accept a sixty-five-year sentence. In time he would come to be known as one of the highest escape risks in the system.

Kirk's first escape was planned in 1980 with Carl Crafton, an older, mild-mannered, softspoken convict, an ex-junkie serving a thirty-five-year sentence for armed robbery of a drugstore in Chattanooga. Crafton, a self-educated man, acted as a counselor, a jailhouse lawyer of sorts in prison.

On the morning of November 17, Tim Kirk and Carl Crafton, who both had kitchen duties, left the dining hall to pick up the garbage in the kitchen. Each carried a large plastic container out to the dumpster parked in back. They stood a minute, watching; then they jumped into the truck and waited for it to move. They hoped the truck would get outside the fence before the compactor was activated.

But before they even made it to the gate, they saw the compactor begin to move down on them. Crafton was a man of slight build and not as strong as Kirk. Kirk called out to him to try to move himself out of its way, but the compactor was larger than it had looked from outside the truck. Kirk scrambled too, burrowing deep into the garbage. The monstrous thing began to squeeze down, pressing, pushing the air out of Kirk, until he felt he would explode. A terrible strangled noise came from Crafton. Kirk struggled to see him. Crafton was unconscious. With the last bit of air and the last bit of strength he had left in him Kirk yelled out, wondering as he did, how much longer it was going to hurt before he wouldn't know anything anymore. And somehow another animallike sound issued forth from him. The thing stopped, all was quiet for a moment, and it began to lift.

Crafton suffered a concussion and a hairline skull fracture; Kirk, a few broken ribs. Three months later, two other men would try it and would be less lucky: one man would be killed; the other, mangled, crippled for life.

For Kirk and Crafton the real punishment was still to come. They were being moved. They would now spend Christmas—perhaps every Christmas for the rest of their lives—at Brushy Mountain State Prison, a maximum-security facility known throughout the Tennessee prison system as the end of the line.

Brushy was where the rats were the size of cats, where because of overcrowding, men would carry their thin, lumpy mattresses that stank of mold and stale sweat up to the gym where four hundred of them would sleep on the floor. More slept in the hallway outside the schoolroom. They shared one toilet and one shower. Brushy was where a man could escape if he could scale the side of a mountain five hundred feet high—a wall of slate that shoots straight up—and then face the sharp rocks and snake-infested bush on the other side. One man tried it and lasted five days. When James Earl Ray, convicted assassin of Martin Luther King, Jr., escaped over that mountain wall, it was the guards with their dogs who finally tracked him.

Brushy was a brutal place, a dumping ground for troublesome and dangerous inmates, the dregs of other prisons. Men were treated like animals, and animals were what many of them became.

Weapons were confiscated every day, and still the entire prison population seemed to be armed. In the lobby outside the administration offices, an array of home-made knives and guns were displayed in a glass case: shanks made from steel slats in the ventilators; screwdrivers sharpened to stiletto-fine points; zip guns; and pistols and other free-world weapons that came into the prison inside books and other packages. Hacksaws and wire cutters were smuggled from the machine shop. It was said about Brushy that a man could get anything he wanted there if he could pay for it, and do anything he wanted but leave.

Located eighty miles northwest of Knoxville in Morgan County, the prison is one major source of income for the community. The other is strip mining. Wartburg, the county seat, has a population of 761. There are five blacks in the county, all members of the same family. They are the only blacks the people of Morgan County have ever laid eyes on. But they hear about the black inmates over there in the hollow from the guards who work there. Almost everyone in those parts has had a relative or neighbor at one time or another who's worked at Brushy. They've all heard stories.

For the past few years a group of black inmates, all from Memphis, all serving life sentences, had taken control of the prison population. They ran an extortion racket enforced with threats of beatings, stabbings, and gang rapes. Two men who called themselves the godfathers, James Mitchell and James Nichols, were both serving sentences of 120 years for first-degree murder. They and their men were housed in D block, a building that was used for both violent offenders and high escape risks. Called Administrative Lockup, it was in fact a prison within a prison. There a man was kept locked in his cell twenty-three hours and fifteen minutes a day, let out only forty-five minutes for exercise.

White inmates were forced to pay twenty dollars a week to the mob. They'd make their weekly payments with money their families sent for toothpaste and soap and stamps. They'd have to turn over their TV sets, radios, tape decks—as well as their bodies—on demand. If they dared stand their ground, they'd be held by two men and beaten by two more. Or stabbed. Or raped.

A new black, upon entering the prison, would be approached by one of the mob, given the name of someone who needed killing or maiming, and told what would happen to him if he failed to carry out orders.

The South still winces from charges of racism; southern prisons, hotbeds of racial violence, are a prime target. Cries of racism bring an immediate response from civil rights groups around the country. As a result, the prison administration began to back off from such confrontations, tipping the balance, some whites feel, and making a Memphis Mafia possible.

At Brushy Mountain housing is divided into wings, called "blocks." Inside the blocks are levels, called "walks," which house ten cells. At the end of each walk, next to the shower, is a locked gate that leads to the walkway.

Kirk and Crafton were put in B block, on 4 walk, one level down and across from 5 walk, where members of the Memphis mob were housed. Their cell had no hot water, no lights, and, for a long time during the coldest months, no heat. They slept fully clothed, wearing thermal underwear, two or three pairs of socks, a hat, and gloves. And still they'd round up all the blankets they could get their hands on. Inside the cell they could take three and a half steps forward; sideways it measured one and a half steps. Food, never hot, was slid under the cell door. Any complaint was met with, "File a grievance with the administration." Periodically, all the men in that block would throw their trays in protest. In general, the attitude of the staff was, "Hell, they're only getting what they deserve. This ain't no hotel."

Hatred for a convict is personal. He is despised, regarded as subhuman, an aberration. And he is feared.

And so he is warehoused, put out of sight. Tennessee's Governor Lamar Alexander, noting the cost of such warehousing—nearly ten thousand dollars a year per inmate—said, "For a dollar a year more we could send them all to Harvard."

Brushy Mountain is out of the public's eye, tucked away miles from the watchdog media. It is run by unsophisticated, uneducated, underpaid men, many of whose fathers were guards in the same prison, who grew up hearing stories of whippings and beatings. To the administration at Brushy, the real enemy is a meddlesome judge.

In 1982, Judge L. Clure Morton would declare Brushy Mountain State Prison unconstitutional, the conditions cruel and unusual punishment. He would call the cells in D block, where Kirk had lived for two years, dungeons. In 1983, D block would be closed down and Brushy turned into a classification center, housing men for no more than three weeks.

Over the years, both in and out of prison, Kirk had constructed a network of friends, followers in a sense, who held him in high regard. He had a presence, a sense of himself that they liked. He was fair; his dealings, at least among thieves, were honest; he kept his word. And when he was approached, as he often was, with a problematic situation, he was a careful and attentive listener. Kirk treated the guards with respect, and he expected no less in return. Other inmates were pushed and prodded; not Kirk. Below the cool exterior, but not so far from the surface, was a man who knew he would do whatever he thought he had to.

An inmate who accepts the fact that he will live out his life in prison can be observed sitting hours at a time, day and night, in front of his TV, if he has one; and when the day's programming has ended, he'll sit there and watch the flickering shadows on the screen. The man who refuses to accept that fate can have only one goal—to escape.

From the moment he knew he was going to Brushy, Kirk had only one thought: how soon and by what means to escape.

He was transferred from Nashville on an old school bus the state used for transporting convicts. There were heavy steel straps across the windows. Kirk wondered if there was a window in the bathroom too. After a while he went to have a look. There was one, and it had only two iron bars on it. Good, he'd remember that.

At the end of December, he fell ill in Brushy. He was taken to a hospital in Oak Ridge where tests showed that he had a kidney stone. Arrangements were made to transport him, on the same bus, to Baptist Hospital in Nashville to have the stone removed. In excruciating pain and running a high fever, he somehow made it to the bathroom. He'd refused the pain medication; he needed to stay awake. Inside his prison jumpsuit he'd hidden a small hacksaw and a jar of black shoe polish. Sweating, the pain so bad he wanted to scream out, he sawed away at one of the bars. It was getting dark and it was raining, which was lucky; the rain would rust the bars where they were freshly cut. Until then the shoe polish would cover the marks. The guards paid no attention to how long he was in the bathroom; they just figured the poor guy was sick. By the time they'd reached Nashville, Kirk had one of the bars sawed completely through and had started on the second.

The next day he was operated on. He was kept in the hospital another full week. On the day he was to be released, the prison sent only one elderly guard instead of the usual two transportation officers. Kirk knew the man and remembered him as something of a nut. On the bus

Kirk told the guard he was supposed to undo his chains so he could go to the bathroom. The guard promptly unlocked all his restraints.

"I looked at his pistol. Damn. I had a bunch of staples and a drain in my gut; otherwise, I could've made it, easy. So I missed that chance."

Back at Brushy, Kirk requested a meeting in the law library with fellow inmates Ricky Moorman and Jack Blankenship. Tennessee prisons are required by law to provide inmates with a room in which to hold legal conferences and to make books available for research. At Brushy the law library was also the pool hall, the chapel, and the room where inmates could meet to discuss their "legal problems." There were two half-empty bookcases over in the far corner. The reading matter consisted mainly of pamphlets donated by church groups—the Union Rescue Mission, Temple Baptist, Good News Testament—and some books, one by Billy Graham, another called *Dealing with the Devil*, a children's book by Kate Greenaway, and a couple of inspirational books, *Living Positively*, *Selected to Live*. The few outdated law textbooks had pages torn out.

Behind the law library was the chaplain's office. A fluorescent-lit oil painting dominated the room. Eight feet tall, it was a larger-than-life Jesus, dripping with lipstick-red blood.

The legal business that Kirk, Moorman, and Blankenship met to discuss that night concerned Kirk's scheduled trip back to the hospital at the main prison in Nashville a few weeks hence for a postoperative checkup. They devised a plan so that all three could be on that same bus to the hospital: Kirk for his checkup, Blankenship with a kidney ailment Kirk would coach him to fake, and Moorman for a back injury that he would soon begin to complain of.

Once on the bus they would take turns sawing the second bar in the bathroom, disguising the cuts with shoe polish. Then, that evening after their doctor's appointments, they'd board the bus again and make their move.

The timing was crucial; they would have to jump off before the bus picked up speed. The interstate was only a half mile from the prison compound, just the other side of railroad tracks.

On May 21, 1981, everything went exactly as planned. One by one they slipped into the bathroom. Blankenship was the first one out the window; Moorman was next. By the time Kirk jumped, the bus had picked up speed and was doing better than fifty miles an hour. He broke his heel and ankle in the fall. Blankenship had already disappeared down the railroad tracks. Moorman was running fast but stopped when he looked back and saw Kirk limping. Kirk called out to him to keep going. Moorman ran back and slipped a shoulder under Kirk's arm for support; together they got a mile and a half before the Metro Nashville police picked them up.

Blankenship was captured in Arkansas three days later, but Moorman and Kirk were shipped back to Brushy. This time Kirk made his entrance on crutches, his leg in a cast.

The atmosphere in the prison had changed. The air was so highly charged that Kirk could feel it on the surface of his skin. It jolted him awake some mornings, and his sleep was fitful. There'd been a steady increase in the incidents of violence since he'd first arrived in December. One by one men who'd been making the extortion payments to the Memphis mob stopped. Emboldened perhaps by Kirk's presence or simply following his example, they stood their ground. Mitchell and Nichols, afraid they were losing face as well as their position as kings of the hill, stepped up their terrorist activities and began to direct them at Kirk's friends.

Carl Crafton was caught one evening as he was coming out of the shower. A jar of boiling Magic Shave was thrown in his face, nearly blinding him. Some days later, one of the mob made a lance by tying a knife to the end of a broom handle. As Crafton walked by, the man shoved it out between the bars. Crafton threw his towel over the thing and twisted it away so that he suffered only minor knife wounds.

TBI agents who police the prison and who are called out there every time a stabbing or a shooting occurs say, "The only people out at that prison who aren't armed are the guards."

Ricky Moorman was hit out in the yard. The guard who "patted him down" on the way out found the knife Ricky had hidden in his clothes. Ricky said to him, "You're not going to send me out there without it, are you?" And the guard, who knew the others were all similarly armed, and who wasn't prepared to do anything about that, let him go. Hours later, Ricky was found stabbed and was taken to the medic for treatment.

Billy Joe Linticum was cornered one day in the pool hall by members of the mob who demanded to know why he was late with his payments. Billy Joe looked around, saw that he was alone, and promised to pay up that next Friday. They jumped him anyway, stabbed him, then climbed out of the window and were gone by the time the prison police got there. They took Billy Joe to the infirmary.

Then in September it was Kirk's turn.

"There was that little voice in my head again that morning. I was out in the yard, hobbling around on my crutches. . . . It was nine o'clock. On the other side of the fence I could see Mitchell and Nichols—all of them there watching me. Hey Tim," one of them called, "come over here; Danny's got something to tell you.

"And even though the little voice in my head warned me, I hobbled on over. I got to the part of the fence where the breezeway was, which was out of sight of the tower. I heard something behind me—a footstep on gravel. There was only time to turn a fraction. I knew what was coming. I knew my best chance was to turn so that the knife would at least miss my heart."

It was a long screwdriver, honed razor sharp, that they used.

"I felt that steel go into my body again and again. It punctured my lung, and I could feel the life drain out of me. When I knew I couldn't stand any more I grabbed at one of them to try to bring him down with me. If only I could get the knife out of his hand. . . .

"Out of the corner of my eye I could see Cowboy, a friend of mine, over there, talking on the phone. He was turning round and round, trying to see what was happening. He turned so fast the cable got all wound around him. He dropped the phone and ran over."

By then Kirk was on the ground and they were stomping on both his legs. Cowboy yelled out for help as he struggled to pull the men off Kirk. Guards rushed over, then the prison police.

Kirk refused to be carried out on a stretcher.

They were going to see that he could walk—with two broken legs now, and bleeding like a hog.

He was taken to the hospital emergency room in Oak Ridge, where a drain was inserted into his lung. He had seven severe stab wounds and casts on both legs. That was noon Saturday; on Tuesday he was back at Brushy in a wheelchair.

Notes were waiting, hand-scrawled: "We know we've put fear in your heart. . . . next time we'll finish the job." "We're inside your head now; we know what you're thinking."

Friends wrote too, asking what he wanted them to do. They were ready, they said, waiting for word from him.

Kirk and Crafton talked it over.

"What're you going to do?" Crafton asked.

"Deal with it," Kirk answered.

"How?"

"I'm not going to ask them to put me on seven or eight walk [a check-in for inmates who wanted protection]. I'll handle it."

"How?" Crafton insisted.

"I don't know yet. Maybe I'll get a gun. It's not time for runnin' though, I'll tell you that. If I run they'll catch up with me one day, and I'll have to deal with it then."

Kirk tried to reason it out. "When a country's at war, they take a man off the street, give him a gun, and tell him what the enemy looks like—then he's supposed to go and shoot him. That's okay, right? Now these bastards, they're laying in wait for me. And all of a sudden I'm laying in the hospital with a lot of holes in me and another broken leg. Am I supposed to pretend it's not happening? Out in the street if you don't want to fight back, you can hop a plane or bus and get the hell away from him. But they got us all locked up in here together. In a place like this when someone tells you they're going to kill you, it's a good idea to take that very, very seriously."

In his cell he began to exercise his arms; then, when the casts came off, he began to work his legs, to build up the weak muscles. He'd do that out in the yard; he wanted them all to watch his progress.

The prison grapevine is as efficient a system of communication as man has invented. It was known among the inmates in segregated lockup that there was a .25 caliber gun out in the prison population. Kirk sent word that he wanted to buy it.

By January 1982, the tension between the two factions had come to a breaking point. During the time Kirk was recovering, getting himself back in condition, the mob had been able to get a .32 automatic into the prison. They'd pulled it on David Reeves out in the yard. He was monopolizing the phone, they told him.

Then sometime during the third week of January, Nichols trapped a new white inmate, a young boy, in the yard, and all six of his men raped him.

On February 6, a Friday, Crafton got a letter from Reeves telling him to alert the others on 4 walk. The mob was getting ready to do something. Larry Wimberly, a member of the Memphis gang, had already bent the lock on his cell door and was walking in and out at will.

Sunday morning Crafton got word the Memphis gang had bent the slam, the steel bar that extends across a whole row of cells and acts as a master lock. Kirk sent another message out to the population, an urgent one this time, to get the gun to him right away. That afternoon it came.

That Sunday night the walks were unusually quiet. Officers Sawyers Jordan, Michael Hall, Obra Seivers, and Richard Oren were on duty. Their station was at the end of the walk, separated from the cells by a locked gate. Each officer was equipped with a two-way radio; on the desk was a telephone to the outside.

Officer Seivers had just returned from passing out bed linens. Inmate Jimmy Carter had just got a telephone call, and Officer Jordan had gone to get him; it turned out Carter was in chapel, so Jordan returned to the desk to tell the caller that.

Crafton had been moved to another walk after the second incident against him, and Kirk's cellmate was now Billy Reece. Reece was "rock boy" that week, the name for the inmate assigned to janitorial duties. Since the rock boy is responsible for keeping the floors of the walk and the shower clean, his door is kept unlocked so he can go in and out of his cell. The gates at either end of the walk are kept locked, however.

At seven-thirty, Reece, mopping the walk outside his cell, called to one of the officers and said that Billy Joe in the next cell needed to see him.

Officer Oren unlocked the gate and started down the walk. When he got to Kirk and Reece's cell, Kirk said, "Don't move or I'll shoot you." Then he reached around and pulled the officer's keys from him.

At that moment inmates Roger Bowlin, Robert Gibson, Blankenship, Linticum, Brown, and Earl Neeley, all armed with knives and shanks, rushed the desk and took the officers' keys and radios. Officer Oren was taken hostage; the others were locked in an area down the walk, away from the desk telephone. As Kirk and the other six inmates started up the stairs to 5 walk, someone called out, "Pick a guard to come up with us. We need another hostage."

Neeley went down and chose Officer Jordan. John Henry Brown took him, and holding him at the neck, knife in hand, said, "We're going up on five walk to kill some niggers."

Neeley squatted down, hiding behind the wall. The cell block fell silent. Neeley reached up and unlocked the gate to 5 walk. It clanged open. One of the men whispered to the guards to walk ahead, all the way to the end, and stand facing the wall.

Then Kirk began to walk, his footsteps echoing hollowly on the concrete floor. He stopped. A moment passed in which it seemed not even a breath was drawn, and suddenly three deafening shots exploded. A scream, a groan, and all was still for a beat. Three more shots rang out. Footsteps sounded again, slow and deliberate, followed by two more shots. Empty cartridges rolled down to the walk below and bounced off the cement.

"Come out from behind that bunk so we can see who you are," Kirk said. Then, "Okay, you're cool." He continued walking, stopped, fired two more shots. All was still again.

"Are you finished?" Gibson called out.

"No, not yet," Kirk answered. He was reloading.

Another round of shots rang out. "Now we're finished."

Someone said, "I don't think this one is dead."

"Well, pull him over to the bars and stab him a few times."

"Someone jammed the locks. If he's not dead, it'll take longer to get in there to get him help."

*   *   *

Gary Neil Tate had worked as a medic at Brushy Mountain for four and a half years. His training as an emergency medical technician made him invaluable in a prison where no week went by without at least one incident of violence. The men, many of whose lives had been saved by his quick attention, had come to trust him.

Tate had come on duty at two in the afternoon that Sunday. The infirmary was adjacent to 5 walk; the door had a window through which he could see almost the entire length of the walk. At seven o'clock that evening he was cleaning up the examining room. With him was Lloyd Neece, an inmate who was helping him, and a guard, Officer Jeffers. When the first shot was fired, Tate rushed to the door and looked out its window. Just inside the gate to 5 walk, he saw an inmate he knew to be Neeley hunkered down, holding a knife and a set of keys. Behind him was Gibson yelling into a two-way radio: "We've took five walk and we got two hostages up here with us, and two more downstairs on four. Don't nobody try to come in or we'll kill 'em."

Tate turned to Officer Jeffers. "Call downstairs and tell them to seal off B Block."

Several more rounds of shots were fired; then the shooting stopped.

Tate looked through the window to his left. He could see Kirk standing in the shower area reloading his gun.

Tate called to Gibson. "Let me speak to Kirk."

"Who's Kirk?" Gibson asked.

"You know who Kirk is. Tim Kirk. Let me speak to him."

Kirk came to the infirmary door with the pistol in his hand.

"I want those hostages that you have, Tim. And I want the weapons too."

"Doc," Kirk said evenly, "we've got to do what we've got to do. I'll surrender the gun and the hostages if you'll promise that none of us will get hurt."

"Nobody's going to hurt you. Just give me the gun."

Deputy Warden Hobbs had just come into the infirmary.

Kirk said, "I'll be back."

Gibson was still talking loudly and excitedly into the radio. Warden Hobbs wanted to know what was said between Kirk and Tate. As Tate repeated the conversation, more shots were fired. They both looked out of the window and saw Kirk standing in front of one of the cells.

Kirk came back to Tate's door and saw Warden Hobbs standing just behind the medic.

"Doc," Kirk asked, "will you stand by your word?"

"Yes."

"What about Warden Hobbs? Will he give his word we won't be hurt?"

Tate looked at Hobbs. Hobbs nodded. "Yes, we'll do as promised."

The warden told Officer Jeffers to open the door.

Kirk said, "Okay, I'll give you the gun first; the others will hand you their weapons." Kirk dropped the clip about halfway out of the gun and started to lay it on the floor. Tate reached down and took it out of his hand.

Then Gibson came forward and laid the radio and his knife on the floor. One by one the men lined up and handed Tate their knives, handles first. Then they walked over to a table against the wall and stripped off their clothes for a body search.

As the men were led away, Kirk turned to speak to Tate. "Doc, when you testify, will you just tell it like it is?"

When Special Agent Bob Newby of the Tennessee Bureau of Investigation got to the scene, he thought how quiet it was. "Normally, it's like a zoo. Whenever the police or TBI walk past the cells, the inmates will yell obscenities and spit at you through the bars. One TBI agent had a pail of urine thrown at him. But that Sunday night, the place was real quiet.

"They were bringing in stretchers to carry out the dead bodies. Nichols bled all the way from his cell to the ambulance, right to the morgue. Just like the proverbial stuck pig. One of the guards said that was the only way he wanted to see that man leave prison.

"Mitchell was lying face up on the floor in a pool of blood. Looking at the way the pillow was arranged at the end of his bunk, I'd say he was lying there reading the book there beside him. It was *The Anarchist's Cookbook*. We found a large toenail clipper sharpened to a fine point on the top of his table.

"Wimberly was just standing there against the bars. He'd escaped unharmed by hiding in the corner of his cell behind two mattresses. We found bullets inside the mattress.

"[Memphis mob members] Jones and Hawkins had both been taken to the hospital. It had taken a while to get the cell doors opened. Electric cord was wrapped around the bars and tied, and the locks were jammed with pieces of paper, matchsticks, and broken-off pieces of an ink pen. Blood was all over their cell. It looked like everything they had was dumped on the floor. A cabinet, a TV, and a pile of laundry were all piled up in the corner as a barricade.

"Two young blacks, nineteen years old, had just been put on that walk two days ago. They were scared to death. They didn't know if they were going to be shot. They hid behind their bunks and mattresses.

"We tried to take statements from the seven. Gibson said, 'We had a job to do and we went and did it!' They were in a jovial mood, like they were pleased with what they'd done. Gibson and Neeley had been attacked from behind with a meat cleaver by one of the Memphis gang. Blankenship was a real escape artist—once while he was on escape, he'd gone and gotten himself a job as a security guard for a while. Not a bad guy, in a way. But Gibson, he's crazy. I wouldn't want to turn my back on him.

"A snitch offered me some coffee. I said, 'I don't know if I want any of your coffee.' 'It's okay,' he said. 'It's only been poisoned once that I know of.' "

The only one who wouldn't talk to anyone was Kirk. He said he had nothing to say.

But inside the prison there was a new king of the hill. Kirk had been attacked and threatened, and he had handled it. He had taken care of business the way a man should. A punk would have asked to be put in check-in, a snitch would have run to the administration; either would have been ostracized even by his own friends. In the prison system there is no lower form of life than a punk or a snitch.

In March, the Morgan County grand jury indicted William Timothy Kirk, John Henry Brown, Billy Joe Linticum, Jack Blankenship, Earl M. Neeley, Roger Hal Bowlin, and Robert Gibson on two counts of first-degree murder and four counts each of felonious assault with intent to commit murder and kidnapping.

Judge Lee Asbury of Morgan County was a craggy, white-haired man in his fifties with crisp blue eyes and skin ruddy from years of fishing the glass-like local lakes. Many of the cases on Judge Asbury's docket originated at Brushy, often six stabbings a month, but this was a full-scale shoot-out that had made the front pages of every paper in the state. He was angered by the shootings. Padding about his office in his stocking feet, his desk piled high with books and papers, he wondered at a system that would throw these men together in one cell block.

"Around these parts," he said to a friend, "pit bull fights are a popular—and illegal—sport." His blue eyes glinted with meaning.

His office was in a back room on the ground floor of a squat brick building across the street from the courthouse.

In the front room where his secretary sat there were two or three men in work jeans, flannel shirts, and red baseball caps, just sitting and passing the time of day, almost every day. They worried about what would happen if those men ever broke out of that prison up there in the hollow. The men sitting around Judge Asbury's office agreed that Brushy was a jungle, "and everybody knows that in a jungle you either got to kill or be killed. But, hell, they should ought to've left them poor guards out of it."

It wasn't until August that attorneys were appointed. Judge Asbury made up a roster of the East Tennessee criminal lawyers he thought most capable of trying a major capital case. All were accustomed to six-figure fees. As court-appointed counsel, each would appear for a token fifteen hundred dollars.

Of the seven appointed, four were from Knoxville. James A. H. Bell, a thirty-four-year-old partner in the firm of Tipton and Bell—formerly Ritchie, Tipton, and Bell—would represent Tim Kirk.

Jim Bell had grown up in Fountain City where his father owned an appliance store. Now he lived with his second wife, Karen, in fashionable West Knoxville, and drove to work in his brown Mercedes convertible. His office, of plush tufted leather, gleaming mahogany, and old lithographs, was on the fifteenth floor of the stately old Hamilton Building. Bell would make national news twice in the next two years. In August 1983 he would defend the Reverend Larry Hamilton, a minister in the Church of God of the Union Assembly whose twelve-year-old daughter, Pamela, had bone cancer; her father had refused medical treatment on religious grounds. Jim Bell would appear on *Good Morning America* in New York, *The Phil Donahue Show*, and *Nightline*.

Under Tennessee law, all seven attorneys were entitled to associate counsel. Jim Bell was destined to make national news the second time when he appointed Mary Evans to the case.

Bob Ritchie was appointed to represent John Henry Brown. At forty-three, Ritchie was considered one of the best criminal defense lawyers in the state and had established a reputation nationally. A country boy from Laurel County, Kentucky, he went into law after first considering a career as a minister. A year after his appointment to the Brushy case, he would be elected president of the National Criminal Lawyers Association. He would be responsible for the formation of a committee that would assist lawyers defending persons facing the death penalty. The committee was formed because of "vengeance from the death penalty's return in 1984," Ritchie explained. "Criminal defense lawyers will never accept the death penalty for a client. There is no fair way to impose it. The system is not sufficiently perfect to use death as a penalty. There ought to be one execution on televison; that would eliminate it forever."

Bob Ritchie told the court he would appoint twenty-seven-year-old Janet Vest as associate counsel.

Chapter Six

On August 25, Mary Evans and Janet Vest drove to Brushy Mountain State Prison. It was noon and blistering hot. They talked about the case they were assigned to, their first major case. They were both adamantly opposed to the death penalty and determined that their clients would not go to the electric chair.

At a quick glance Mary and Janet seemed similar, their lives parallel. They were fourteen months apart in age; both were attractive, blond, well dressed, befitting the two prestigious law firms they worked for. Janet had grown up in Johnson City, Tennessee, population fifty thousand. She was the youngest of three children whose father worked as a building inspector and real estate appraiser. He was also a city commissioner. Janet got her degree in Corrections and Social Work at East Tennessee State University, then went on to the University of Tennessee Law School.

At a closer look, the similarities ended. Janet was just under five feet tall, with a small-featured, almost kewpie-doll face, and she liked to chatter. Mary had no small talk. Janet's social behavior was conventional. She did not—as Mary was known to do—go around spreading stress. A pleasant "good morning" did not in any way compromise her principles. Mary reserved her wishes for a good morning for the very few close, loyal friends who, to her way of thinking, deserved one. As one friend put it, "Let's face it; Mary Evans just doesn't do charm."

Janet's voice was light; the words rushed out in an almost childlike way. Mary's husky voice was flatter, her humor dryer.

As they neared the rural hamlet of Wartburg where the green rolling hills gave way to mountains, bluish in the distance, they could see the tall jagged mountain called Brushy. At the bottom of the mountain sat the medieval fortress incongruously painted yellow—the prison. It was a grotesque fantasy that lay before the two young attorneys.

At the main gate they were asked for credentials and told to wait. Some minutes later, a white pickup truck appeared. The driver was a heavy-set woman in a tan uniform. She got out and walked toward them. Her hair was shoe-polish black, closely cropped and shaped to a V in back; her lips were painted vivid red.

She took them, one at a time, into a shack just inside the gate and searched them, her hands roughly feeling their bodies for weapons concealed inside their clothing. Her red mouth twisted into a smirk when Mary reminded her that they were attorneys.

They were allowed to bring their briefcases but were told to lock their purses inside the car. They climbed into the truck to be driven up the hill to the main building. Mary's anger smoldered as the truck bounced along the unpaved road.

At the next checkpoint, they were met by armed guards who issued visitors' tags and escorted them down a narrow hallway, past the warden's offices, and on to the next set of gates.

The floors now were no longer carpeted. The pungent smell of disinfectant stung their nostrils. Steel gates clanged and clanged again, echoing inside their heads.

They came to a breezeway that led to the prison yard. To the left were two small conference rooms where attorneys met with clients. Mary and Janet stared past the set of trap gates that opened onto the yard. The temperature had soared to well over ninety that day. The men wore jeans without shirts. Scars and tattoos were visible; bandannas were tied around their foreheads to keep sweat from their eyes. Three or four were at the basketball net, half-heartedly shooting baskets; others sat idly in groups of two or three on the cement ledge that rimmed the steamy yard.

"In here, girls." The guard unlocked a conference room door and Mary and Janet entered. It was large enough only for a desk and two chairs. The door was half-windowed, with wire mesh covering the glass.

Kirk was standing in his cell looking over the letters that had been written to him regularly since the shooting. He celled alone now, using the top bunk as a kind of desk to spread his papers on and lean up against as he made notes.

Last night word had come down the prison grapevine that a bunch of young women attorneys had been appointed to work on their cases. Remarks had been called out up and down the walk until the wee hours.

The letters he was rereading were from convicts in other prisons throughout the state. Some were from blacks, assuring Kirk they understood it was not a racial incident, as the papers were saying, that they believed it to be an act of self-defense. Others were threatening letters that had been intercepted and had found their way to him.

What's happening Bro Adell?

How's life treating you? Fine, I do hope. Well, as for myself I am doing fine far as health is concerned, but that's about all a nigger can say at this moment, because they have the brother back on Administration Lock-up for stabbing one of those white boy's friends that did that shooting in Brushy. I stabbed him about ten times in the neck and back, they thought he was dead, because he tried to go up the steps and fell out. I really don't see how he pulled through that, maybe he had a rabbit's foot with him. Yes, I came from Brushy—Reeves and Ricky Moorman jumped me. When we got to Nashville I had to have thirty-two stitches putted in my nose, but it wasn't about any shit because it will be another place and another time. I started to take that punk out a hundred times when we was on 5 walk because of that shit I heard about him. He won't be so lucky the next time, because I am sure about what part he played now. Have you heard anything from my sweet lady yet? When you do tell her I still love her. She is the sunshine of my life.

> Take care,
> your friend,
> "O"

P.S. Holler at my friend in 4 cell.

Another one was marked, "Knock on floor three times to let me know you got this."

T.K.:

Sent word to you I wanted a legal conference. Also sent it to Administration with NO response. I can understand the reluctants to talk with anyone Black, when so much shit being kicked around. Also requested Carl to assist me in a legal conference that he refused. Let me state clearly I have NO intent to capitalize off ya'll situation, I can never assist the justice system in any manner, nor would I attempt to advance my cause at the expense of ya'll. I know the administration is trying to have me kill. I know other Blacks that I broke ties with are trying to cross me out my life with lies. I know some Blacks in population had spreaded rumors and lies because they are paranoid of me. Blacks that I once associated with want me dead because I would not be a tool and take care of things that's irrelevant to me. I tried to get moved upstairs last week or so, because I knew it wasn't racist and wanted to set the example for all. I don't see anyone burning in the chair at this stage. They are using that as a fear tactic to keep things from gettin out of hand. . . . So be it, I'm a warrior and don't play games with people's lives. Now you know where my head's at—so anymore gossip around my name, please ignore it.

[signature crossed out]

Kirk looked up from the letters as a guard appeared at his cell door to tell him he had a visitor.

"Who?"

The guard gave him a crooked grin and winked. "She says she's your attorney."

Kirk glared back. "I'll be right with you," he said, and he gathered up his papers.

There were two women sitting, their backs to the door, in the conference room. Kirk looked at them through the window as he waited for a guard to come unlock the door. The one on the right wore her hair pinned up. She was bent over, looking for something in her briefcase. At the sound of the key in the lock she turned.

A shiver passed through him; his skin prickled. Kirk felt he was looking at a face he knew. And even before she spoke he knew how she'd sound.

John Henry Brown came into the room then. Stiffly, and with a certain awkwardness, the two young attractive women introduced themselves to the two not unattractive men whom they would be representing on first-degree murder charges. The four sat down across a table, each man facing his attorney. Kirk looked away, fixing his eyes on something across the room while he collected himself.

She had asked him a question. He realized he hadn't heard her name.

"Ma'am?"

"I asked you what your original sentence was."

"Sixty-five years for armed robbery."

He looked at her. I know who she is now, he thought. She is my punishment. Whenever it was that I formed the picture in my mind of the woman I needed to find, it was always this one sitting here in front of me now.

She was hunched over her papers, taking notes. Evidently he was answering her questions.

John Henry and his attorney were talking now, and Mary was listening.

For all the years I didn't care about the rules, Kirk thought, she is my punishment. Rules are for weak people, I always believed. Now I pay.

John Henry was explaining, "They knew they had a problem when Tim didn't die."

"What happened?" Mary asked Kirk.

Kirk forced his attention to answering her questions, nervously stealing glances at her when she was looking at the others. He described the events that led up to the shooting. "I had to protect my life. What would you do?"

"I don't know," she said. "I don't know all the facts."

"I didn't want to do what I did, believe me. I thought about my family—the news would be hard for my mother

and father to take. But it was a war there was no retreat
from. There was nowhere to go."

"But couldn't you have told someone? The administration?"

He tried not to smile. "Uh, that sort of thing just isn't
done here. It'd be better to just let them kill me."

Silence fell over the four. Mary reached for the indictment papers and began to read. The little short one—as
Kirk would come to call Janet—picked up her pencil and
wrote nervously. They both looked so young, even in their
lawyer clothes. Fresh-scrubbed, hair shiny clean, sitting
here in this dingy room. Kirk wondered if the smell wasn't
getting to them. He didn't notice it anymore, but visitors
always asked what it was. Disinfectant, industrial strength,
he'd tell them, mixed with the stench of rotting souls.

Kirk spoke quietly, his voice gentle. "When you're
put in places like this, what they want to do is strip away
every last bit of dignity a man has. That way society feels
justified. 'See,' they can say, 'they're animals, so we're
right to treat them like animals.' Actual physical life be-
comes less and less important living in these garbage cans.
It's what little dignity you can hold onto that's important."
He paused. "That, and being able to see the truth."

Seven hours and twenty minutes after they'd got there,
the lawyers were at the main gate signing out.

Janet started to ask Mary what she thought but she
stopped. Something in the way Mary looked kept her
quiet.

As they were driving away from the prison grounds,
Mary glanced in the rear-view mirror at the yellow fortress reflected there. "I feel," she said in a barely audible
voice, "I feel like I shouldn't ever go back."

"What?" said Janet. "What do you mean?"

Mary didn't seem to hear the question.

Kirk lay awake most of that night, too agitated to
sleep. Every time he'd close his eyes, her face was there.

The worst part of it all, he thought, is that she'll only be in my life a little while; then she'll be gone.

He waited all the next day for a guard to come tell him she was out there. With each hour that passed he grew more irritable, paced his cell, wishing he could scream out. That night he let himself slip into a depression. She wasn't coming back. It was too tough a case for a fledgling lawyer. Women shouldn't have to come into such a place anyhow. In his mind he listed all the reasons, preparing himself for the worst, until finally he slept—a heavy, dreamless sleep.

But then, incredibly, when he woke the next morning he knew she would come that day. He didn't know how he knew, but he did. He scrubbed his face, combed his hair carefully, and at ten o'clock when he heard the footsteps nearing his cell, the words were in his mind before the guard spoke then. "Hey Kirk, your lawyer's here."

Mary and Janet had brought a tape recorder and a camera with them, to begin their interviews with the guards and the other witnesses. They also intended to photograph the inside of the prison to illustrate the conditions. Mary began by firing a series of questions at Kirk, glancing only briefly across the table at him, then quickly lowering her eyes to her papers. Janet began to talk to John Henry and, for an instant, as though by accident, Mary's and Kirk's eyes met. Kirk drew in a breath.

For the last thirteen years he had disciplined himself to shut down feelings. In prison, feelings are dangerous; they weaken the spirit and threaten the mind with thoughts that cause pain. Now, however, a powerful wave of feeling rushed over him, catching him by surprise. It made his chest ache.

Cautiously, he looked up. She was half smiling at something.

"Let's go and see about those witnesses," she said to Janet as she packed up her papers. And they were gone.

*   *   *

After that day they began conferring separately. John Henry and Janet met in a separate room; Kirk and Mary were alone.

Bit by bit conversation slipped from the business at hand to life in general.

"What made you decide to be a criminal lawyer?"

"I wanted to help people who can't afford high-priced lawyers. Not everyone who's arrested is guilty as charged, but everyone deserves proper representation. This is a system where some get justice and some don't. It just depends on your bank account."

He asked her if she thought Jake Butcher would win the gubernatorial race.

"I don't care who's elected," she said. "I don't vote."

She had strong feelings about the death penalty though, and about prisons, especially this one. She hated hypocrites and phonies. Most of all she hated weaklings.

To Kirk, the boundaries between convicts and the free world were sharply drawn. It was "us" against "them." Convicts were the underdogs who "told it like it was" in the lingua franca of the underground, the subculture, and "they" didn't understand it. Even if they knew the words they still wouldn't get it.

To him, "they" were the nine-to-fivers whose lives were empty and who were too dumb to ask why. "They" were the drones who had no control over their lives because the ones in power saw to it they never got control. The ones in power were either very smart or very lucky. "We" were freer in prison than the dumb drones out there.

Kirk spoke in slow, rhythmic, melodious tones—thoughtful but easy. He didn't deny what he'd done; he took full responsibility for it.

"Lady, I'm just a thief." But he hastened to add that until he was forced into open combat with that group out there—he gestured to indicate the ones he'd killed—"I've never been involved in a single incident of violence."

He assured her he would never use his gun when he stole unless someone tried to stop him from getting away. "And that would be just plain dumb, because if you try to interfere with a man's business, you're likely to get hurt."

Crime was a big industry, he explained. Look how many people got rich. Lawyers, judges, wardens—look at all the corrupt officials who fed off crime. Politicians, police chiefs . . .

"Damn," he said, "why couldn't I have had an attorney like you when they gave me the sixty-five years? Look at all the work you're doing on this case. I know there're attorneys out there who work this hard for their clients, but they're sure as hell not court-appointed. I'd never have gotten all this time if I'd have had someone like you."

Wartburg in Morgan County has only one stoplight for its one main street. The stately old courthouse is up a good climb of steep, cracked steps. A walkway cuts across a wide expanse of lawn, past a Civil War monument or two, to the pillared entrance.

It was a brilliant October day; the blistering summer days that had lingered on into September were finally gone, and the air felt fresh. It was the sort of day when one would expect to see a smattering of townsfolk strolling down to the general store or just standing, passing the time of day.

But there was to be an arraignment at the courthouse at noon, and Wartburg looked as though it was getting ready for war. Uniformed men were arriving by the truckload, armed with rifles, machine guns, and pistols. State and local police, the Tactical Assistance Team, and townsfolk gathered, slack-jawed with wonder, and lined the street.

Then the Mercedes began to arrive, and some other

fancy cars no one could identify by name. The townsfolk gawked at the parade of Knoxville lawyers in their citified suits and ties—and the women lawyers! They looked like actresses on the TV screen.

As the courthouse bells chimed the noon hour, the prison transportation bus pulled up. The men and women of Wartburg drew their children to them and fell silent as the notorious seven were about to be taken down off the bus.

A few of the attorneys had lingered at the top of the courthouse steps, enjoying the autumn sun. They turned now toward the bus. Jerry Becker suddenly spotted his client, Billy Joe Linticum.

"Hey," he yelled, "will you get a look at that!"

The seven were all wearing the regulation bright orange Day-Glo jumpsuits made of heavy-duty canvas. But Billy Joe's had been chopped off just below the knees. Jack Blankenship was wearing a University of Tennessee orange-and-white football cap; John Henry Brown had cut his coveralls too and wore orange-and-white striped socks.

Bewildered titters from the crowd were drowned out by the clanking and clattering of seven pairs of manacles, belly chains, and ankle restraints.

Flustered guards hurriedly searched the men for scissors or a knife. To their dismay, they found nothing to explain how seven accused murderers from the most secure unit in the most maximum-secure prison in this part of the United States, who'd been strip-searched before they left, had managed to cut their pants!

The men were led up the courthouse steps; they filed past the crowd, looking as if it were all some part of a college fraternity initiation rite. Becker laughed out loud. "Bermuda shorts?"

Billy Joe grinned and winked.

One day in late October as Mary and Janet were being escorted to B block to an interview room, they came to an area at the bottom of the steps that was flooded with four inches or so of filthy rainwater from a recent rainstorm. Mary refused to walk through it and ruin her shoes. Instead, she demanded some other room be made available to them. The guard said he didn't think there was another room free. Mary glared at him. "Then I'll wait until there is one," she said, refusing to move.

Janet hesitated a moment, then tried to step across it, drenching her feet and shoes. Kirk observed the little drama with a sense of pride that his was the lawyer who wouldn't give in. A few moments later the guard reappeared. He'd found another room for them.

Mary had been spending hours, three and four times a week, at the prison, investigating conditions. She looked into the histories, prison records, and psychological profiles of the victims. She interviewed dozens of other inmates, some of them witnesses to the shooting. Sometimes she'd be there as long as eleven hours at a time. Gradually a picture of life at Brushy Mountain emerged. There was evidence that the administration had known that tensions between the two factions were about to erupt.

Mary transcribed a taped interview with inmate David Wolfenbarger:

Wolfenbarger is serving a ninety-nine-year sentence for murder out of Knoxville and is in 7 on C block. David told us a history of extortion and other horrors at BMP taking place since about 1976. He said that it all started when they brought Mitchell, Hawkins, Iceman, Conally, and Nichols together at BMP.

Around two years ago, David came around the gym. Mitch told him that starting on State Draw Day (the day on which inmates get their "draw" of an amount up to fifty-five dollars) that Mitch wanted fifteen dollars every month for the privilege of living in population. David told him he was crazy. Mitch told him to "go get your shit" (meaning knives or other weapons). David repeated that he was crazy and walked away. He told John Henry what happened. John Henry told him to tell Mitch to kiss his ass and not give him a damn thing. He said basically the war started around that period of time. David noted that they really hated John Henry Brown. He also knew about the hit list. He said it came down about maybe two years ago and had at least thirty names on it, that the guards were definitely aware of the list. In fact he believes he was told about the list by a guard. He was told to be careful, that the guards were basically on their side and knew that the black guys were nothing but trouble.

David witnessed the stabbing of Tim Kirk by Wimberly and Johnson. He said that at that time he was working in the kitchen so he was looking out the kitchen window down on B block exercise yard and he saw Victor Johnson and Larry Wimberly just come up and jump on Tim Kirk. Cowboy (Donnie Wolverton) jumped in to help. David said from what he could see there was no provocation; they just came over and started sticking him.

David said there was a lot of extortion going on—a lot of people were paying these guys, but they didn't want the other whites to know they were weak, so they tried to keep it quiet. It was even more trouble for them that way. He said that when young ones came in—eighteen years old or so—they either had to take up with the blacks sexually or get checked in (protective custody) or fight them for their lives.

He said that rumors were coming down through population every day that the niggers

were going to saw out of their cells and take out
John Henry and Billy Joe in D block. That was
even before the February 8 trouble. He notes
that another time some of the black guys jumped
on John Henry and Billy Joe on 2 walk (Janet
probably has more detailed notes on this since
John Henry is her client).

In Mary's memo describing her interview with Captain Sammy Carson of the Brushy administration, she
wrote:

It is to be noted first that Captain Carson is a
witness listed on the presentment by the state,
but he did not wish to be tape-recorded, so I
merely took notes while interviewing him. . . .
Captain Carson seems to be a fairly articulate
and friendly individual, but he is extremely eva-
sive. You are always given the impression that he
knows a lot more than he is saying, and of course
he did not want to be taped, which generally
gives one the impression that he has something
to hide. Captain Carson seems especially protective of the area regarding whether or not he and
other members of the administration, including
Warden Davis, were aware of the potential trouble between the defendants and the black group
before it occurred. Obviously, this is due to the
fact that if they were aware, nothing was done,
and I suppose it would make the Brushy Mountain administration look pretty bad that they had
not done anything to try to stop the trouble.
Therefore they are very reluctant to talk about
why cell changes were made in terms of putting whites and blacks together on the same
walk, when they are known to be enemies. He

seems, as far as I can tell, to be about third or fourth down in the line of command, but it's mysterious who exactly is in charge up there anyway.

Mary and Janet taped a joint conversation with Steven Jacks, a counselor at BMP, on September 28, 1982, at 1:05 P.M.

MARY: Steve, do you have any idea why you are listed on the presentment as a witness?

STEVE: . . . because I was a counselor to the block.

MARY: What exactly does a counselor do?

STEVE: Not a whole lot.

MARY: Ha ha.

STEVE: We mostly just run errands for the inmates, make telephone calls, check on their time and money. Try to help them with their problems.

MARY: Okay, at various times you have been counselor for both Kirk and John Henry Brown?

STEVE: Right.

JANET: What role did John Henry Brown play in this whole thing? How long have you known him?

STEVE: Since he's been at this institution. I guess it's been three years.

JANET: What's your impression of him?

STEVE: He's pretty respectful towards the staff. He doesn't take much off the convicts, you know, he doesn't go after them unless they come after him. He's got a bad history of carrying a knife around. Locked him up more than once for having it.

JANET: Why do you believe he played such a role in this? Does he seem to be some type of leader?

STEVE: That's a good question. I don't know if he was the leader of this or Tim Kirk was, but they all had so much time it didn't make no difference to them; they were going to be here for the next thirty years. As long as these two groups were here one or the other was going to be after each other all the time.

JANET: Why do you think John Henry seems to sort of protect younger, weaker convicts?

STEVE: It could be that he's got a son in prison, and John Henry has been in prison all his life and I guess he kind of figured how it was when he first came in.

MARY: Okay Steve, have you known that this has been tape-recorded the entire time we've been talking?

JANET: Wait a minute; I have one more question.

MARY: Let me finish this.

STEVE: Right.

MARY: And it's been with your permission?

STEVE: Right.

MARY: Okay.

Mary and Janet continue to question Steve Jacks about the events that led up to the shooting on February 8. In one of Mary's conversations with the staff, she was warned that Tim Kirk was one of the worst escape risks they had. She was told that he would do anything to escape.

One day in October, Kirk looked at her and said, "Hey, put away those papers a minute; I want to tell you something."

He watched her as she put them away. "I want you to know how much I appreciate all the work you've been doin'. If I had a lot of money, I'd give it to you. But hey, lighten up. There's really not that much you can do for me. Look, even if we win the case I don't meet a parole board for thirty years, so it really doesn't matter, don't you see?"

She frowned. "No, I don't see. What about the death penalty?"

"My life's not in your hands; get that out of your head. It doesn't matter whether they give me life or the death penalty. All I'm interested in is getting out of prison, any way I can. If there's any way to escape, whether it's today or tomorrow or next week, I'm going to take it. A man's got to be prepared to risk his life for his freedom.

"There's a strong possibility I might not be at that trial. I owe it to you to tell you that. I have another weapon and I intend to position myself to get away, and it might happen before that court date. So I really hate to see you do all this work, because you might have an empty chair in that courtroom."

She started to speak. He held up a hand to stop her.

"I don't care to hear any more about the case. It takes my mind off what I've got to do. As far as I'm concerned the problem's been dealt with. Lay it down; leave it alone. I was justified in what I did regardless of what any court of law says. Let the court go ahead and do whatever they're going to do with it. I'm going to go on about what I was doing when those bastards stabbed me. I was walking around on a broken leg from when I was trying to escape. I'm living in conditions the judge said were unconstitutional, that are unfit for human habitation. So it seems to me I have a constitutional right to remove myself from these unconstitutional conditions any way that I can. That's the way I feel. I don't know how Joe Blow feels or how Joe Public feels, but that's how I feel."

He almost grinned at his own logic, but Mary was clearly disturbed. In her mind, the loss of a life was more important than anything she could comprehend.

Regardless of what he said, she would continue to build his defense. In her notes, she wrote, "The defendant told me that he is very interested in escaping from prison, that he has always tried to escape on every occasion that he could find to do so."

When Jim Bell sent papers to be signed by Kirk requesting an appeal in the event the jury found him guilty and sentenced him to death, Kirk ripped the papers in half. "I'm not going to beg them for my life," he snapped to Mary.

Chapter Seven

November marked the end of the World's Fair which had come to Knoxville in 1982, bringing eleven million tourists from around the world. The party was over, and Knoxville was beginning to feel like the morning after.

Tourists cleared out of the city's hotel rooms. In their wake came two hundred faceless men from around the nation, silent about their business, and working into the night before strolling back down through the silence of Church and Gay streets. They were examiners of the Federal Deposit Insurance Corporation, and their target was Jacob Franklin Butcher, forty-six, known throughout Knoxville as Jake.

Jake Butcher had come out of the hills north of Knoxville fifteen years before with his brother, C. H. Butcher, Jr., known by his initials pronounced in the local vernacular as "Saitch." Their father, a cigar-chewing country banker who had come out of the Depression, had begged them not to go to the big city. "Them bluebloods will never run with a man who's plowed a mule," he warned.

Indeed the bluebloods of Knoxville, most of them Republican and conservative, did look down their noses at the Butchers. But they could hardly ignore them.

In fifteen years the brothers had built a banking empire that controlled twenty-seven banks in Tennessee and Kentucky, including Knoxville's two biggest. They presided over assets totaling $3 billion, and little happened in Knoxville without feeling their hand.

Jake Butcher had run for governor of Tennessee as a Democrat twice and had almost won in 1978. He had been the chief architect and chairman of the World's Fair, jaunting around the world to seek foreign participants. Tall, silver-haired, movie-star handsome, he was a churning bundle of energy whose tongue could not keep up with the speeding thoughts in his brain. Because of that, he spoke in sentence fragments, spewing them out in the flat mountain accent.

Butcher lived with his wife, Sonya, a former Broadway and Hollywood actress of B-grade movies, in a $2 million mansion north of town prophetically called Whirlwind. Often he commuted to work in a helicopter, landing on top of the twenty-seven-story glass tower of his bank that dominated the Knoxville skyline. Across the street, his brother was starting an even larger skyscraper. At Whirlwind, they often entertained celebrities like Jimmy and Rosalyn Carter and Walter and Joan Mondale. It was a homegrown Horatio Alger story.

But the two hundred faceless men were concluding that there was a far different vision of Butcher. On Valentine's Day in 1983, they closed his United American Bank in Knoxville, and in the following year a dozen more Butcher banks failed. As the dust cleared it became apparent that the Butchers had made more than $600 million in loans, many of them to each other.

Two years later Butcher would admit that he had used forged signatures, fake companies, and other means to steal more than $40 million from his banks, and he would be sentenced to twenty years in prison.

But the two-year downhill ride on the roller coaster had just begun in March 1982, and Butcher's story sent the lunch crowd at the Bistro, many of them close friends of Jake's, reeling. Someone remembered a statement Jake had made once: "The only way you can lose money when you have a bank is to shovel it out the back door."

Around the corner at Joanne and Earl's, the blue-collar crowd saw it differently. "Always knew those Butcher boys was crooks, just like their daddy was. Ev'body knows he was a damned land robber. Hope they go ahead and throw their asses in jail."

In the first week of November, Mary moved into Janet's two-bedroom apartment in a complex twenty minutes from downtown. In their hilltop apartment, Mary and Janet compared their inmate clients to people like the Butchers who flout the law and never seem to spend a day in prison.

They'd become obsessed with their cases, contacted anti-capital-punishment groups from around the country. Each week they filed new motions with the court, drew up new affidavits to be signed by still more witnesses Mary continued to turn up. Guards who at first had refused to talk to her gave in when it was finally clear she wouldn't quit hounding them.

Lunch dates were forgotten. Mary almost never went to her parents' home on weekends. Saturdays she'd put on a pair of jeans and spend the whole day and evening, sometimes until after eleven, at the prison. Twice when she got home at midnight, she found John Lockridge's card slipped under the door, an angry reminder that they'd had a date.

Mary and Janet had gone down to Nashville to the main prison to interview people the state had listed as witnesses. Among them was black inmate Hugh Briggs. That interview left them with a clear sense of the kind of danger their clients faced if a jury found them not guilty and they were returned to prison.

MARY: Okay, now Hugh you realize this conversation is being tape-recorded, and that's with your permission?

HUGH: Yeah.

MARY: Okay, uh, as we were just talking about the February eighth incident at Brushy Mountain, uh, I was just showing you that your name was listed on the presentment as a possible state witness. Do you have any idea why your name is on this presentment?

HUGH: No, I don't.

MARY: You have no idea whatsoever. Were you on the walk that night?

HUGH: I was laid up drunk.

MARY: Well, let me ask you this, did the TBI talk to you after?

HUGH: Not up there. I tell you what they did, they got me and sent me over here. I think it was about a week after, they come and got me out of bed at twelve or one at night, and put me on a special bus and brought me down here to Nashville.

MARY: Do you have any idea why they did that?

HUGH: They said it was because they had information that I had a pistol.

JANET: What did you say to them?

HUGH: Told them I didn't have one, I never had one, nobody never seen me with one, and wherever did the information come from.

JANET: Did they check—

HUGH: Well, around that time I was supposed to be the big drug dealer up there, and everything else, you know.

JANET: Did they shake down your cell?

HUGH: Yeah, they tore my cell up.

MARY: Never found any gun?

HUGH: No.

MARY: Okay, and then what happened after you got down here?

HUGH: Then I stayed locked up for three weeks. Warden Rose called me out and talked to me. Says he was giving me a break and not gonna keep me in lock-up. I was trying to explain to him that I didn't need to be locked up in the first place. Eventually he went on and let me out. As long as I'd be a good boy and keep my nose clean and all this kind of stuff. I said okay, but I'd do the things I been doing for the last ten or twelve years, you know, and I ain't had a write-up yet, you know, so—

JANET: What are you doing time for?

HUGH: Right now? Murder and robbery.

JANET: How much time you got to do?

HUGH: Three hundred and eighteen years.

MARY: Okay, now did—you were starting to talk about the TBI, that they came down here—

HUGH: They asked me did I know anything about it—I said no. Do you know the people that was involved, and I said yes. I know John Henry and Billy Joe, and I know everybody that was involved. I also know the people that got killed. They asked were you enemies with them—no. White or black, they asked— nope, I didn't have nothing to do with it.

MARY: Um-humm.

HUGH: 'Cause I was up there at Brushy for a disciplinary write-up. I got a murder charge while I was there, twenty-five years for killing another inmate.

JANET: Was it with a gun?

HUGH: Uh-uh. Knife.

JANET: Who would want to put you in this position? Do you have any idea?

HUGH: I've got a thousand enemies, just like I got a thousand friends. That's the way of life here.

JANET: What if they asked you if you knew anything about the trouble between the whites and the blacks? What would you say?

HUGH: I've already said that it was the blacks' fault. John Henry and them tried their best to dodge it—for years and years. It didn't just start right there, the shooting, it went on two or three years before that.

JANET: Do you think it was racial or just these particular blacks?

HUGH: No, it couldn't have been racial. . . . they passed black cells and they didn't shoot.

JANET: Right.

HUGH: Particular blacks, yeah. Just as it would have been if they'd had a pistol. They wouldn't have shot every white dude they see'd, they'd have shot the particular white dude. You know, whoever gets the first jump. . . . wasn't no racial thing.

JANET: Why was it John Henry Brown and Tim and those guys were the ones that ended up taking it into their own hands?

HUGH: Because they wouldn't put up with it. Tim got stuck, and he wasn't even involved in it. He went up on the yard one day and he got stuck. He didn't have nothing to do with it.

MARY: Just drug him into it.

HUGH: You get a situation where something has to happen and it just did. Uh, you tell yourself and you tell the other people okay we went too far. I mean we can't make friends here, we can't call it off, so now from here on in when we meet, somebody's got to go. In order for me to survive I gotta kill you, or in order for you to survive you gotta kill me. That's it. . . . I'll tell you what I call it. Even if it was did in a way that makes everybody else frown, I call it self-defense.

JANET: That's what we call it.

HUGH: Really, I mean just plain simple self-defense. Either a man's gonna kill you or you gonna kill him. Now how you do it, I don't guess that's important. The thing is that you gotta do it. You know if you stick him with a knife he's dead, or if you throw him off the walk he's dead, or if you shoot him he's dead, if you poison him he's dead, so I mean it's just something that's got to be done.

JANET: What's gonna happen now, do you think? Regardless of the trial, most of these people are still doing—like you said—life plus—

HUGH: What's gonna happen is that even if they get out of this case or whatever, they still got people that they're gonna have to hurt or they're gonna hurt them.

JANET: Do you think they can keep them apart? Do you think the administration will put them together?

HUGH: No they can't keep them apart; them people got too much time. They got three places they can send a man with fifty, sixty, seventy, a hundred years, and each one of the people involved got over a hundred years. We all know once you been up to Brushy they don't want you here, they don't want you at Fort Pillow, they don't want you at Turney Center, or nowhere, because once you been to Brushy you're undesirable. You only have to get one or two write-ups and they'll send you back to Brushy, so we all always wind up back up there together. Even the ones that are not supposed to be around each other. I mean most of us we can have a little disagreement and can talk it out after time goes by. You just leave me alone and I'll leave you alone. But see, in this situation there that ain't gonna work.

JANET: It's gone too far?

HUGH: Yeah, it's gone too far. People have already died, people's already made threats, and people's made promises. So we gonna just have to finish it out one way or the other.

During one of their interviews, Kirk explained to Mary how the warden could control the world behind the walls. Inmates he didn't like, who were uncooperative or too independent-minded, could be dealt with most effectively by putting them on a walk with their enemies. That way human nature would take care of the problem for him.

"This is the real world you're seeing. I guess it's a little different from what they taught you in law school. In the real world, justice serves only those in power, and it's spelled *just us*."

John Lockridge had been suffering from high blood pressure and frequent nosebleeds. He was scheduled to go in the hospital for tests. Kirk was aware of their relationship; sometimes in the evening when Mary was visiting them and they'd lost track of time, Lockridge would call the prison. A guard would knock at the door, tell her she had a call, and she'd be furious. "I don't like him checking up on me," she said. But when Lockridge went to the hospital, she was there for him, even missing a court date. She spent the day at the hospital reading to him.

Still, she explained to Kirk, the relationship was empty.

One evening Kirk asked her, "What do you think would have happened if we'd met—say in Knoxville, instead of in here?"

"I think wherever we met it would be the same," she answered.

Each night when he'd go back to his cell, he'd pace the floor wondering, Is she saying what I think she's saying? I've been in prison for thirteen years. I don't know anything about what's in a woman's mind. Is she really feeling the same way I am? How could she be?

Yet when he told her he liked the way she looked when she wore her hair down, she started wearing it that way.

He could spend whole days thinking about her. The days would fly by until she came back. And then she'd smile at him and he kept that smile inside of him; it lit his steel-gray world.

In early January, Mary walked into Jim Bell's office and told him they had a serious matter to discuss. It was about what he liked to call his "toothpaste method" of trying a case. "What you do is, the night before a trial, you take all the information your associate gives you and squeeze it into your ear."

Mary reminded him that in Kirk's case a man's life was at stake. Bell's toothpaste method wouldn't do. She believed she could get Kirk acquitted if he, Bell, would step aside. She wanted to try the case herself.

Bell recalled that he was outraged. As he saw it, this was a major capital case and Mary didn't have the skill or the experience to try it. Furious, Mary argued back that he hadn't done a lick of work on the case, that all he was interested in was keeping Kirk from the electric chair, whereas Mary saw a way to win the case with a solid self-defense argument.

The fight between them raged on until Bell ended it by firing her. If she wanted to, he said, she could finish doing the leg work, without pay.

Mary's only hope then was Judge Asbury. Maybe he could be convinced that Mary should be appointed lead counsel. Bell agreed to put in a conference call to him. Judge Asbury heard them each out and made his decision: Bell would continue to represent Kirk, but Mary could sit at the defense table if she wished. As to their dispute about how the case should be handled, they would have to settle that between themselves.

On January 14, Mary spent six and a half hours at the prison with Kirk. She told him about the fight. He listened very carefully as she, near tears, replayed the scene for him. His eyes blazed with anger when she told him she'd been fired. He got up and knocked at the door to summon the guard. He and his attorney needed to make an urgent phone call, he said.

When he got Bell on the phone, he told him, angrily, that he wanted him off the case. He intended to make a formal request to the court that Mary replace him as lead attorney.

That night when she got home she drew up her résumé:

MARY PENTECOST EVANS

PERSONAL DATA:
Address—1434 Northshore Woods, Knoxville,
Tennessee 37919
Phone—(615) 691–9530
Birth date—12/17/56
Marital status—Single

WORK EXPERIENCE
Legal
Law clerk, University of Tennessee Office of the
General Counsel, Suite 800, Andy Holt Tower,
Knoxville, Tennessee, for a period of eighteen
months during law school.
Responsibilities: Upkeep of law library, research,
some preparation of pleadings and other legal
documents. Primary focus: civil rights and educa-
tion law.
Law clerk, Lockridge and Becker, P.C., Sixth
Floor Park National Bank Building, Knoxville,
Tennessee 37902, for period of eight months dur-
ing law school.
Responsibilities: Same as above, and in addition
extensive investigation, and client interviewing
and contact. Primary focus: general civil practice
and some criminal work.
Current, June 1981—Associate, Tipton and Bell,
Attorneys, 1515 Hamilton Building, Knoxville,
Tennessee 37902.
Responsibilities: Engaged almost exclusively in
criminal defense work. I have had experience in
every aspect of a criminal case, including investigation, dealing with clients, trial preparation, us-

ing an exhaustive trial notebook method, and trial practice. I have practiced in sessions courts and in the criminal courts, handling my own cases, and also working closely with the other two attorneys of the firm on their cases. My work has included almost every type of criminal case, including misdemeanors, drug cases, theft crimes, fraud crimes, and murder including death penalty cases.

WORK EXPERIENCE
Nonlegal
Various part-time jobs to finance my undergraduate and legal education.

EDUCATIONAL BACKGROUND
Legal
Graduated June 1981 from The University of Tennessee College of Law, J.D. degree.
Honors and Activities: Member Student Bar Association, Phi Delta Phi legal fraternity. Completed Criminal Advocacy and Advanced Criminal Advocacy at the University of Tennessee Legal Clinic, which involved handling a wide variety of indigent criminal cases in general sessions court during basic and criminal court during advanced course.

Undergraduate
Graduated August 1978 from The University of Tennessee, Knoxville, B.A. degree.
Major: Philosophy
Minor: English
Honors and activities: Graduated with High Honors.
Member Alpha Lambda Delta, scholastic sorority; Philosophy Club.

ORGANIZATIONS:
Member of Knoxville, Tennessee, and American
Bar Associations, Tennessee Association of Crim-
inal Defense Lawyers, Knoxville and Tennessee
Trial Lawyers. Active in Lawyer Referral Service
and Knoxville Barristers.

MISCELLANEOUS:
Am willing to relocate anywhere in the United
States.

REFERENCES WILL BE FURNISHED PROMP-
TLY UPON REQUEST.

One of the places she applied for employment was
with the attorney general's office in Anderson County.
Attorney General James Ramsey, tall, good-looking,
Dartmouth-educated, found Mary "cold and a bit hard. I
especially didn't like the way she bad-mouthed her current employer. Matter of fact, I thought she was a bitch,"
said the man who, seven months later, would be her
prosecuting attorney.

She also applied for a position with the public defender's office in London, Kentucky, one hundred miles from
Knoxville. Mary said she was currently working on a major
death-penalty case and wouldn't be free until that was
over. Thirty-six-year-old Paul Zurkuhlen, directing attorney for the London, Kentucky, office of the Department
of Public Advocacy, was impressed with her criminal-law
background.

"I found her to be worldly wise for someone her age.
She was pragmatic about what a defense lawyer can and
cannot do. When I asked her why an attractive single
woman wanted to move to a town of four thousand she
said, 'Because I want to do trial work.'

"Then I asked her, 'If you were king what would you
do with someone charged with murder?'

" 'I'd turn him loose,' she said, 'because I'm crazy about them.' "

Even though Zurkuhlen thought that answer was "kind of weird," he decided that she was better qualified than the five other applicants. He told her to report for work on April 1.

The "magnificent seven," in collaboration with a few of the other inmates scheduled to testify at the trial, had worked out a spectacular escape plan: A pistol would be hidden in the bathroom at the courthouse. One of them would go in, get the gun, and take Judge Asbury as a hostage.

Carl Crafton, who sometimes called a newsman at Channel 2 News, knew a film crew was planning to arrive by helicopter to cover the trial. Another of the "seven" would hold a gun on the helicopter pilot while as many as possible climbed aboard and made their escape. The rest would escape on foot or in cars.

The grapevine had it that Mary Evans was in love with Tim Kirk and that "they were having privacy"—a prison euphemism for making love—during their prolonged visits. Tim, who'd got women to bring into the prison drugs or money or whatever he needed, could probably get Mary Evans to assist in the escape. Tim had a friend on the outside who offered to get a Mac-10 machine gun to her; she could bring it to the courthouse in her briefcase.

On January 14, Mary signed in at the prison at 12:16. A guard passing by the windowed interview room noticed them huddled together, almost—but not quite—out of view. Months later when the guard told of having seen them together, he explained his permissiveness by saying, "What the hell, a little privacy now and then makes 'em easier to handle."

Mary told Kirk about the new job.

"Just suppose," he said, weighing his words, keeping

his gaze steady, "I was able to get out of here, and I turned up on your doorstep in Kentucky. What would you do? Would you run me off?"

"No," she said finally, "I wouldn't."

"That's what's in my mind. It's what's always been in my mind, from the beginning."

Mary told him she was going away for a while. She wanted some time to think. She told him she might take a trip to San Francisco with John Lockridge at the end of the month.

Kirk tried not to show that it hurt. He knew he had no right, no call on her. She was free. If she had to be with someone to find out what she felt, he would handle it.

But when she reached up and kissed him on the cheek as she was leaving, and he watched her walk down the hall and disappear through the gate, he felt—for the first time in his life—real fear.

"For the next five weeks," Kirk said, "it was all just one long day. I kept thinking maybe she'd just stay gone. It got so I couldn't even stand to listen to music. I just pulled back inside myself like a hurt animal out in the wild. Even the guards stayed away from me. Man, it was bad. I didn't know anything could hurt that bad. I'd keep thinking, shit, this was the worst day of my God-damned life, and then I'd wake up and there'd be another one just like it. And another one after that."

During the night the temperature dropped to several degrees below freezing, and for the next three days Knoxville was paralyzed by the worst ice storm in years. The trees looked like glass figurines of silver and mauve. Streets and pavements glistened like mirrors, impassable by car or on foot.

In the prison, men slept dressed in every piece of clothing they could round up, including hats and gloves. Pipes froze, and they went without water. They hadn't had a hot meal in over a week.

On the fourth day the sun shone, and by afternoon the ice began to soften and Mary and John Lockridge were able to get to the airport.

In San Francisco they stayed at the Hyatt Regency on Union Square and went to some of the city's best-known restaurants. One day they drove over to Sausalito and had dinner at Alta Mira, a hilltop restaurant that overlooks the bay and the Golden Gate Bridge, and saw in the distance, rising up out of the water, Alcatraz.

It was on a Friday, February 25, at a little after eleven o'clock that a guard came to Kirk's cell door.

"She's here," he said.

Kirk turned quickly so the guard wouldn't see the sudden flush that must have reddened his face.

"Give me five minutes, will you, Jerry?"

Mary stood waiting for him. Kirk said later he'd never in all his life seen anyone more beautiful. They stood silently, smiling into each other's eyes.

They talked that day for eleven hours, stopping only to go to the food vendor machine to get a snack and a soft drink.

They spoke of ways they might arrange to continue to see each other after the trial. If his various escape plans failed, Kirk might be able to get transferred to Eddyville Prison in Kentucky under the interstate compact penal system. Mary offered to do some work on his Memphis conviction in her spare time, to try to get him a new trial. Sixty-five years for armed robbery was outrageous; if they could get that reduced, and they won this case. . . .

But somehow, no matter how they tried to figure out legal means that would allow them to see each other as frequently as they now decided they must, their conversation inevitably drifted back to escape.

While she had been away, the attorneys for the defense had filed a motion with the court for psychological examinations for the seven codefendants. Kirk had de-

clined. He thought it was a waste of time. Their only
defense, he maintained, was self-defense. But John Henry
Brown had been taken to Knoxville for testing by psychologist Kathy Broughan; the night he got back, he told Kirk
about it.

"They removed the restraints, man."

"All of them?"

"All of them."

Kirk thought about that. Now he said to Mary, "I
think I'm going to change my mind about having a psychological evaluation. I think I might like to have one."

"All right," she said.

"But I want to be up front with you," he said, watching her face carefully as he spoke. "If I see a shot when
I'm taking that test, I'm gonna go for it. Understood?"

Unflinching, she met his gaze. "I'll arrange it."

He lay thinking that night, running the conversation
over again in his mind. No, he said to himself, she *couldn't*
have understood what I was saying. She's a *lawyer*, for
Christ's sake, an officer of the court. I must be losing my
mind.

He thought about all they'd said during the eleven
hours they spent talking. She had told him how much she
liked being with him. That she felt she could relax and let
down the façade. She said she'd never been able to talk to
anyone in quite the same way; with him she was able just
to be herself.

And he'd told her he felt the same way. With her he
didn't have to be the mean, tough convict, Tim Kirk; that
she had a way of seeing through all that, to the man he
really was.

Then she had confided that she'd lost faith in the
justice system. She'd begun to see how the scales could be
tilted with money. Her life, she said, was empty. It wasn't
about anything. What goals did she have? Money? A big
house, car? No, she said, all she really needed was a man
she could care about, a kid, and a dog. All her life she'd

been looking for something with meaning. So far everything she'd found was hollow, didn't have any substance. Her life was so sheltered when she got her degree; she'd had no idea how much she would come to despise the law profession. Her eyes wandered past him, focusing on some distant mental picture, and she said, "Maybe if I gave them back my law license, they'd let me go."

Kirk got up and paced his cell. Go where? What was she saying?

During the month of March, Mary went to the prison almost every day. They got so used to seeing her at the checkpoint that some days she walked right by, without signing in or being searched.

Michelle Evans, a twenty-eight-year-old FBI agent, had been assigned to the Oak Ridge division, which included Brushy Mountain Prison. Her duties were to investigate civil rights complaints, money-order scams, and credit-card frauds and to question inmates suspected of having knowledge of federal crimes committed outside the prison.

Tall and willowy with long chestnut-colored hair, she looked more like a fashion model than a fed. But Michelle was third-generation law enforcement. Her father had left the FBI in California to practice law in rural Tennessee; her grandfather was a homicide detective with the Los Angeles Police Department. In July 1981, Michelle would marry Fred Evans, an FBI agent recently transferred from Newark, New Jersey, to Knoxville.

She hated going up to the prison. She always tried to cram as many interviews as possible into as few visits as she could. She'd come to hate the whistles and catcalls. She and Fred had to have their home phone number changed periodically lest the inmates drive her crazy calling. They always had a reason, of course, but at the bottom of it was their desperate, depressing loneliness.

One day early in March as she was about to sign in at

the front gate, she saw what looked like her signature, "M. Evans." Thinking the log book might have been opened to the wrong page, she looked at the date at the top of the page. It was correct.

"What's this?" she asked the checkpoint guard, wondering if someone was using her name. She started flipping back through the pages.

"That's the attorney, Mary Evans."

"What's she doing, coming here so much?"

The guard said, "And that's not the half of it either, what you see there. Half the time she slips by without signing in."

"She must be nuts," Michelle said, noticing the ten- and eleven-hour visits.

The guard wrinkled his nose. "She's somethin', all right, but I don't know's you'd call it nuts." Then he went on: "That girl don't care what the rules are; she just pushes her way through. And when you say somethin' to her, she's like to throw a fit. Says she'll call the judge, and the commissioner, and the governor. We just tell her go ahead. 'Ma'am, you can go ahead and call the President of the United States, we're still not gonna let you tell us what to do.' "

Michelle shook her head and hurried on about her business. In a matter of weeks she would be the case agent on her first UFAP (unlawful flight to avoid prosecution) case, and it would be Mary Evans she'd be tracking down.

Mary asked the Rural Legal Services for a psychologist in the area who did the kind of evaluation she needed. She was given the name of Gary Salk in Oak Ridge.

That night she told Kirk she was ready to make the appointment. Did he want her there with him?

They were sitting under the harsh light of the small interview room off the breezeway. It was late and unusually quiet. A single guard sat at his desk at the other end of the hall.

Kirk looked at her for a long moment before he spoke. "I told you what I might do when I get there."

Mary cocked her head to one side, a look of mock wonder on her face.

"You really are dense, aren't you?"

"Why? What are you telling me?"

"Tim, how dense can you get?"

Slowly, he asked her, "Is what you're telling me that you're going to help me get away?"

"Well, what've we been talking about all this time? We want to be together, don't we?"

"But for how long? You can't just throw away everything for a fling. I've spent a lot of years in these prisons, and I've seen a lot of people leave. Most all of them wind up coming back."

"We'll take what we can get. That's all anybody ever has, anyway."

On Thursday, March 24, at eleven o'clock, Mary telephoned Doctor Salk at his office. She explained that she was representing a man in Brushy Mountain who was accused of murder and that she'd like to come speak to him in person about testing.

She also explained there was a time problem, since the trial was only a week away. He gave her an appointment the following day.

She got there at one o'clock. Mary looked the office over very carefully, asking the doctor about exits and entrances, other offices in the building. She explained that those were things the guards would want to know ahead of time. Then she raised the question about the handcuffs.

"Mr. Kirk will arrive in chains and manacles. Of course you'll want them removed."

It hadn't occurred to the doctor before, but yes, he might be giving him some tests in which he would have to manipulate some pieces.

"What about the other chains and the leg irons?"

"Sure," the doctor said, "I guess so."

Mary went out to the prison the night before the scheduled appointment at the psychologist's. Kirk was on edge. He spoke rapidly, moving around the room, shoving his chair out of the way.

"Look," he said, "it doesn't have to be like this. We could still do it the other way."

They had discussed Kirk's leaving her there with the guards, bound and tied the same way, and meeting when he'd gotten somewhere.

"Don't you see," he said, "my fucking life is over; it's wasted, thrown away. The only way I'm ever going to be out there in that world is runnin'. You've got your whole future, a family. *Think*. You don't have to be right out there on front street like that. You can come meet me a couple of weeks later, when the heat dies down."

But Mary argued, "What's the difference if I go with you now or turn up missing later? Don't you think they'll figure out where I've gone? And do you think it would be any easier on my folks if I said to them, 'Gee Mom, gee Dad, my client's escaped, so I'm going to have to leave now, to go be with him.' Do you think that would hurt any less?"

"But before you just jump off into this thing I want you to think of this. We could get an hour down the road and get arrested, and there goes everything, your career, your freedom, all for one hour."

"Then that'll be one more hour than we've got now," she said with finality.

Chapter Eight

It was four-forty-five, rush hour. The red Toyota stopped at a busy intersection to wait for the light to change. Mary glanced nervously to her left as the police car pulled to a stop beside her. Her fingers tapped the steering wheel. Quietly, soothingly, Kirk said, "Isn't that fine? He's doin' what he's supposed to be doin', and we're doin' what we're supposed to be doin'. . . . all just sittin' here waitin' for the light to change, obeyin' the law. See? Now the light's green."

Mary glanced over at him. There hadn't been time, back there in the doctor's office, to see how he looked in the clothes she'd bought for him. During their visits in the prison, Kirk sometimes used to say, leaning his chin on his hand and cocking his head, "Why would someone like you want anything to do with a varmint like me? I'm just a grubby ol' convict."

Now she said, "You're not bad-looking, for a grubby ol' convict, you know that?"

When they got to the other side of town, the residential area where the rendezvous spot was, Mary picked up speed. Kirk kept glancing down at the speedometer. "Don't go over the limit," he said—as he would continue to say whenever Mary was at the wheel. Really, Kirk preferred to do the driving. That was why he had taken the doctor's wallet: not for the twenty-five dollars but for the IDs. He needed something until he had a chance to create his own.

"Watch your speed," he said again.

Mary gave him an odd look. "I'm only doing forty." She turned onto a dirt road that led to a secluded spot deep in the woods. The getaway car was waiting. In the front seat were a man and a woman, friends of Tim's identified here as Jim and Alice. Tim had known them for years and had put Mary in touch with them when the escape plans had begun. The couple waved to Mary and Tim to hurry.

Suddenly there was no time to gather up all the stray items inside the car, things the police would find that might provide them with information: the road map of Kentucky, for instance. It was somewhere in the side pocket or glove compartment. . . . And there was the paper bag from the hardware store with the receipt inside for the Tucktape. Where was her bankbook? She'd opened an account in London, Kentucky, with six hundred dollars her father had given her, to start her off on her new job.

"There's no time for that now. Let's go," Kirk commanded.

They parked the Toyota on a quiet dead-end street in the Scenic Woods subdivision, off the Norris Freeway at the Anderson-Knox county line, and got into the back of Jim and Alice's car.

The getaway car headed out, Jim at the wheel. They scooted across the county line, following the back roads that threaded in among the East Tennessee hills.

Every few minutes one of them would run the radio dial to tune in the news. Finally at six-fifteen a program was interrupted with this bulletin: "A Brushy Mountain Prison inmate escaped this afternoon with his Knoxville attorney, Mary Evans. Police say William Timothy Kirk is armed and considered dangerous. It is not known whether Ms. Evans is being held hostage. The two left the Oak

Ridge office of psychologist Gary Salk where Kirk was being tested. Kirk, serving sixty-five years for armed robbery, faces trial next week on charges of murdering two fellow inmates. Ms. Evans is his court-appointed lawyer in the case."

Following that announcement came another: ". . . one more incident of violence at Brushy Mountain Prison today at two-thirty. Inmate Jerry Wear was stabbed to death by his cellmate, Ricky Moorman—"

Mary gasped, looked over at Kirk. "Turn that off," Kirk said. Then to her, "I don't want to hear any more about that place tonight."

Twilight fell around them; each hour that passed, each mile they put behind them seemed another victory. It was as though they'd reached as high as they could and grabbed a handful of time right out of the sky, and now it was theirs.

Jim and Alice lived in an old Victorian farmhouse, one that sat up on top of a hill. A wide front porch, a white painted railing, and lace-curtained windows were caught in the beam of headlights, then disappeared into darkness again as the car pulled around to the back.

Kirk walked through the warm, homey kitchen. The living room, with its stone fireplace and comfortable-looking furniture, looked to him like a picture in a storybook.

Someone switched on the TV, but neither Mary nor Kirk wanted any such intrusion. They said goodnight to their hosts and went upstairs to the room they had been told was theirs, just at the top of the stairs.

It was wallpapered in a pale floral print. White curtains hung at the windows. Against the wall stood an old chest of drawers with a marble top, and before them was a large brass bed.

They slept late the next morning. Kirk had awakened a few times during the early hours, sat bolt upright for a moment, until satisfied it wasn't all a dream—he wasn't back in his cell; Mary really was there asleep beside him—and then closed his eyes and let himself sleep some more.

Jim and Alice had delayed breakfast for them. Mary went into the kitchen to help, and Kirk, eager to feel the ground beneath his feet, walked outside. The sun was shining high in the sky; birds sang out from their perches in the trees. "And I am where I'm supposed to be today too," he said, enjoying the rightness of it all. Then he realized what day it was. Good Friday. A very good Friday.

A plow and a tractor out by the woodshed reminded him of home. He pretended for a moment he had traveled back in time, to a time before the prisons and all that he had seen, all that had ever happened. He walked around to the front of the house, photographing it in his mind. He wanted to remember it exactly as it was.

They had their breakfast at a table in a large, sunny kitchen. Afterward Mary and Alice brought out packages of pink hair rollers and bottles and jars. They set to work. Kirk was told to shave his beard.

"What if you don't like the way I look without my beard?"

"I'll never notice. I'll be too busy looking at your curls."

"My what? Oh no, you don't."

By afternoon, Mary had brown hair, cut in layers, and bangs. Kirk had an Afro.

They discussed when and how to get to North Carolina, their first stop. It had to be explained to Kirk that without credit cards he couldn't rent a car.

"What happened to cash? Is it outdated now?"

Jim said he and Alice would be pleased to drive them.

The fugitives' ultimate destination was Florida, where Kirk had arranged to meet a former street partner who was holding five thousand dollars that belonged to Kirk. But before they started moving around they thought it best to pick a place and wait for the earthquake they

INTERSTATE FLIGHT—AIDING AND ABETTING ESCAPE OF PENITENTIARY INMATE, AGGRAVATED ASSAULT

WANTED BY FBI

Entered NCIC
I.O. 4936
7-12-83

MARY PENTECOST EVANS

FBI No. 615 986 AA8

ALIASES: Mary Mayo Pentecost, Mary P. Evans

NO FINGERPRINTS AVAILABLE

Photograph taken 1982

A Federal warrant was issued on April 5, 1983, at Knoxville, Tennessee, charging Evans with unlawful interstate flight to avoid prosecution for the crimes of aiding and abetting the escape of a penitentiary inmate and aggravated assault (Title 18, U.S. Code, Section 1073).

IF YOU HAVE INFORMATION CONCERNING THIS PERSON, PLEASE CONTACT YOUR LOCAL FBI OFFICE. TELEPHONE NUMBERS AND ADDRESSES OF ALL FBI OFFICES LISTED ON BACK.

Identification Order 4936
July 12, 1983

Mary P. Evans

DESCRIPTION
AGE: 26, born December 17, 1956, Knoxville, Tennessee
(not supported by birth records)
HEIGHT: 5'4" to 5'5"   EYES: green
WEIGHT: 103 to 118 pounds   COMPLEXION: fair
BUILD: slender   RACE: white
HAIR: blonde, brown roots   NATIONALITY: American
OCCUPATIONS: attorney, cashier, law clerk, reservations clerk
REMARKS: prefers expensive restaurants and accommodations
SOCIAL SECURITY NUMBER USED: 408-11-2045

CAUTION
EVANS IS BEING SOUGHT IN CONNECTION WITH THE ESCAPE OF HER CLIENT, WILLIAM TIMOTHY KIRK, AN INMATE FROM THE TENNESSEE STATE PRISON SYSTEM. IDENTIFICATION ORDER 4935. SHE ALLEGEDLY ASSISTED IN THE ESCAPE IN WHICH THREE CORRECTIONAL OFFICERS WERE TAKEN HOSTAGE BY PROVIDING A .25-CALIBER AUTOMATIC WEAPON TO KIRK, BY WHOM SHE MAY NOW BE ACCOMPANIED. EVANS REPORTEDLY HAS SUICIDAL TENDENCIES. EVANS AND KIRK ARE BELIEVED ARMED WITH A .25-CALIBER AUTOMATIC AND THREE .38-CALIBER REVOLVERS AND SHOULD BE CONSIDERED ARMED, DANGEROUS AND ESCAPE RISKS.

William H. Webster
Director
Federal Bureau of Investigation
Washington, D. C. 20535

COURTESY OF WILLIAM Y. DORAN, SPECIAL AGENT, FBI, KNOXVILLE, TN

INTERSTATE FLIGHT—AGGRAVATED ASSAULT, ARMED ROBBERY, ESCAPE

WANTED BY FBI

WILLIAM TIMOTHY KIRK

FBI No. 961 369 E

ALIASES: William H. Kirk, William Kirk, William T. Kirk, William Thomas Kirk, William Tim Kirk, Gary Clive Salk, Gene Wiggins, Lloyd Eugene Wiggins, Jackie Yarbrough

NCIC: 20PI17DO1413XI01DI13

20 L 25 W IOO 14
M 4 W III

Photographs taken 1972   Photographs taken 1979

William T. Kirk

A Federal warrant was issued on April 5, 1983, at Knoxville, Tennessee, charging Kirk with unlawful interstate flight to avoid prosecution for the crimes of aggravated assault, armed robbery, and escape (Title 18, U.S. Code, Section 1073).

IF YOU HAVE INFORMATION CONCERNING THIS PERSON, PLEASE CONTACT YOUR LOCAL FBI OFFICE. TELEPHONE NUMBERS AND ADDRESSES OF ALL FBI OFFICES LISTED ON BACK.

Identification Order 4935
July 12, 1983

DESCRIPTION

AGE: 36, born January 22, 1947, Sikeston, Missouri
HEIGHT: 5'11" to 6'
WEIGHT: 177 to 190 pounds
HAIR: brown, shoulder length
BUILD: medium
EYES: brown
COMPLEXION: fair
RACE: white
NATIONALITY: American
OCCUPATIONS: brick layer, boat rigger, forestry, laborer, machine operator, steel worker, tree trimmer
SCARS AND MARKS: tattoos of arrow pointing down and a rose on left arm; arrow pointing up and the initials "T.K." on right arm
REMARKS: may have full beard and mustache or may be clean shaven. Has worn eyeglasses but may not be required for corrective vision.
SOCIAL SECURITY NUMBER USED: 346-36-4788

CRIMINAL RECORD

Kirk has been convicted of carrying a concealed weapon, burglary, armed robbery, robbery with a deadly weapon and concealing stolen property.

CAUTION

KIRK IS BEING SOUGHT AS AN ESCAPEE FROM THE TENNESSEE STATE PRISON SYSTEM WHERE HE WAS SERVING A LENGTHY SENTENCE FOR ROBBERY WITH A DEADLY WEAPON AND CONCEALING STOLEN PROPERTY. KIRK MAY BE ACCOMPANIED BY MARY PENTECOST EVANS, HIS COURT-APPOINTED ATTORNEY, IDENTIFICATION ORDER 4936, WHO ALLEGEDLY ASSISTED HIM IN HIS ESCAPE WHEREIN THREE CORRECTIONAL OFFICERS WERE TAKEN HOSTAGE. KIRK AND EVANS ARE BELIEVED ARMED WITH A .25-CALIBER AUTOMATIC AND THREE .38-CALIBER REVOLVERS. CONSIDER BOTH INDIVIDUALS ARMED, DANGEROUS AND ESCAPE RISKS.

William H. Webster
Director
Federal Bureau of Investigation
Washington, D. C. 20535

COURTESY OF WILLIAM Y. DORAN, SPECIAL AGENT, FBI, KNOXVILLE, TN

Psychologist Gary Salk in the office from which the escape occurred. PHOTO: ROBIN HEAD INTEMANN

Tim Kirk's *in absentia* trial for murder.
PHOTO: ROBIN HEAD INTEMANN

Mary Evans, after her capture, being
brought back to the Anderson County jail.

PHOTO: JOE STEWARDSON, *THE KNOXVILLE JOURNAL*

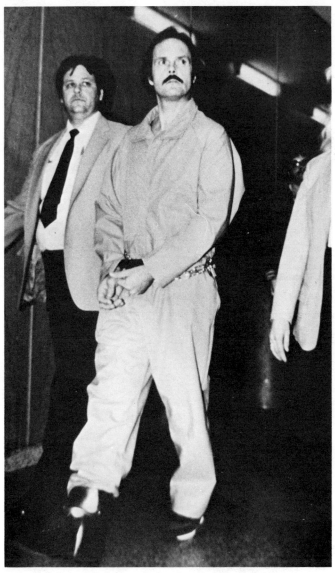

Tim Kirk being led out of courthouse after his
arraignment hearing. PHOTO: SKIP O'ROURKE, *THE KNOXVILLE JOURNAL*

Mary Evans at her bond hearing, shortly after
capture, August 1983. PHOTO: SKIP O'ROURKE, *THE KNOXVILLE JOURNAL*

Tim Kirk on his way to sentencing hearing after
his capture. PHOTO: RUTH ELIASON, *THE OAK RIDGER*

B. H. Pentecost, Mary's father, leaving the courthouse after the sentencing hearing. PHOTO: RUTH ELIASON, *THE OAK RIDGER*

Mary with her lawyer Bob Ritchie (on her left) and psychiatrist Robert Sadoff (on her right). Behind are her parents. PHOTO: MIKE DUBOSE

Mary, wearing Tim's jeans, on her way to the
Women's Prison in Nashville. PHOTO: MIKE DUBOSE

Mary at her parole board hearing, November 1985.
PHOTO: SKIP O'ROURKE, *THE KNOXVILLE JOURNAL*

seemed to have caused in East Tennessee to quiet down. Surely in a few days there'd only be a tremor or two, and they could begin to travel.

The place they decided on was Statesville, North Carolina, a small city on the bus route to Florida. Since neither of them had any connections in the area, it would be an unlikely place for the police to begin their search. They'd also found out that a golf tournament was being held there. The Ramada Inn, the only fair-sized motel in town, would be busy, providing them with a crowd they could blend into.

They were given a driver's license that had once belonged to a Robert Farmer of Knoxville, a convict currently serving time in prison. They were also given two valises and a bulletproof vest. Then their friends checked them into the motel while they waited in the car. Between them they had twelve hundred dollars, including the five hundred from Ricky Moorman's brother, Ron. Assured the pair had made it safely to their room, Jim and Alice left them and took off.

For the next few days they floated along on a high. Everything had gone as planned, no one had got hurt, and they'd left no loose ends for the police to pick up and piece together. Best of all though, they'd both broken free. Kirk was free of the squalor and meanness of his dark world—it was almost enough for him just to stand outside and look at the traffic.

And Mary didn't have to be the Mary Evans for whom she couldn't seem to find a place—not in marriage, not as a lawyer. She had a new name now, a new haircut; she could be anyone she pleased—or no one in particular.

They shopped for clothes, walking to a nearby factory outlet store that was like a huge warehouse. They would get brand-new wardrobes.

It was spring. They were in love, not only with each other, but with the person reflected in each other's eyes.

But the story didn't seem to be dying down. Everywhere they went they saw their names: in every newspaper-vending machine and coffee shop and candy store where they stopped to buy cigarettes. "Woman Lawyer Aids Escape," "Brushy Inmate, Lawyer at Large; Escape Car Found," "Escapee Seen as 'Con Man'," "Friends Describe Mary Evans as Cool, Aloof." On the evening news, pictures of them flashed across the TV screen. It was a mug shot of Kirk they were using.

"Now ain't that the meanest, ugliest varmint you ever saw? How could you run off with that face?"

Mary was genuinely upset. The media were portraying Tim as a vicious killer who would likely leave her in a ditch somewhere when he was finished with her. She knew her parents must be terrified for her. "We'll have to make contact with them somehow, Tim. At least to ease their minds a little."

They decided that as soon as they began to move, they'd get a message to Mary's parents.

Mary was learning what people had thought of her all this time. "*Bullshit*," she swore back at the television after one such comment. "They don't care what they say, do they?"

Kirk was mainly interested to hear about the "sightings" the media were reporting, to find out what direction their search was taking them. "How do you like that? Each station has us going in a different direction."

They were truly dumbfounded when the network news came on, and they discovered they'd become national curiosities too. "All we did was leave; what's the big deal?" Mary asked.

Jim Ramsey, district attorney general in Oak Ridge, had from the beginning requested assistance from the FBI. He was told that until the fugitives were positively sighted in another state, the FBI couldn't get into it. On Tuesday, April 5, Ramsey got his wish. A man in Warren,

Arkansas, spotted a couple fitting Evans's and Kirk's descriptions in a late-model blue Toyota with a Tennessee temporary license in the rear window. The car was headed north on Arkansas Highway 15. A TBI agent speculated that the car was heading in the general direction of Palatine, Illinois. Two of Kirk's sons lived there in the custody of his former mother-in-law, Mrs. Harriet Foy. Captain Sammy Carson, a prison supervisor, told the FBI that Kirk had been in contact with Mrs. Foy on four different occasions and had stated that he intended to come see her and the children.

A federal warrant was obtained, and a flyer was printed, with a recent photograph of Mary, her hair falling in lovely, loose waves to her shoulders, a faint smile on her lips. Beside it her vital statistics were listed. Hair: blond, brown roots; Occupations: attorney, cashier, law clerk, reservations clerk; Remarks: prefers expensive restaurants and accommodations.

Below a heading "Caution," it warned: "Evans reportedly has suicidal tendencies. Evans and Kirk are believed armed with a .25 caliber automatic and three .38 caliber revolvers and should be considered armed, dangerous and escape risks."

Soon after, the *Knoxville Journal* printed its own artist's version of the Wanted poster, ten inches high, on the front page. They used a different photograph of Mary, one with her hair pulled back, looking very much like a debutante. Next to her was a mug shot of Kirk, his hair long and unkempt, his beard and mustache shaggy, his eyes half closed in a sinister expression. Beauty and the beast.

Heading the FBI's investigation was Michelle Kilgore Evans. She began by talking to the guards in Kirk's unit, who'd seen Mary almost daily before the escape. "We weren't surprised. We knowed somethin' like that was bound to happen. Just wait till they get caught. Be kinda interestin' to see how she'd do in one of these places."

When asked about Kirk, the guards agreed that he

minded his own business, did his own time, and never messed with people unless they messed with him.

Michelle Evans spent the first month gathering background information on both Kirk and Evans. She began by interviewing Kirk's past associates, some of whom were in other prisons. She spoke to police officers who'd arrested him, his family, his ex-wife, and other girlfriends.

In her personality assessment of him, Kirk was an anomaly. "He's supposed to .be a bad-ass, but a lot of people talk about him like he's some kind of hero."

TBI agents who had been called to the prison on the Thursday of the escape were later convinced the stabbing of Jerry Wear had been planned ahead of time as a diversionary tactic. Prison staff, occupied with the new outbreak of violence, were busy locking down the prison. No one noticed that the transportation officers hadn't returned at four-thirty when they were expected.

Another aspect agents considered was that up until the night before, Moorman and Wear were cellmates, but after Wear met with Blankenship's defense attorney, Charlie Susano, and returned to his cell, Moorman had asked to be moved, and was. The next morning Wear called his sister and told her to come see him, that "they" were going to kill him.

The same inmate who'd told the FBI about Kirk's initial escape plans told Michelle Evans what he knew about the stabbing on the day of the actual escape:

> On the day Tim Kirk escaped, Jerry Wear was killed. Tim Kirk passed a note to Ricky Moorman that said Jerry Wear needed killing and that he [Kirk] was gone but would be back in sixty to ninety days. I saw the note and Ricky Moorman flushed it down the toilet.
>
> At exercise time, Ricky Moorman was passed a knife by Jack Blankenship, and Ricky Moorman ran over and stabbed Jerry Wear. David Reeves

was not involved in the murder of Jerry Wear. Jerry Wear was not armed with a knife at the time Ricky Moorman stabbed him. Carl Crafton gave officers a knife that did belong to Jerry Wear, but he [Crafton] got it from Ricky Moorman, who got it from Ricky McDonald, who got it out of the shower.

Since Kirk's escape I have seen letters that were written by Tim Kirk. These letters were sent to Larry Hacker and were brought in by visitors. Kirk has said in these letters that he was in High Point, North Carolina, and he would come back to get the other inmates when he gets his people together. Kirk also told me prior to the escape that he was going to start hitting armored cars. Tim said Mary Evans wanted to help with hitting armored cars and that Mary told him that she wanted to be like Bonnie and Clyde all over again.

Larry Hacker's contact to the outside is a man they refer to as the "ol' man." The ol' man has a girl who goes between William Timothy Kirk and the ol' man and passes the information to the inmates. I don't know who the man or woman is.

In addition to this statement I am willing to tell authorities how things are smuggled into the prison.

Then Michelle entered Mary's circle, starting with her family and working outward to friends, associates, classmates, and acquaintances.

On Easter Sunday, four days after the escape, John Lockridge called his mother from New York to wish her a happy Easter. He hadn't heard the news; he'd been out of touch with his office since he left Friday morning. When his mother told him, he caught the first flight back to Knoxville.

On Friday, April 8, FBI agent John McGivney took a statement from John Lockridge.

"He stated that he'd known Mary Evans since she was a senior in law school and that they'd remained close personal friends. After they met they began a very intimate relationship. They remained lovers until approximately two months ago. He advised that this relationship evolved into his divorce and that he was divorced thirteen months ago.

"When he first met Mary she resided on White Avenue. When they became intimate friends she would often spend the night with him in his A-frame home at 7301 Crystal Lake in Knoxville. They also often took trips together. He found that whenever he had a little extra money he would contact Mary and they would go have a good time. He has taken her to New York, San Francisco, Washington, D.C., West Palm Beach and Coral Gables, Florida, and numerous places in North Carolina where they spent various amounts of time together.

"He does not know exactly just when he began to notice a problem developing between him and Mary, but he does know that after she was assigned to the William Kirk case she talked more and more about him. On one occasion he asked her to describe Kirk. She sensed he was jealous; he denied it. On another occasion he asked her if she was having sex with Kirk in the prison, and although she did not admit it, she did not appear to deny it with conviction.

"He recalled that on the weekend of the Southeast Conference Basketball Tournament he and some friends went to Birmingham, Alabama, to attend the tournament. She did not accompany him since she really did not care for any kind of athletics. He called her practically every night while he was there. On the evening of March 12, he called and found her in a very upset state of mind. She was screaming about the fact that she had too much on her, that she needed money, and that she was hungry. This made absolutely no sense whatever. He reminded her that he had given her thirty dollars prior to leaving for the tournament. He asked her what she had done with the thirty dollars; she said she still had it. He told her to go over to the A-frame and get some steaks out of the freezer. She asked him if that would really be all right. The entire conversation was insane since she knew she could have anything in his house simply for the asking. He advised that when he returned home from the trip she apologized for the way she acted on the phone but she gave no explanation for the way she talked.

"Lockridge gave her two checks amounting to $1000 simply because she asked for the money. (One check was for $300; another for $700.)

"During the week of March 22, he had invited some friends of both of them to his house for dinner, Katie and Harrison Ambrose. Katie is a law clerk for the current U.S. magistrate, Robert Murriam. [Lockridge] said that after the Ambroses had arrived and Mary still hadn't shown up, he called Brushy Mountain Prison to see if she had left there yet. He talked to an individual by the name of Williams, who stated that she was still at the prison. Some time later Mary called him from the prison to say that she got his message and that she would be at the house shortly. In the meantime it had gotten very late and he and the Ambroses went ahead and had dinner. After she arrived, she was apologetic. Lockridge said he was extremely tired and went to bed. Mary and the Ambroses stayed up for a while and he does not know what time they left that evening.

"He had a date with Mary on the following evening, Friday, March 25; again she was not at home at the time of their date. Again he called Brushy Mountain and found she was still at the prison, so he left his card and went on to the Cow Palace. She arrived there sometime later; she appeared totally unconcerned that he was dancing with another girl. He stated that this was unusual for her since she had exhibited jealousy in the past.

"After she arrived they went out to dinner together, but she stated she was tired and wanted to go to bed early. Saturday afternoon, March 26, he picked her up early in the afternoon and they had lunch at Friday's. Again she appeared very withdrawn from him. On Tuesday, March 29, they had another date, and she agreed to let him spend the night at her apartment. They were intimate that evening, which was very unusual in the relationship for the preceding two months. The next morning, March 30, he left for New York and contacted her as soon as he arrived there. He called her collect at approximately 11:00 A.M. and they had a very good conversation. He stated that this conversation was the best they'd had in the past two months; it encouraged him that the relationship was no longer on the wane. The following morning, which was March 31, he again called her at approximately 10:45. This call was also collect. At this time he advised Mary that he would be through with his case in New York earlier than he had anticipated, and he suggested they get together and go somewhere for the weekend. She told him she was moving to London, Kentucky, the following Friday and that her dad and her brother were helping her move and would probably spend the night in London with her. She ended the conversation by saying 'I love you, John.' He stated that this was unusual, definitely not her style.

"He advised that she is a very intelligent young lady but that she has somehow placed herself in the position of being the champion of the underdog and sees all her clients as being victims of society.

"He advised that in January 1982 he was at home with his daughter and that he received a phone call from Mary. She said she'd taken some pills and had tried to commit suicide. He then called Katie and Harrison Ambrose. They took her to St. Mary's Hospital, where she was treated and released. Subsequent to that she went to Kathy Broughan, a psychologist, and has been treated by her ever since."

Agent McGivney quizzed Lockridge about the specific places he and Mary had visited, places she might choose to return to while on the run.

The FBI agent learned about trips to San Francisco, Sausalito, New York, Coral Gables, and West Palm Beach.

"The first trip he ever made with Mary was during the summer of 1980. It was July or August; he took her to Washington, D.C. They stayed at the Madison Hotel during this trip. He also recalled they stayed at the Georgetown Hotel on one occasion. On the day Reagan was shot at the Hilton Hotel in Washington, D.C., they were staying at that hotel. It was a business trip; [Lockridge] had gone there to see Senator Howard Baker, but he was unable to see Baker that day because of the shooting episode.

"He took Mary to Asheville, North Carolina, on two or three different occasions. They always stayed at The Inn On the Plaza Hotel, and they usually ate at the Grosvenor's Restaurant.

"On one occasion they went to a state park in Clemmons, North Carolina, and stayed at the Old Reynolds House. She loved this old house and had a marvelous time. He said he would not be surprised if she returned to that location with Kirk.

"When Mary was married she apparently went camping with her husband on several occasions.

"They also stayed at the Terrace Garden Hotel in Atlanta once, during the Peach Bowl of 1982. While they were there Mary visited a friend whose first name was Elaine. She mentioned to him that Elaine was a good friend. [Elaine] sold her Fiat automobile for $6,000 and went on safari in Africa. He allowed that this apartment is undoubtedly available since Elaine was divorced, and they were apparently very close friends.

"He recalled that Mary's former husband had access to an apartment or cabin in Hilton Head, South Carolina.

"He took Mary to Pompano Beach, Florida, and they stayed in a woman's condominium. He explained that he and this woman had exchanged residences for a three-week period so that the woman and her husband could visit the World's Fair. . . . The condominium was located on Crystal Lake Street next to the Crystal Lake Country Club. He said that Mary might possibly still have a key to that condominium although she only spent one of the three weeks there with him.

"Concerning close personal friends that Mary had, he mentioned Cynthia D'Andrea, who works at Miller's department store in Knoxville, and Lisa Shivers, a nurse at East Tennessee Children's Hospital was another close personal friend, and that Lisa and her boyfriend had once accompanied them on a trip to Asheville, North Carolina.

"Bill Smith, a friend who works at the UT print shop, was also a good friend. This individual sings professionally under the name of Rocky Davis at the Round-up Club out on Asheville Highway.

"He recalled that Mary once mentioned to him that there were some cabins near Townsend, Tennessee, known as the Elkmont Cabins. They were a part of the Smokies which was on land lease. He said that these cabins were available to her first husband, that they had camped there in the past.

"Concerning a former client of his who had an apartment used by him and Mary, he identified this individual as Dick Wellons. Wellons had been convicted of drug trafficking and was currently in prison. He stated that he [Lockridge] and Mary had used his apartment on one occasion. The apartment is located near Norris, Tennessee, and is currently owned by Knoxville attorney Bill Banks. But he doubts very seriously that Mary could locate that apartment at this time."

*   *   *

In high school many considered Mary a snob; they said she would only deign to talk to the rich kids. Yet at the same time Michelle learned that Mary liked to hang out with the Vestal crowd, kids from the roughest neighborhood in Knoxville.

As a lawyer Mary was said to be a champion of the underdog; when she traveled she liked her accommodations to be first class. Mary liked to wear an old pair of jeans and a shirt, but they were designer jeans and silk shirts. One of her friends said, "If Mary was in a bad mood, John would have to hang some more gold around her neck—to cheer her up."

Yet her few close friends spoke of her in loving, glowing terms. One of them, who asked for anonymity, told a reporter for *The Washington Post*, "Mary wasn't cruel; she was good-hearted. She always had a feeling for a guy who had a hard time. She's a very complex person. The key to understanding Mary is the relationships with the men in her life. Her husband was your basic high school football hero, gorgeously built. She was a high achiever. It was a complete mismatch. Her father was very domineering. He treated her like an oldest son. Women need to feel needed, especially if people around them are more powerful and established and don't need them," she said, referring to Mary's relationship with Lockridge.

Michelle didn't feel she knew who Mary was any better after three months than when she began. "Mary's five different people. Make that ten."

So she gave up trying to figure Mary out; she just wanted to track her down. She sent special bulletins to the cities Mary had visited, circulated flyers, and warned all of her friends that if they failed to report any contact with her, they'd be guilty of a felony.

On April 10, at twenty past ten in the evening, Mary's friend and law school classmate, Katie Ambrose, answered her phone. It was Mary, calling collect. Harrison Ambrose got on the extension.

"How is everybody?" Mary asked.

"Everybody's very upset and concerned," Katie said.

Harrison asked her outright if she had gone willingly or if she was coerced. Mary made a sound like a laugh and said she was in no danger. "Is your phone safe?" she asked, matter-of-factly.

Harrison said it was, but he told her the FBI was on the case and could eventually trace the call.

Katie Ambrose clerked for Magistrate Robert Murriam, the judge who had issued the UFAP warrant. Mary teased her that it was her boss who'd sicced the FBI on them.

"Okay. The reason I'm calling is to ask you to relay this message to my father, to John, and to Janet: Tell them I'm sorry, but I'm safe and well. And I've never been happier in my life."

Katie Ambrose was stunned. "Mary, I can't tell your father that!" she said. "He's convinced you've been kidnapped. It'll destroy him."

There was a brief silence on the other end; then Mary said, "Deliver the message."

Harrison argued that she might feel safe, but how could she be certain Kirk wouldn't use her as a hostage?

"I don't think there's any possibility of that," she said calmly.

Harrison tried to ask her about the reported sightings in Illinois and elsewhere, but Mary wouldn't answer, and after a moment, she rang off. The Ambroses notified the FBI.

The call was traced to the Trailways bus station in Columbia, South Carolina, but a check by the FBI failed to positively identify Evans or Kirk.

On April 11, the Anderson County grand jury indicted Mary Pentecost Evans and William Timothy Kirk on nine counts each: four counts of armed robbery (the guns from the guards and the money from Dr. Salk), four counts of aggravated kidnapping (the charge for holding a person at gunpoint), and one count of escape.

Michelle Evans was in her office, talking on the phone, when she heard someone knock. She hung up and went to the door. The man standing there was tall, gray-haired, and dressed in a business suit. Rather stately, she thought. He introduced himself as Mr. Pentecost, Mary's father, and asked if he might talk to her. He addressed her as "Mrs. Evans." She showed him to a private office in the back.

Michelle had heard that Mr. Pentecost was driving the Knoxville agents up the wall; they had told her about their last telephone conversation with him, a day or two before. Pentecost was supposing, for example, that his daughter was being held hostage by drug dealers on board a boat off the coast of Venezuela. If hostage negotiations were necessary, he wanted to be flown there to handle it.

The tired and exasperated agent had said, "Look, Mr. Pentecost, you're just going to have to face the fact that your daughter may not be a kidnap victim. It's very likely she aided Kirk and took off with him." Without a word, Pentecost had banged the phone down.

Michelle looked at this man. She knew his lifetime values, all he'd held dear, had been torn from him. She let him talk. He told her he wasn't satisfied with the way the Knoxville office was handling the case. He was worried most that Mary would get caught in a shoot-out.

"My daughter isn't a criminal," he said. "She's an officer of the court. Do you have any idea how hard it is to go through law school? How much work it is? She is proud of her achievement." His voice dropped, his eyes grew bright with tears. "We are a Christian family—" The words broke off.

"Mr. Pentecost," Michelle said, "all we want to do is get your daughter back to you safely." She promised to keep him apprised of any new developments.

It was a promise Michelle would find very hard to keep. A week later a body was found in Cleveland, Tennessee, at the bottom of a quarry. The girl had been beaten, her face disfigured beyond recognition. She had no ID, but she was blond, had on jeans and a red top, and was the same height as Mary. Michelle waited for dental reports to come back, hoping the newspapers wouldn't get wind of it and that Mr. Pentecost wouldn't call.

No sooner did they get a negative identification on that one than another body turned up, this time in Anderson County, on TVA property, not far from where Mary's car had been found.

On April 14, the FBI began an extensive manhunt involving more than one hundred agents in the forty states that either Evans or Kirk had visited or had contacts in. Florida authorities were put on the alert. Tom Evans, Jr., Mary's former husband, was living in Pompano Beach; agents interviewed him. Kirk's oldest half brother had a home in Sarasota, as did one of his sisters; both of them were called on by agents. They were told that failure to notify the FBI should Evans or Kirk contact them would be a felonious act and punishable as such.

On April 20 a sighting was reported in Pennsylvania: "White female in her thirties, weighing about 110 pounds, blond, clean-looking, entered a Howard Johnson's motel with a scruffy 'bozo' white male in his thirties, weighing about 190 pounds, brown hair. No luggage, car, driver's license, credit cards. Woman did all the talking; man stood to the rear of the lobby. Address given was Philadelphia. Next morning the couple requested room service. Maid came in to clean room as man and the woman were in the process of taking off. They ran past her when she attempted to call the manager. Couple jumped into a light blue car. Left room looking like a pigpen. FBI agents responded, conducted interviews, took photographs, etc. Results, negative."

Michelle Evans received a report of another sighting

in Nebraska. The report read: " 'Classy' girl entered bar with 'motorcycle-type guy.' Girl fit description of Evans. She carried large canvas-type bag, wore jeans, blouse with green vest, ordered Lowenbrau. Man was aloof, kept looking around, nervous. Waitress tried to question them about where they were from. Couple said they were just passing through. Next day, photos were in the newspapers, owner of the bar recalled that the photos were similar to the people at bar on previous night. Waitress confirmed the identification. FBI followed up. The location was near a prison where Kirk was once incarcerated, Jefferson County Correction Facility, in Missouri. Results, negative."

On April 29, two people were sighted at Wallburn Mall, Boston, Massachusetts. "White male and white female, driving a blue car with a white top, whipped into a parking space. The woman ran out of the car to a phone booth at the side of the mall. Her description matched that of Evans. The male waited in the car. Scraggy hair, tattoo on forearm, facial details matched Kirk. Observer noted the car had Knox County plates but didn't write down number. Observer was willing to undergo hypnosis. Had seen photos in newspapers, recognized Evans and Kirk. No other witnesses."

Two sheriff's deputies picked up a prisoner in Nashville whom they were to escort to California. At the Nashville airport the prisoner, a former inmate at the main prison in Nashville, spotted a man he swore was Kirk purchasing two airline tickets to Ontario, California. Behind him was a five-foot-four blond, same description as Evans. The inmate became so adamant that the couple were Kirk and Evans that the deputies noted the flight number and followed the two people until they'd boarded the aircraft. Then they notified FBI in Dallas. A check with airline officials failed to identify any passengers using aliases. Investigation, negative.

On April 21, Governor Lamar Alexander offered a reward of five thousand dollars for information leading to their capture. On April 29, the Pentecosts issued a written statement to the papers:

> We want to express our love for Mary and our complete confidence and faith in her. We have waited, hoping and praying for her safe return. We continue to wait, hope, and pray. While she may not get this word wherever she is, we know it is of some comfort to her knowing in her heart that not only her family but also close friends who really know her believe in her.
>
> We know that some are logically and objectively searching for answers to what happened and why. We do not understand others who seem to have forgotten what our system of justice provides relative to innocence and guilt. We abhor the reports which appear to assume Mary's guilt in this matter. Much of what has been reported is inaccurate and without foundation. We know Mary. It is our belief that she will be vindicated when all the facts are known.
>
> We have faith in Mary and we have faith in God. We are gravely concerned for her safety and appreciate the continued prayers of friends and caring people everywhere for her safe return.
>
> Mary, you are in our every thought and prayer every moment. Hold on and look up.

Chapter Nine

It wasn't until April 11 that Mary and Tim felt safe enough to board a bus. They traveled at night, stopping twice, once at Columbia, South Carolina, where Mary had made the call to the Ambroses, and again to get something to eat.

It was two o'clock in the morning, and there was a one-hour layover. They were headed across the road to an all-night diner when a man stepped out of the shadows and stopped them. Kirk's hand instinctively went to the gun he was carrying in his pocket.

"Hey man, want to buy some weed?"

Kirk grabbed Mary's arm. "No, no," he said quickly, "I never use the stuff." He hurried them away, fully expecting a narcotics agent to jump out of a doorway.

They got to Sarasota early in the morning and checked into an Econo-Line motel, using the names of Bob and Sharon Farmer. The first thing they had to do was get themselves some names. But to do that they'd need a car to get around in and a place to live. They rented a 1973 Mercury Montego from Poor Ole Joe's ABC Used Car Rentals. Poor Ole Joe asked a lot of questions, and Kirk was uneasy using the Robert Farmer ID. What they needed, he explained to Mary, were names with no histories, no

Social Security numbers, driver's licenses, or records of any sort. The place to find them was in the cemetery, on the headstones of young children.

It took the better part of an afternoon, but finally they found four names: Robert Allen Allred, a nine-year-old boy who died in 1962; Judith Ann Metcalf, an infant who died on the very day she was born; Lisa Jo-Ann Richard, a two-year-old; and Tammy Renee Haskins, who lived for one week in July 1963.

Since it was too late to go to the Bureau of Vital Statistics to try to get birth certificates, they decided to go to a real estate agency instead. That morning there had been some apartments listed for rent in the local paper; Mary had circled the ones that looked interesting. The best ones had to be seen through an agent.

The real estate agent was friendly, asked few questions, and showed them a bungalow Mary loved. It was across the causeway, on Siesta Key, right on the beach road. A colony of sorts, it was popular with artists and young couples who were—or weren't—married. Against his better judgment, Kirk agreed to take it, under the name of Farmer. He asked the agent if he knew where he might cash a cashier's check for three thousand dollars. It, too, was made out to Robert Farmer, and he had no ID other than the driver's license to back it up. The agent was very helpful; he sent Kirk to his bank and gave him the name of the vice-president there. He told Kirk to be sure to tell the official he was renting one of the bungalows in Siesta Key.

Mary waited out in the car. After twenty minutes she went in to look for him. Twenty minutes after that, she went in again, certain this time that something had gone wrong.

In fact Kirk and the vice-president of the bank were sitting chatting. Kirk explained that he was a carpenter, that he and his wife lived in North Carolina. A week ago, their house had burned to the ground, all of their papers with it. Luckily, they had their driver's licenses with them, or they'd really have a problem. They'd driven down to Florida to recover from the trauma. This check for three thousand dollars was the first of the insurance checks they were waiting for. In the meantime, he said, both he and his wife liked the area so much they might just decide to stay and rebuild their home there.

The man, taken with Kirk's sincerity, told him he'd be happy to have him as a neighbor, and Kirk, realizing that Mary must be a nervous wreck by now, brought the cozy chat to an end. He got the check okayed, cashed it, shook hands warmly, and left.

Mary was the one to convince the people at the Bureau of Vital Statistics to issue birth certificates. She introduced herself as Sharon Farmer, a student of genealogy, while Kirk watched from a safe distance. She came away with four certificates. Mary also breezed through the driver's written and road test; Kirk struggled with the application; then, because it had been six years since he'd driven a car, he had trouble parallel-parking. That gave Mary no small pleasure. Kirk was an avid tease; now it was Mary's turn.

A few days before, they had been walking past a furniture store when Kirk had spotted a piano through the window. "Let's go in."

"What for?" Mary asked.

"I don't know. I feel an urge to look at furniture," he said, leading her directly to the baby grand piano. "I think I might want to buy this piano, for instance, but I want to hear how it sounds first. Play it for me, will you?"

"Are you crazy?" Mary asked.

"I hear you're a fine pianist."

"Where'd you hear that?"

"I read it in the papers. They say music was one of your majors."

She grunted. "Come on, let's get out of here."

"Not until you play for me."

"In front of all these people? Tim, quit it!"

He had her going now, and he liked to see her mad. "Hey," he said, "who knows when I'll ever have a chance to hear you play?"

"Tim, I'm leaving."

That night they were getting dressed to go to a movie. Mary handed him a pair of jeans she had bought for him when they were putting wardrobes together.

"Are these for me?" he asked, looking at the embroidery on the pockets.

She nodded. "They're yours."

"What's with the butterflies?"

Mary laughed. "They're not butterflies."

"No? What are they?"

"They're not anything. It's just a design. They've been making jeans like that for years."

He looked doubtful but put them on.

When they got to the movie theater there was a line. They saw men in pairs, many of them wearing similarly embroidered jeans. Tim exploded. "Faggot jeans! You bought me God-damned faggot jeans!"

Mary burst out laughing. "No, they're not. They're what people are wearing, not just fags."

"C'mon, we're leaving." He knew that no amount of explaining would make her understand what was going through his mind: How would he look to his friends back there behind those walls?

Before they left the motel, Kirk made a long-distance collect phone call to a number in Tennessee.

In a statement given to the FBI, William Reece, whose phone number appears in Mary's address book under the name "Wheels," described the conversation he had with Kirk on that day.

My son Billy Reece was an inmate at Brushy Mountain Prison until his release on approximately August 21, 1983. For a time he was a cellmate of Tim Kirk. I met Tim Kirk on one occasion while at Brushy Mountain Prison to see Billy. Kirk asked me if he could arrange to have his elderly father fly down here and would I help pick him up at the airport and take him to Brushy to see Tim. I told him I'd be glad to for I knew that they'd probably never get to see each other again. As it turned out, I never did have to go get his dad—I don't know if they ever got together or not. That's the only time I have ever seen Tim Kirk. I've talked to Kirk a few times while he was in prison because he'd been given my number by Billy and he always called to thank me and Carrie for the boxes we'd send him and Billy. I don't recall when I'd get these calls but I know one of them was around Christmas.

I remember seeing on TV about Kirk and that Evans girl escaping together. About two or three weeks after that, the phone rang and when I answered, the lady said I had a collect call from Sarasota, Florida, and I said well go ahead. When Tim came on the phone, he said how was I and how hot was it. I told him he better get further and faster because the governor had put out a reward for him and the girl. Tim just laughed. He asked how Billy was—how he was getting along.

I asked how Mary was getting along and Tim said she had her butt turned up to the sun laying in the sand. I don't recall that he said anything else about her. He said it was nice and warm down there and that she liked it there so they were just going to stay there for a while. I asked what he was doing and Tim said he was just lying around taking it easy. I reminded him we were on long distance so we wound up the conversation and I wished him well.

I have never met or talked to Mary Evans and I have not furnished Kirk or Evans with a car or in any way helped them escape. I have no knowledge as to how they might have left the state. I have no idea why the name "Wheels" would appear in any place alongside my phone number. All I can remember or suggest to explain this is it was a means of remembering me in someone else's mind.

On April 13, Mary and Tim moved into the bungalow. The monthly rent was four hundred dollars. Kirk paid it in cash, in advance.

Mary's dream was finally a reality: she had a cabin in the woods where she could just be. More, this cabin had a beach a mile and a half long, to walk along and hunt shells; she could swim or simply lie in the sun and do absolutely nothing.

Even Kirk was starting to relax a little. One day he said, "Isn't it like someone came into that room up at Brushy and said, 'Well now, how would y'all like it to be when you get there?'"

Mary planned meals and shopped for food and cooked. Kirk enjoyed going to the grocery store with her, and wanted to sample everything on the shelves, buy one of each. Mary, who was an organized shopper, would ask him, "What're the mushrooms for?" "I like them," he'd answer with a boyish smile. "Tim, we don't need mushrooms," she'd say, and put them back on the shelf. Or olives, or sardines. And sotto voce he'd say, "Baby, have a heart. If you knew the crap they call food up there. . . ." And up and down the aisles he'd go, staring at the jars and cans as though they were rare jewels. Then he'd look around and catch Mary putting something back.

In the evenings after dinner they'd walk along the

water's edge and talk about how they wished this time would never come to an end.

"Tim, promise me we won't get caught."

"I can't promise you that."

"I know you can't. But I wish someone could. What'll it be like for me if I have to go to prison?"

Tim felt as if his heart would break in two. He put his arms around her, hiding the tears that welled up in his eyes.

One night she sent him to the store for some soft drinks. When he came out, he saw a tiny black kitten struggling to get itself up onto the curb where an ice cream cone had dropped. Kirk lifted it and the kitten began to lick the ice cream. Then, satisfied, it rolled over on its back, and Kirk saw it had a little white star underneath its chin. He walked to his car, opened the door, and nearly stepped on the tiny thing. It had followed him and gotten under the car. Kirk hesitated a minute. "No good," he said; he'd always had a superstition about black cats. Except that this one did have a white spot. Anyway, cats were never his favorite. But it was funny the way it was looking up at him. He scooped it up, sat it on his lap, and drove home.

Mary came to the door when he knocked. "Where's your key?" she asked.

He handed her the paper bag. "Here, take this."

She jumped back when the bag began to move by itself.

"Don't drop it," he said.

"What is it—Oh Tim! Oh, wait." She started out the door.

"Where're you going?" he called after her.

"Be right back. We need milk!" And she was gone.

She had talked about getting a cat but then said no, it wouldn't be fair. How could they think about keeping one when they might have to pick up and run at any minute? But this one seemed to have dropped down out of the sky.

He became Tim Kirk's kitten, slept on the top of his head, sat on his knee when they drove. They'd never heard of a cat who could stand to be inside a car, but this was one travelin' cat, they thought. He stayed with them almost to the end.

They went to the movies one night to see *A Boy and His Dog*, a post-nuclear-holocaust story set sometime after the turn of the next century. "Right about the time I become eligible for parole," Kirk noted.

In the movie, society had moved underground, rebuilt itself, and was tightly ruled by a superstructure called the Council. Bands of men roamed the surface of the earth looking for food, stray females, and supplies. All alone, except for his dog, was a boy, not from the city, who survived by his and his dog's wits. The dog had supernatural powers and could sniff out food and warn the boy of impending danger; they communicated telepathically.

A girl had been sent from the underground city to lure the boy down there; the structure needed fresh sperm for their reproductive bank because all the men in the city were sterile. The girl fell in love with the boy. They spent the night together, but when he woke she was gone. The boy had to find her. The dog warned the boy not to go down to the city, that no one had ever returned from there. He went anyway, found the girl, and spirited her off. They barely escaped with their lives. She had defied the Council; if she ever returned, they'd eliminate her.

When they came back to the surface, the boy found his dog starving, nearly dead. The girl had become bossy and possessive; she told him to leave the dog. The boy wouldn't do that and, as the movie ended, the boy and dog were seen walking off, the dog fed, revived, and

happy. "Thanks," he said to the boy. "You're a real pal."
The girl was nowhere to be seen.

All through the movie Tim and Mary poked each
other as they recognized the many parallels.

"The dog is my sixth sense," he said.

"And the Council is Knoxville and the legal profession," she said.

Mary had toured the John Ringling mansion in Sarasota, with Tom when they were on their honeymoon. She
had described it to Kirk on the drive down to Florida with
such fervor that he was eager to see it. It was like a palace,
she said.

When they got there, Mary was in a hurry to show
him the formal gardens, but Kirk was more interested in
the house itself, in the actual *things* that millionaires had.
If a millionaire wanted a bed that was so big it wouldn't fit
through the door, he hired workmen to take the bed apart
and reassemble it in his bedroom. If he wanted his dining
room to have walls of tile, and American tiles wouldn't do,
he sent to Europe for ones he liked better. And millionaires' wives didn't keep their clothes in closets; they turned
whole rooms into closets for their clothes. Kirk noted with
interest the threadbare oriental rugs.

Mary was telling Kirk how this whole mansion was
built by John Ringling for his adored wife, Mabel, but
Kirk was only half listening. He was thinking that John
Ringling had made his millions by putting freaks and wild
animals in cages and having people pay money to come
look at them.

When they got back to the bungalow, Kirk took out
the camera he had bought the day before. Other times
when he had been out of prison, either on escape or on
parole, he had wound up regretting that he hadn't any
pictures to remind him. He didn't tell Mary that; he just
said he felt like taking pictures.

They posed for each other: Kirk in shorts and sandals, shirt open, his hair neatly trimmed and still curled, clean-shaven except for the mustache, leaning against a palm tree. Mary stood, bare-legged, in scant shorts and a T-shirt, smiling shyly into the camera, looking like a little girl. Then Kirk photographed them together, by extending the hand holding the camera as far as he could, and holding Mary with the other. Mary nestled in close, her face almost blending with his.

Kirk was still worried about the Farmer ID. "It won't stand a check," he said. "If I get stopped for runnin' a red light, I'm back in prison."

"So don't run a red light."

"Damn it, woman, don't you hear me? We've rented this place in one name, we got driver's licenses in other names—I'm not going to be able to stay out unless I start building a foundation under me. People are supposed to have bank accounts, checking accounts—"

In fact some of the people he had counted on to help him were shying away. At first he thought it was only the imaginings of a hunted man, but finally someone came out with it.

"It's not that I'm not happy to see you, man, but that's an officer of the court you've got with you. I mean what happens when the honeymoon's over and she's facin' jail, and they say tell us who it was helped you or we'll throw your ass into jail? No tellin' what she'll do then, man. What's she doin' this for, anyway?"

For Kirk, a man who lived by his loyalties, the sudden withdrawal of his closest friends threw a cloud over his existence. He began to hesitate to approach people he needed to see. Even the people whose house they'd stayed in and who had driven them to North Carolina were really saying—now that he thought about it—"Look, we're glad to help you get on the road, but that's it."

When Mary was told why some of the people Kirk had counted on were backing away, she became furious. How could anyone not trust her after what she'd done? What more did they want? The idea that his friends actually feared her was more than she could take.

One evening as they were sitting down to dinner, they heard a news announcement on the network broadcast: "Judge Lee Asbury of Morgan County in East Tennessee has ruled that escaped convict William Timothy Kirk, indicted for the shooting murder of two Brushy Mountain inmates, will stand trial for first-degree murder regardless of whether he shows up for the proceedings or not. The trial, which had been scheduled for April eleventh, has been set for April twentieth."

Mary and Kirk stared at each other, stunned. "How can they do that?" Kirk asked. "I didn't know they could do that. You're my lawyer, tell me. What's the deal?"

"I never heard of anything like this before. I don't know."

"I mean what happens if they find me guilty and sentence me to death in the electric chair? How they goin' to do that without me bein' there?"

It was about the first week of May that Kirk noticed a change in Mary. Sometimes she looked like a kid whose day at the fair was over; the balloon in her hand had slipped away from her and was riding away on the wind. Where once he'd been able to assure her that their needs would be taken care of, that there were people standing by ready to help them, now it all sounded like empty promises made by a man who had only dreams.

They'd bought a car, a silver Thunderbird, and now they were running out of money. He'd told her from the beginning that was the danger, that people always start making mistakes when the money runs out.

He sensed the day might come soon when he'd have

to start thinking about stealing again. They'd talked about getting jobs, but how could they? How could they get jobs under one name and live under another? They could move on and be rid of the Farmer name for good, but they'd already paid the May rent. Given how short of money they were, that would be silly.

The more Kirk studied the dilemma, the more tangled up in it he found himself. One night, after a day at the beach, blissful for Mary, but one of torment for him, he went to where she sat reading.

"I've been thinking," he said, "if you went back to Knoxville now, it will have been just a little more than a month—it might not be so bad for you. You could say I forced you, that I threatened your family—"

She looked up at him, eyeing him peculiarly, and twisted her mouth in an expression of irritation. "Go away. I'm reading."

"Look, the truth of it is, it just isn't any good. I don't feel the same anymore. I'm sorry, but that's the way it is."

This time her eyes wandered slowly to him. She studied his face carefully.

In high gear now, his voice gathering strength as he went along, he said, "Look, whatever it was we had for a while is gone. Lately I haven't even been able to see what attracted me to you in the first place. It's only fair that I tell you I don't think I feel like making love to you anymore. What I want to do is drive you to the airport, put you on an airplane, and get you out of my life. You're excess baggage now."

He watched as the words found their mark and saw her go pale, then redden as tears began to form in her eyes. She got up and went into the bedroom, threw some clothes into a bag, and gathered up whatever things were in the bathroom.

"Have you checked the flights?" she asked.

"There's one you can make."

"Let's go then."

She sat woodenly in the car until he pulled up to the curb. He gave her the cash for the ticket, which left him with thirty dollars.

There was a pay phone near the door. She went to it and stood there a moment or two, her bags at her feet.

Kirk watched her. He was unable to drive off. He felt encased in something that wouldn't let him breathe.

She turned and faced him, hands jammed deep inside her pockets. Then she reached down to pick up her bags and walked toward him.

Tears sprang to his eyes as she yanked the car door open. "I'm not going," she said.

"Get in the God-damned car." He put his arms around her and pulled her to him. Words tumbled out amid tears. "I didn't know what else to do," he said. "I just thought if you went back now maybe you wouldn't have to go to prison. I was so confused, I don't know how I let this happen. I just wanted you to stop loving me, go on back home hating me."

A few days later they were walking past a mall in Sarasota when Kirk spotted an armored car that had pulled up in front of a jewelry store. The uniformed guard, a pot-bellied, florid-faced man, lumbered down out of the van and walked into the store. Ten minutes later he came out holding a large canvas bag in each hand. He set the bags on the ground while he unlocked the rear doors. All the while the driver sat, bored and sleepy-eyed, behind the wheel. He never once looked around.

Kirk watched that car every day for the next two weeks, memorizing its movements. Then he and Mary drove up to North Carolina to a place in the mountains where several of his past associates visited. He told them about the armored car and the pudgy guard. They agreed with Kirk. It sounded like a sweet set-up.

For Kirk and Mary it was especially sweet. After this one job they'd have the money to go to the Cayman Islands, and from there—if they wanted to—to Europe. Or maybe they'd like to go somewhere like Oregon. . . .

They made the trip from Florida to North Carolina a few times. Kirk liked being in a car with Mary; he felt safe and enclosed.

On one of these trips, the kitten lay curled beside them on the car seat. Kirk drove and with his free hand stroked the animal as he talked about his family, saying how he wished he could understand why he had turned out the way he did, when he came from such good people. "Nobody beat me, or acted mean to me. They didn't spoil me, or neglect me. They're just good, honest hard-working people. Just ordinary, you know?"

"Yeah," she said, watching the flat Florida landscape slip by. "Like mine."

"Different as we are, that's one thing we have in common, isn't it? We both got born into the wrong families."

"Or maybe they gave birth to the wrong kids."

She turned to him. The kitten had woken up and had rolled over onto his back. Tim was tickling his tummy, and the kitten was trying to grasp hold of Tim's finger. It was Tim the kitten woke up each morning, pawing his cheek gently till he opened his eyes. And Tim would say, "Guess you want me to put somethin' in your bowl, right, pal?" Poor nameless thing. They knew he wasn't theirs to name. He was just riding with them for a while; then he would have to find his own way. Mary felt badly about that, but Tim pointed out, "Hey, we're leavin' him a whole lot better off than we found him."

Mary was still watching him. "Do you believe in God?" she asked.

"Yeah, I do."

"I mean really, deep down?"

"Yeah. Do you?"

"Yes," she said. Then after a while she said, "You really are a nice person, aren't you?"

"I don't know, Mary," he said quietly. "I don't know."

During the month of May, the operators of the Marina Grocery in Badin Lake, between Raleigh and Charlotte, North Carolina, positively identified Mary Evans as the young woman who'd been in the store at least nine times. Poor Ole Joe remembered that three car payments were mailed from that area. When the car was returned it was noted that Kirk had put 750 miles on it.

The FBI had two agents at the lake. One had his son with him on a small fishing boat; the other posed as a hiker. When the FBI got word that Evans and Kirk had been spotted, the bureau even called the SWAT team to tell them to get ready to storm-troop the area. But then a few more days passed without another sighting by the agents, and the SWAT team was called off.

Kirk and Mary returned to Florida with two of Kirk's friends to get ready to hit the armored car. But the very next day a bank in downtown Sarasota was robbed. The police issued an all-points bulletin in which the thief was described as a white male, 190 pounds, six feet tall, with a mustache and longish brown hair.

Kirk cursed his bad luck. Some double of his had gone and robbed a bank, and here he was renting a bungalow under the name of a convict in a Tennessee prison. And nosy Poor Ole Joe over at the car rental place had only to pick up a phone and check the number on the driver's license he had on record to start the ball rolling. Or the rental agent, for that matter. Or the talkative vice-president at the bank, who might easily think back after hearing about the robbery and wonder about the Robert Farmer who came in with a cashier's check and fit the description the police were broadcasting.

They had no choice. The whole west coast of Florida would soon be swarming with FBI agents looking for someone who looked like him. They got in the car and started driving across the state and north, to the east coast.

Chapter Ten

Kirk's trial had been separated from that of the other six codefendants. Judge Asbury ruled that Kirk had voluntarily absented himself, thereby severing his case from the others. Furthermore, an affidavit from Deputy Warden Otis Jones had warned the court of the possible danger. "All of these inmates on trial have a history of violence, prison disruptions, escapes. Trial of all six with Kirk at large would pose a great security risk."

Judge Asbury appointed Creed Daniel of Knoxville to replace Mary Evans as Jim Bell's cocounsel.

Bell registered his objection to the court's ruling to try the case in Kirk's absence. The court noted his exception and assured the defense, "Mr. Kirk is certainly welcome to attend the trial if he wishes to do so."

During the voir dire, Jim Bell said to a prospective juror, "Creed [Daniel] reached over here and said I've got my arm around Tim. Tim is not here. Now, does that make any difference—Tim not being here?"

"No, sir," the juror answered.

"Okay, we've got a chair over there that says reserved for Tim Kirk. We're not trying to be funny about it, but that's just to show Tim isn't here, and it's a problem for us, 'cause it's like trying this case with our hands cuffed, see—"

"Yeah."

"We're kinda the underdog. But, ah—you know, we can't confer with our client if we—ah—bluster around here a little bit, and stumble—ah—you would understand that, 'cause we don't have the assistance of our client."

"Yes, sir."

"Okay. You won't hold that against us, and this lawyer from Rutledge, Creed Daniel?"

"No, sir."

Bell finished his questioning by saying, "I've asked you a bunch of questions. I haven't asked you nothin' that made you mad at me, and you don't want to sit on this case, have I?"

"No, sir."

Bell finished by telling the potential juror that he'd like to see him be foreman of the jury. He was roundly scolded by the judge for that remark.

Also acting as cocounsel for the defense was Neil Cohen, a University of Tennessee law professor who had written a *Tennessee Law Review* article on trial in absentia.

"This will be the first capital case in United States history in which a defendant is to be tried in absentia," Cohen told the court.

Creed Daniel, in his statement to the court, said, "It is incumbent upon the state to show there is a living individual. Has the state in its proof shown they have a living person? We maintain that charges against the defendant require some proof he is living."

Attorney General W. Paul Phillips said for the prosecution, "If he is alive, then all charges will stand. If he is dead, he will not be prejudiced."

Criminal Court Judge Lee Asbury overruled the motion to dismiss the case. Privately, Judge Asbury's explanation was, "Hell, Kirk had availed himself of all the rights and privileges of the court. He filed motions; we held hearings on those motions. No one has deprived him of his right to be present. I consider this an attempt to thwart the process. Any way you look at it, the principles don't change. He was invited; he chose not to be here. Mr. Kirk is held by the court to have waived his constitutional right."

Tim Kirk's empty chair was the focus of attention, a blunt indictment of the proceedings. Spectators sat in six rows of benches. A huge calendar portrait of General George Patton looked down on them from one of the yellowish wooden walls. A 1960s sunburst clock whirred away the minutes above the heads of the men and women of the jury.

Judge Asbury's white hair glowed holy-card-like around his face, lighted from the sun filtered through shuttered windows behind him. Four portraits of former Morgan County judges sat in judgment with him from the wall to his left.

On April 27, the defense rested its case with the forty-minute testimony of Brushy Mountain inmate Carl Crafton. Slight, angular frame, wire-rimmed glasses, short, neatly cropped hair—he had an almost professorial look.

Jim Bell's boyish face was serious, but his eyes twinkled in anticipation. He had expected the seven women and five men of the jury to fall in love with Carl Crafton. He started slowly, speaking in his deep good-ol'-boy country accent.

"Please state your name for the benefit of the court and for the jury."

"My name is Carl Crafton."

"Yes, sir. And Mr. Crafton, where do you live?"

"Ah—presently at Brushy Mountain State Penitentiary."

"All right, sir. And what block are you living on?"

"B block."

"All right. So the jury will know something about you, how old are you?"

"I'm forty-six."

"And how long have you lived at Brushy?"

"I've been there since November twenty-third, 1980."

"All right, sir. And would you tell us, so that the jury will know, and just to be entirely open, why you are in prison?"

"For armed robbery of a drugstore in Chattanooga, Tennessee. . . ."

"All right," Bell said. "Now, did you know William Timothy Kirk?"

"Yes, sir. I knew him very well."

"And how did you know Tim, and how did you come to know him?"

"Ah—I met Tim at Nashville, at the Nashville Penitentiary."

"How would you describe your relationship with Tim?"

"As very close friends. . . ." Crafton smiled.

"All right. Now Mr. Crafton, did you know while you were at Brushy Mountain other individuals such as Mr. Roger Bolin? . . . A Mr. Neely? . . . A Mr. Gibson? . . . John Henry Brown? . . . Mr. Linticum? . . . Mr. Blankenship? . . ."

Crafton nodded at each name and answered, "Yes, sir."

"All right. Now, did you know a James 'Nick' Nichols?"

"Ah—yes, sir."

"Did you know a James 'Mitch' Mitchell?"

"Yes, sir."

"Paul Hawkins, and the rest of the individuals whose names are on the chart?"

Bell indicated the large printed chart for Crafton and the jury.

"Yeah, I knew every one of them."

"All right, sir. Now, Mr. Crafton, before we get into the situation about things at Brushy, I would like for you to acclimate us—or get us adjusted to life in the penitentiary. . . ."

"Yes, sir. Well, the atmosphere has changed. It changes like, through the years there's been a new concept about prisons and people have changed and new-type prisoners are coming in. In the last four or five years, they're changing. Ah—in the last six or seven years, it seems that—ah—groups—they'll gather in groups, more than they would as individuals prior to that."

"All right."

"Ah—there seems to be a lot more violence than what there was back in the fifties and around in there."

"How long . . . have you—of the years that you've lived on this earth have you been in prison?"

"Twenty-three calendar years . . ."

There was a murmur in the courtroom as people tried to relate such a long period of years to their own lives.

"All right, sir," Bell continued, ". . . as a person within the walls of a prison, are there individuals who talk and act as an adviser to the other inmates or convicts?"

"Yes, sir."

"All right, would you explain that to the jury?"

"Well, sir—through the years, like for instance myself, I only had an eighth-grade formal education. So I completed high school—"

"In prison?" Bell interrupted.

"Right. And enrolled in different colleges. Ah, Lee Junior College at Baytown, Texas, and Roane Community College here in Tennessee. Ah—ah—psychology/sociology courses here in Tennessee. And in Tennessee composition, Western civilization, history, and things like that. . . . During the period of time it kinda prepares us to be counselors, or advisers, or—mediators in the prison. . . ."

". . . what does that person do?"

"Well—in the past—like in the late sixties and early seventies, it was mostly petition the courts for redress on prisoners' rights issues. Ah—in the last two or three years it's been a strategist more than a counselor. . . . How do we survive in this situation—and us—it's kinda been like a small war in the last two or three years, to be truthful with you. . . ."

"All right. Now, Mr. Crafton, what role did you have in the prison as a mediator or counselor at the present time?"

"Well, I think that, ah—it's referred to as a legal adviser. It's sanctioned by the administration, and I'm allowed to have an hour conference with any inmate who requests it, in the evenings. . . ."

"Now, Mr. Crafton . . . did you have that same capacity on or about February eighth . . . and how long have you acted in that capacity?"

"Well . . . really . . . for the last fifteen years, but I've—at Brushy Mountain, from the day I got there."

"What was the situation there, immediately prior to February eighth? . . ."

"Well, I'd rather—much rather start from the day that I was received at Brushy Mountain, to clarify it."

"All right."

Carl Crafton adjusted himself in the witness chair and then continued.

"On—ah—December twenty-fourth, the day that I came to the prison, I was placed in D block, which is administrative segregation unit, isolation, on one walk, seven cell. And—ah—that evening at shower time, when I came out of the shower, I was walking back to my cell, and an inmate stopped me."

"And who was that?"

"A black inmate."

"Who?"

"Iceman."

"Iceman?"

There was a smattering of laughter from the spectators.

"Right."

"All right. And he's known as Robert Jones?"

"Right, that's correct."

"All right, sir, go ahead."

Crafton corroborated what the prison population knew only too well.

"Ah—he asked me if I would pass something to the next cell, and I said yeah, I will . . . he had ah—what we call a stinger—it's an element, a heating element for heating water, like for coffee or so forth. He had it in a quart jar, plastic quart container and ah—it was a shaving substance that only blacks use, called 'Magic Shave.' "

"What does it do . . . ?"

"It burns. Has a stinging sensation. Anyway—"

Bell interrupted. "Does it do that to the skin of a white man?"

"Right, uh-huh. A white man's skin is tender, or whatever. I don't know really what it is, about the pigmentation of the skin that causes it not to harm a black, but it does harm a white."

"All right."

"Well, he had it boiling, and he had been boiling it while I was in the shower, and when he turned around he throwed it on me."

"All right."

"So—I sensed something was—a little nervousness about him—and the walk was quiet. And since I didn't know these people at the time, I didn't really know what had been going on at Brushy Mountain. I didn't know I was in danger."

"All right, after the incident, Carl, did you, in your capacity, make inquiries . . . ?"

"Ah—the officers that were on the walk, they saw this incident occur. They removed me from there and placed me on four walk in D block in with another inmate that said he knew me, and he would like for me to move in there with him. Ah—I related to the man on four walk what had occurred on one walk, and asked 'em who is this guy; is he just a nut? And they began telling me what had been transpiring at Brushy Mountain for a couple of years prior to this. . . . these people use the fear factor to extort money from other inmates. To establish this fear factor they had to injure someone, or they . . . couldn't collect nothing. And it was a lucrative practice in Brushy Mountain to collect this extortion money."

The jury reacted visibly, glancing at one another.

"What kind of things would be extorted?"

"Ah—well, I know of inmates there who have ah—one had his mother sell a house, send the money out to Memphis to this guy—Roger Bolin had his family sell some property and send it to James Nichols's family—"

The members of the jury gasped.

"Why, that's incredible," Bell said. "Is that true, or not—"

"They extorted the people's family—"

Judge Asbury interjected, "Refrain from making any comments, Mr. Bell. Let the witness testify. . . ."

Carl Crafton glanced at the judge and then went on. "Well—the way they would begin to extort—the way they did me, first I received some notes. 'If you're going to live here, you're going to pay.' "

"All right. You personally got those notes?"

"Certainly . . . every one of us received those notes, at one time or the other."

"Now who were the notes coming from, the particular individuals?"

"Ah—James Nichols, he would sign because he was the one that was the leader, him and Mitchell were the—kinda like the 'godfathers' of 'em. The rest of 'em were puppets. That's all they were."

"All right."

"Pull a string and they would do it. . . . I know of several that were paying like twenty dollars a week; whatever they could get from their families."

"Why? Why would somebody want to pay you twenty dollars a week, would you tell us? . . ."

"To live."

"To live in Brushy Mountain?"

"Certainly."

Jim Bell paused for a moment to give the jury time to react.

"Now—Mr. Crafton," he continued, "what other things are we talking about in terms of extortion?"

"Well, I know of inmates who ah—were forced to give their televisions up, and their radios and things like that. . . ."

"What else?"

"Well—I think that there's probably been several give up their manhood in that prison; extorted for that, for sexual favors . . ."

Crafton stopped and lowered his eyes for a few seconds. ". . . now like Roger—he's paid them for a couple of years, and then he quit because Billy Joe Linticum and Johnny Brown—John Henry Brown—advised him that they would ride with him, if he would quit paying, because they were getting too big with it. They were beginning to touch people that weren't supposed to be touched. You know, people that had been in prison for several years and had maintained a pretty good reputation, didn't mean anybody any harm. And they would ride on him in his cell, man."

"All right, now the people that I've listed here on the right . . ."—Bell indicated the list of names to Crafton and to the jury—"were they the ones that were engaging in what you mentioned, causing people to lose their manhood?"

"Yes, sir. They even raped each other. Now Jones there raped Donnie Currant on two walk. They—they rape each other if there's not anybody else around. . . ."

There were quick, flushed expressions on the jurors' faces.

"Now let me ask you about things involving new individuals, young, timid, white men who come to a prison. I ask you to tell the jury what would happen to them, when they got to Nichols and that bunch."

"Well, they wouldn't last long." Crafton shifted in his

seat. "They were older and they think youth represents beauty, and they would probably assault him, and they would certainly rape him."

"Well—could not one—if you were Tim Kirk or if you knew this was going on . . . why couldn't you pick up the phone and call Nashville—or make a complaint to the law enforcement agencies, or tell the guard . . . ?"

". . . if you did do that, then you would be ostracized by the entire prison population . . . for being an informer. They certainly wouldn't have respected that, and you couldn't survive there."

". . . That person is known as a snitch?"

"That's correct, yes."

". . . What happens to a snitch? Where does he go?"

"He'll either go to check-in, to a self-protection walk— and if he remains in population he's, as I said, ostracized, and I believe that's the worse punishment that he could receive. Where no other inmates would talk to him. Ah—he couldn't even hold . . . a general discussion with anyone."

"Now, Carl, do those things really happen here in the valley—?"

Crafton spoke up immediately. "It happens in every prison. . . ."

"All right. . . . Tell us about violence in Brushy Mountain that you're aware of, and based on your experience as the mediator and that sort of thing. Will you tell us about that?"

"Well, recently, in the last few years, it's been like an overkill every time when a couple of 'em will grab a guy and they will stab him eight or ten times. And that's what it is; the psychological thing of the overkill. They hold him to the ground and keep stabbin' him. Everybody says Tim Kirk was stabbed six times. He was stabbed seven times."

Carl Crafton looked around the courtroom, strong emotion blazing in his eyes. "How many times does he have to be stabbed before he goes back on 'em, man? That's what the point is. They broke his leg, laid him on the floor and stomped his leg till they broke it. Hospital records will verify it. How many times do you have to get stabbed before you're justified in reacting?"

Bell looked with purpose at the men and women of the jury and then turned to Crafton.

"All right—well, let me ask you this. What about—besides Tim—who would do things like that?"

An edge of anger came into Crafton's voice.

"What do you mean who would do things like that besides Tim . . . ?"

"Well—who would be the victims besides Tim . . . ?"

Crafton relaxed. "Roger Bolin was stabbed twelve times; Billy Joe Linticum stabbed once; Ricky Moorman was stabbed once. . . ."

"Now let me ask you this, Carl—other than those seven, Bolin, Kirk, Neely, Gibson, Brown, Linticum, Blankenship—did this group restrict themselves to this group?"

". . . they didn't even restrict themselves to a race; they attacked—they had the entire prison situation out there in their hands, under their thumbs, blacks and whites."

". . . what is your attitude about it?"

"Well—I'm—I'm strictly—I never get involved in violence. . . ."

Bell walked to the exhibit table and started to show the knives and other weapons from the prison.

"Now, Carl, I want to show you—what's been introduced as exhibits . . ."

"Oh—that's a kitchen knife that's been worked down. And those others are vent knives."

"Vent knives. What's a vent knife?"

"Ah—the air chamber behind the cell, has a vent. . . . it's covered by a vent that has approximately inch and a half flange around it, and that's what those are made from."

"All right. And this is a free-world—"

"Lock blade. . . . Those are quite common in the prison now. At one time there was more homemade knives."

"How do free-world weapons, from outside the walls, get inside the prison?"

"I can't answer that question."

". . . you're right. . . . are there other weapons that are used?"

"Yes, sir."

"Pistols?"

"Yes, sir."

"What about other weapons?"

"Well, you have the zip guns."

"What's a zip gun?"

"It's a firearm that's manufactured out of a pipe, or a tube. There's usually a rubber band on it to fire it, with a nail in it, or something like that."

". . . Carl, can you relate to us . . . as a matter of history about what led up to the events of February eighth? . . ."

Crafton paused to collect his thoughts. "Well—the pool room incident was ah—came about because of Billy Joe Linticum decided that he wouldn't pay another dollar. That's what he told 'em . . . every one of 'em were there. So ah—they jumped him. And ah—so he said yeah, well I'll have your money Friday, you know, trying to wait till he could get him some help. And John Henry was in the visiting gallery at that time, and he wasn't there to help him—"

"John Henry Brown?"

"Uh-huh. Right. He had committed himself to ride with him, if he would resist this, you know. And they were advising other prisoners, if you'll stop it—if you won't make the first payment, then there won't be any more—we'll correct. Ah—some of 'em continued to pay it. . . . it's a lucrative business. . . ."

"So then did something happen at the pool room?"

"Yes, sir. There was a fight there between the black gang and these whites."

". . . How many whites were involved?"

"Well, I really don't know—it was more than they caught, you know, two or three of 'em got out windows or out the door, whatever. I don't know how many."

"How many blacks were involved, to your knowledge?"

"Ah—more than that group there." Crafton pointed to the charts. "There was more to both sides."

"Were you yourself ever the target of an attack by the gang?"

"Only with that 'Magic Shave.' They tried to blind me. . . . they tried to—stab me with a knife tied to a broom handle . . . he ran it out, well, I threw my towel over that."

"Ran it out of what?"

"Out his bars—between his bars. It was like a lance, trying to lance me, and I dropped the towel on it, and twisted it, and just—actually ran, and then the officers came in and removed me from the—and the doctors treated me. . . ."

"What other information were you receiving and what general knowledge did the population at Brushy know?"

"Well, that their life was in danger unless they paid, because there was a lot of examples of what they would do. You know, when they stabbed Roger, they just kept stabbin' him. It was an overkill, twelve times."

Spectators in the courtroom murmured among themselves as they imagined the attack.

"They said he lost more blood than they had ever seen anyone lose in that prison out there, and they were lucky they saved him. We had a medic at that time by the name of Tate that was good. He would get in and stop that blood flow fast. . . . But he's not there now. And now we've lost prisoners recently because we don't have that type of help there. He was a Navy medic, and he knew what he was doing, and regardless of who it was he'd go. We didn't lose hardly any prisoners then. . . ."

An obvious change had come over the jurors. There was sympathy in their faces now. Jim Bell was having his way: the jury was falling in love with Carl Crafton.

Crafton continued speaking. "Two days before, I received a letter from David Reeves. He was on five walk, and he told me to tell everyone down there to barricade their door on four walk, that the blacks on five walk were going to make an attempt. He didn't know when, but we'd better be ready for 'em. So then we began sending messages to population that we needed a weapon, and we didn't get it till Sunday. That's the reason these rumors about the administration knew it was going to happen. . . ."

"But they didn't know—"

Crafton spoke quickly, with feeling. "Yeah, they knew by God, it should happen. . . . But we didn't know it till Sunday morning, that it was going to happen. And I asked Kirk why—why am I going to be left out of this? And he said because you have a chance to get transferred and back into Nashville where you can receive visitors and things like that. He said you're older, and you're not in good physical shape. And that's the type of person he was. He looked out for his friends. He's an exceptional person. . . . I would like to project that image of him not being an animal."

"Well, I understand. We'll talk about that in a minute. We'll talk about Tim Kirk as a human being. . . . Let's go on into this. . . ."

"So we passed notes among us down there and discussed what was happening. Tim celled in nine cell—there is only ten cells on that walk. . . . If they come in on the walk, we're going to lose the first two or three men in the first two or three cells. They have a thirty-two automatic. If they can come in on that walk, they're going to catch them by surprise because they can fire into those people fast. Now the rest of us down the walk, seven, eight, nine we'll be fairly safe, as Tim can step out on the walk, he's the rock man, and fire back with a twenty-five. So it came down, like strategy, what did we do. Did we go ahead and forfeit these three men, in these first three cells; do we go ahead and let them get killed, just for our own self-preservation. We know we're safe down here on the end. . . . It was extremely tense. I saw the men go from smiling, laughing, individuals that I'd known two or three years past to very quiet and subdued and oppressed people. . . . I saw their personalities change. I talked to 'em every day through the years, these different people. I saw the atmosphere of the prison change."

The courtroom was very quiet.

"Carl—with Mitchell and Nichols and their group, what about the guards, were they armed—what did they do?"

"You know—I really don't know what they could do. The officers there at that prison are kinda like, they're going to maintain the order . . . they will try to break up a fight. But so often they can't get there. Like we were in a cage when Tim was stabbed. There was no way anyone could get there to stop it."

"No witnesses."

"No officers witnessed it. At that time we didn't have any officers over the yard, over the exercise yard, in B block exercise yard. Ah—they would try to—they picked their spots before they made a hit, you know. There was several occasions where—there is so much that's not reported. There's just beating you know, where two or three of 'em would grab him and a couple of 'em would work him over good, and then he would say he got hurt on the basketball court. He had to say that."

Jim Bell asked how messages were sent within the prison.

". . . it's done like this. Ah—take a bar of soap and put it in a sock, tie a string around the sock with a note inside of it, and use the soap as a weight, and drop it out the screen and drop it down to one walk. One walk would take the note out, put it on the end of a stick, run it across through the air chamber in the back which is approximately four and a half feet distance, into the cell, opposite walk. Then the guy upstairs, he'll say, got a note for you, Carl, so I drop this sock down, tied on a string, and he puts the note in it, and I pull it up to my cell, and I read it. So it takes a little bit of time for that note to make the trip. . . ."

There was loud laughter in the courtroom.

"How would you describe it in terms of life . . . in terms of fear and . . . those human emotions that one always feels. How would you describe it?"

"That would be the most difficult thing in the world to describe. It's something—it boils in you, and you have—anger—ah—you'll try to find out—figure out some way that you can maybe manipulate around it, you know, to try to pacify this situation, but . . . there's no way that you can. There's nothing that's going to satisfy these people but an act of violence, or the money. . . ."

". . . I want you to relate to the jury, and other inmates that may not testify . . . I want you to relate to the jury how—what the code is within the walls about testifying . . . what's the rules?"

"Well—ah—in our discussions last month about giving testimony in the courtroom, it seemed like everyone was concerned about whether we could mention a name of a convict that was still living or not."

"To avoid being a snitch?"

"Right. And whether this would subject us to any type of—violence there at the prison, or whatever. . . ."

"Let me ask you this. We were talking about Tim a minute ago. Was he the type of person that if a fellow needed a handkerchief, or needed his glasses took care of, or his health, about his heart attack, whether it was a heart attack, or high blood pressure, whatever, what would he do in a situation like that?"

"He'd definitely assist him if he could."

"Did it make any difference who it was?"

"No, it really didn't. No, it didn't. That's what was strange about their stabbing Tim. He was a stranger to these people. They didn't know him. They couldn't have possibly known him other than just rumor, or that he came with me from Nashville. Ah—we'd attempted to escape from Nashville Prison and ah—that's the reason we were transferred to Brushy Mountain."

"How did you all attempt to escape?"

"Ah—in a Dempster dumpster."

"They started compacting—"

"Yeah—and it's a pretty tight spot in there," Crafton said, grinning. "Darndest hug I've ever had in my life, let me tell you . . ."

Laughter filled the room. But Crafton's face was serious again.

". . . he saved my life," Crafton said. "He's nothing but a hero out there in that prison today. And it seems so strange to us—this comes up quite often in our conversations. You know, where were all these people when Tim Kirk was stabbed? Where was all these investigators? Where was this jury and this court? And where were all—why all at once now? . . . Roger Bolin was stabbed twelve times; Tim was stabbed; the extortion has been going on for two or three years; they've been stabbin' people. The hospital records at Oak Ridge will verify it. That ambulance has made many a trip. Where were all these people then? That's what we want to—that's what we're wondering about. All at once you want to kill Tim Kirk, one of the—"

Carl Crafton's voice, and his emotion, had been growing stronger. Bell tried to interrupt.

"Now—if—"

"Well, I get emotional about it because I live with these people, and I see what's going on, and I see what's going on here. And I'm wondering how you could sit in judgment on a man when you know that—"

"Don't go into that, Carl."

"—how many times have you got to get stabbed?!"

"Now—"

"Well, I have to."

"No, you don't."

"All right."

Everything stopped for a long breath. Finally, Bell spoke quietly to Crafton.

". . . to the best of your ability, have you shared with the jury that which occurred prior to the incident of February ninth, 1982?"

"Well, just as straight as I can be, and that's all I can do. . . ."

Carl Crafton left the witness stand.

The state put on a total of fifteen witnesses, among them Dr. Gary Salk, the three transportation guards, Dr. Robert Bigelow, who treated Kirk for stab wounds after the February 8 attack, TBI agent Bill McBee, and Herman Davis, warden of Brushy Mountain Prison.

Warden Davis, a powerfully built man in his fifties, looked every inch the part of a sheriff or warden in a rural southern prison. His manner with the defense was openly hostile. On cross-examination, Bell asked the warden if he'd met Robert W. Ritchie and had a conversation with him at 3:45 P.M. on March 21, 1983, relative to this case.

"I don't recall," the warden answered.

"Do you deny it?"

"I didn't deny it; I don't recall it," Davis answered tersely.

"All right. Do you recall talking with Mr. Ritchie about this case?"

"There's a good possibility I did."

Judge Asbury instructed the warden to answer "yes" or "no." The warden's answer was, "I don't recall."

Bell, keeping his anger in check, asked, "Did you tell

Mr. Ritchie that Mitchell, Nichols, Jones, Hawkins, and Wimberly and others had been involved as a gang, engaged in robbing, extorting, and raping other inmates?"

"As I recall I informed Mr. Ritchie that the groups, both sides, were considered dangerous to the effect that they had to be kept locked up in the penitentiary."

"All right, but that's not what my question was."

The warden stared him down. "I know what your question is, but I can't answer to that extent. I don't recall."

"You met Mary Evans, did you not?" Bell asked.

"Who's that?"

"Mary Evans," Bell repeated.

"Mary Evans?"

Members of the jury eyed the warden skeptically. Her name and photograph had been front-page news across the state for nearly a month.

"Do you know Mary, did you meet with her?"

"Where?"

"Brushy Mountain Prison, on September twenty-eighth, 1982, at two-fifteen P.M. in your office at the prison?"

"I possibly could have."

"All right, sir. You told her, did you not, that you had some indications before February eighth that an incident might take place because the records reflect that there were problems between the blacks and the whites?"

Bell continued to ask the warden about that conversation, and the warden continued to be unable to recall. The next question brought the angry response Bell expected.

"Do you recall Mary Evans asking you, relative to advance knowledge, that the shootings were going to come down? And that you refused to do anything about it; you just blamed it on a few guards who wanted to get their names in the paper?"

"I did not," Davis replied.

"You deny that?"

"I deny that."

"Under oath?"

The warden hesitated, glaring at Bell. "Make the statement again," the warden said.

"Did you tell Mary Evans, when she asked you about whether or not you had advance knowledge relative to an article that appeared in the Nashville paper, that the shooting was going to come down, and you refused to do anything about it, and you told her it was just a few guards wanting to get their name in the paper?"

"I had no knowledge whatsoever the shooting was going to come down—"

"Did you tell that to Mary Evans?"

"—And as far as the guards getting their names in the paper, I don't recall telling Mary Evans that."

"Do you deny it?"

"I deny it."

The defense called John Reddick, a Brushy Mountain records clerk, to the stand. He stated that members of the group identified as the Memphis mob were able to arrange transfers from one state correctional facility to another. Reddick said that the records showed that transfers of four of the "mob" were secured on three occasions.

In response to this, Attorney General Paul Phillips said, "It is odd to me that individuals who were helpless, locked in their cells, and shot at from the outside would be characterized as a mob. Especially when the seven around them who take hostages and start an attack are characterized as victims. That's an odd characterization to me."

The implications of the case were weighed carefully within the walls of Brushy as betting ran rampant among the inmates. Odds were heavy on the possibility of acquittal, a deadlocked jury, or a life sentence. Very few were betting on the death penalty. They had a connection to a Las Vegas line on the outcome.

*　　*　　*

In their final arguments defense attorneys Jim Bell and Creed Daniel asked the jury to put an end to prison disruption: "On behalf of a man whose life will be in your hands," Bell said, "I ask you to send a message to Nashville about this case of human events. That as citizens you don't want a mob to do the things done at Brushy Mountain. I'm pleading with you to bring peace to the valley."

District Attorney General Paul Phillips answered in his closing argument, "As long as inmates take things into their own hands we can never have peace in the valley. Peace in the valley will come all right when the law is upheld behind those walls." Referring to the psychological test given Kirk moments before his escape in which he revealed that he thought "rules are for weak people," Phillips said, "They [the inmates] are going to have to learn that rules are for strong people too. We use rules as the basis of civilization." He also criticized the testimony of Carl Crafton. "You can't say that a man who testifies against the system and for another inmate came here in danger of his life. You don't put your life on the line when you testify against the system, and for an inmate. When you put yourself beside the hero. A person who has shown that he can take the law into his own hands and thwart you. You're supposed to be here today deciding the fate of Mr. Kirk for what occurred up there on five walk. But Mr. Kirk has already thwarted you. He's not here to tell you, because he has forfeited his right to be here by his escape. He said, boys, guards, you know what's hanging over me. You know I have nothing to lose, so he decides, since law is for weak people, you weak people, you jury of Morgan County, you weaklings, you go ahead and carry out your law. I'm strong. I'll take a gun; I'll hold it on some guards. I'll tape their hands and legs up, and then I'll send you a postcard from Canada or Mexico, or somewhere like that, weak people. Because your law, that's for weak people. I don't need your law. I ask you, the jury, to send a message to the prison in the form of a severe sentence for Kirk."

In Judge Asbury's instructions to the jury, he said, "Many men are naturally of weak nerve, and under certain conditions the most innocent person might deem a trial too great a risk to encounter and therefore seek safety in flight. And it is for the jury to say what weight, if any, shall be given to the alleged flight of the defendant."

At 10:30 on the morning of April 29, after a total of eight and a half hours of deliberation, the jury delivered its verdict to the court. Kirk was found guilty of two counts of manslaughter, three counts of intent to commit voluntary manslaughter, and one count of aggravated kidnapping.

Chapter Eleven

The main street that the Daytona Western Union office was on was filled with fast food places, gay bars, and biker bars. It was August 17. At four in the afternoon it was suffocatingly hot. There hadn't been any rain for a week, and still the moisture hung heavy in the air.

Kirk sat waiting down the street and across from the Western Union office in a dented white Ford station wagon while Mary went in to pick up the money order. He'd opened the door on the driver's side to let out some of the heat; his foot dangled to the ground.

He watched her in the side-view mirror as she headed for the office and smiled at the sight of her in his blue jeans. They'd both gained weight in the last few months. He'd grown right out of his jeans: Mary had grown herself right into them.

For the past two and a half weeks they'd been spending their days marking time, waiting for money. They played cards and backgammon, went to the dog races. Mainly they spent their time on the telephone trying to raise enough money to tide them over.

They'd stopped talking about getting a plane and pilot to fly them to the Cayman Islands. A couple of months back, when they had the necessary $960, they'd put it off.

Kirk felt there were too many questions that they had no answers to. What would they do when they got there? How would they live? Did they really want to try to get to Europe? Maybe they should wait a little longer, till the heat died down. Mary wanted to go to Canada or Oregon right away, and find a little cabin in the woods.

Kirk hated having to remind her again and again what lay ahead of them—for her—if they got themselves caught. Each time he did she'd look wounded. Mary was now hearing about waiting for the second time, this time not from a conservative-minded husband but from a man who'd spent his whole life taking risks.

She had become irritable and moody in recent days, which Kirk blamed on circumstance. Being hunted was like having a pack of dogs at your heels, he said, running you into the ground. But it was indecision that made her impatient.

They were heading northeast, away from the Sarasota area, still undecided where to go, when they saw the signs marked "Daytona." It seemed the logical place to stop. There were the dog tracks, beaches; they could spend a few days while they made phone calls and waited for money.

But Kirk had a bad feeling about Daytona from the day they pulled in. "Something doesn't feel right," he said.

"Then let's leave," Mary said, with just enough of a challenge in her tone that he let it drop. It seemed to Kirk that from that moment, every decision they made turned out to be wrong.

They looked for a motel that was back off the highway and near the Western Union office, and cheap. Room 160 at the Daytona Best Western was $14.98 a day, weekly rate. They registered as Robert Allen Allred and Lisa Jo-Ann Richard and paid in cash.

It was the smallest room in the motel. Although it was on a corner, it had only one window that overlooked the parking lot and garbage dumpsters. It was drab, the walls painted an ugly brown. There was a king-sized bed that squeaked, mildew on the shower curtain, small threadbare bath towels, and the constant sound of jets screaming overhead. In the lobby was a dimly lit lounge that had a jukebox and a bar.

The Daytona Beach Kennel Club was a minute away, just across the highway. The admission was fifty cents, and bets started at two dollars. The track was open every night and some afternoons.

Mary and Kirk began going regularly, Mary making two- or six-dollar bets, always at the same window where a gray-haired man who resembled her father sold her the tickets. He remembered that she never smiled, except once when she won. Then she ran and threw her arms around a scruffy-looking man with a bushy mustache and long hair.

One day Kirk noticed two men seated directly in front of them. He nudged Mary and nodded in their direction. He was reminded of another time seven years before in Memphis, at the dog tracks, when he was arrested, taken into custody in handcuffs, and later sentenced to sixty-five years for armed robbery.

He was about to tell Mary to get ready to slip out when one of them took out his wallet. As he opened it to get out his ticket, Kirk could see the Drug Enforcement Agency badge. The man was a narcotics agent.

On July 17, they received their first money order. Mary went to the Western Union office to pick up the hundred dollars her friend Cynthia D'Andrea had wired from Knoxville to Lisa Richard.

A flurry of phone calls were made daily by Kirk and Mary to friends and associates they thought could be trusted. Kirk called friends in Memphis, members of his family, and a friend who took the call at a pay phone at the State Line Market on the Tennessee-Mississippi border.

Mary called Cynthia several more times, talking sometimes as long as an hour in an effort to raise money. She also called Janet Vest. Janet was distraught; if she helped Mary she'd be throwing her own law career to the winds.

On August 11, a money order was sent to Robert Allred from Memphis in the amount of three hundred dollars. For some unexplained reason, the Western Union clerk, Coreen Darcey, took notice of the man who claimed it. Two days later at ten-fifteen in the morning, a money order for forty-five dollars arrived made out to Robert Allred. This time when Kirk went to pick it up, the clerk stalled him, certain now that his face matched that of the man on the FBI poster above her head. She called the local FBI office. Kirk signed for the money and left. The clerk watched him from the window but did not see him get into a car.

On August 17, Mary called the Western Union office to find out if a money order had been sent in either name. She was told one had arrived for Lisa Richard.

At four o'clock that afternoon, the precise time of their escape 139 days earlier, Mary entered the Daytona Western Union office. She put her purse on the counter. As she was about to sign for $350, six FBI agents jumped into the office, guns drawn, and yelled, "Freeze, Mary, FBI!"

Her face went white. She stood paralyzed while one of the agents grabbed for her purse with his free hand and dumped its contents on the floor. Another snapped handcuffs on her wrists. Then, holding her by the arm, he rushed her out onto the street.

At the same time another car full of agents had pulled up beside Kirk and dragged him out of the car.

"It's all over, you son of a bitch. Get on the ground and place your arms behind your back." A search of Kirk's pockets produced eighty-seven cents.

Mary looked down the street and saw Kirk lying face

down on the street, spread-eagled. One agent was holding a gun to his head; another was handcuffing him.

As they were herded into separate cars, they looked at each other. "Don't tell them anything," Kirk said quickly.

They were driven a hundred miles to Orlando, where Bob Ritchie and Janet Vest were waiting. A brief hearing was held that afternoon in a heavily guarded Orange County courtroom in which they both waived extradition rights.

As soon as the extradition hearing ended in Orlando, District Attorney General Jim Ramsey of Anderson County (where the escape had taken place) filed a motion in criminal court to increase Mary Evans's appearance bond from $100,000 to $500,000.

Two FBI agents, Don Collins and Bill McBee, police officer Jon Shipley, and Larry Davidson, an investigator with the attorney general's office, drove to Florida to escort the fugitives back to Tennessee.

It was a twelve-hour trip home. At first Mary glowered at her captors each time they tried to make conversation. Then as the caravan of state cars rolled along the highway, she began to relax. She apologized for not having showered, and for her disheveled appearance. She commented on the paperback romance she'd bought when they stopped for snacks. "This is really the pits of literature," she said, putting it down. They offered her magazines, which she leafed through.

"Are you happy to be going home, Mary?" one of the men asked her.

"Not really," she said.

In the car behind hers, Kirk agonized. "If we'd had more money, we'd still be free." His gaze shifted to the window, to the landscape—and freedom slipping past him. "I'm afraid Mary's whole life will be changed by this," he said.

A pack of cigarettes was held out to him. He lifted his manacled hands and took one, accepting the light that was offered. "Thanks," he said, and he inhaled deeply. The smoke stung his eyes. "I've ruined her life."

The caravan stopped in Henderson, South Carolina, for gas. In a blazing sunset, chained and unable to embrace, Kirk and Mary stood close, their hands touching. The guard who was watching them turned away, misty-eyed, to give them a moment's privacy. Later, he said, "She's a woman in love, that's all."

Dozens of curious spectators were gathered outside the Anderson County Courthouse that Friday night to get a glimpse of the famous fugitives. Deputies kept the crowd across the street from where the cars would arrive. Thirty rifle-toting police officers were on hand; one officer tended a leashed attack dog.

The jail is tucked away in a third-floor corner of the courthouse in Clinton, the county seat. This East Tennessee town, population 5,245, is thirty-eight miles from Knoxville.

Kirk arrived first, at eleven-twenty, Mary a moment or two later. Weary and bedraggled, she got out of the car, her head turned away from the media cameras. Kirk too kept his head lowered as they were rushed inside into the elevator.

Bob Ritchie had arrived at the courthouse just before eleven. He told Sheriff Dennis Trotter he wanted to see Mrs. Evans as soon as she arrived.

"No," the sheriff said, "my orders are no one sees the prisoner until Monday morning."

Ritchie told the sheriff that his client had a constitutional right to counsel and asked to use the telephone to call the judge.

Trotter, who had been picked Tennessee's outstanding sheriff in 1980, would be convicted four years later for selling cocaine, marijuana, Quaaludes, and Valium from a roadside tavern that dealt openly in drugs and prostitution.

He scowled at Ritchie and led him to the "day room," where he could wait for Mary.

Benna Mae Seivers, the sheriff's secretary, a small woman with pearl-gray hair, a warm smile, and a strong sense of public duty, took a dim view of attorney Mary Evans.

"I'd been reading about her, of course, and I even remember seeing her once at this courthouse, for a motion hearing on another case. But I sure wasn't prepared for what I saw that night. She looked like a cull from under the Gay Street bridge," she said, referring to the Knoxville bridge that crosses the Tennessee River where a dozen or so homeless live. "Her hair was stringy; it hadn't been washed. The roots had grown out. She had on an old black T-shirt, dirty jeans, and a cigarette hanging out of the corner of her mouth."

On the way into the room where they were to be booked, Mary and Kirk were able to meet briefly in the back hall just outside the jail. They stood, helpless, their hands manacled to chains around their waists. Kirk's eyes brimmed with tears. Mary cried softly, lifted her face to his, and kissed him.

" 'Bye, honey," she said.

He nodded. " 'Bye," he said quietly, and was led away.

Mary was put in a hot, windowless cell with four metal bunks. The dimly lit cell was closed off by a heavy steel door instead of the customary bars, with only a small opening of thick, reinforced glass. Mary would stay there for four nights.

Sunday morning before regular visiting hours, her parents came to visit. They were allowed forty-five minutes with her in the day room. People visiting other prisoners had fifteen minutes to talk through the cell door window.

The sheriff's staff resented her celebrity status. When

Mary complained about the food, Ritchie arranged for her to order something out. When the temperature soared into the high nineties, Mary demanded a fan, and got one.

Even the matron exhibited symptoms of celebrity fever. Monday morning she stopped at Benna Mae's office and with a nervous little laugh said, "You know, Benna Mae, she was right nice to me back there. I don't think she's really mad at us for locking her up."

"Well now," Benna Mae answered, her voice tinged with sarcasm, "isn't that a relief!"

"She acted like we were nothing," Benna Mae explained. "She was arrogant. Looked down her nose at us like we were backwoods rednecks here in Anderson County. She acted like all this was just temporary, she'd soon be finished with us."

The Pentecosts arrived at the courthouse Monday morning for the bond hearing and took seats in the back row. Silent, their faces expressionless, eyes straight ahead, they looked somehow as though they were in church.

Spectators were searched at the door. Reporters from the *Philadelphia Inquirer*, *The Tennessean*, *The Washington Post*, *Rolling Stone* magazine, *People* magazine, *Newsday*, AP, and UPI filled the front three rows. *Good Morning America* had contacted Ritchie to ask if Mary's parents would appear on their show. Ritchie declined for them.

Female county employees said they'd come to see what *he* looked like.

Mary, her hair freshly washed, and wearing the light-blue blazer her parents had brought, looked tired and pale. She sat at the defense table between Ritchie and Janet Vest and never looked in Kirk's direction.

Anderson County Criminal Court Judge James "Buddy" Scott presided. Born and raised in Oak Ridge where his father had worked for Union Carbide, forty-five-year-old "Buddy," as everyone called him, was a plain-spoken man of simple, home-grown values. His sympathies were clearly with Mary's parents.

When her father took the witness stand, Mary cast her eyes downward and bit her lip. Bob Pentecost spoke with emotion.

"As God is my witness I have no doubt my daughter would appear for all court proceedings if she is allowed to post bond. My daughter is very close to her family and we are very anxious to get her back home." He told the court he was willing to put up property valued at $176,280 owned by him and his wife for bond. "I will use everything I have to get my daughter bailed out of jail."

District Attorney General Jim Ramsey argued for an increase to $450,000, four times the original amount.

"It has been speculated Mary has forfeited her law career; she has already forfeited more than one hundred thousand dollars. A law career is worth more than that. She has violated public and professional trust."

Jerry Becker, a partner in the law firm of Lockridge and Becker, for whom Mary had clerked the summer before her last year of law school, testified as a character witness.

"Mary is a person who cares very deeply about equal justice. She was very, very insightful in her work. The firm grew to trust her research and opinions on law." He described her as a self-starter and very creative in her analysis of the law. "I believe without hesitancy that she will appear if allowed to post bond and return to her parents' farm."

After listening to ninety minutes of testimony, Judge Scott increased her bond to $450,000, and Mary was taken back to her cell.

The next day, August 23, an uncle and aunt of Mary's, James and Mary Sue Robinson, posted their property valued at more than $800,000 for Mary's release. Should Mary fail to show up for court proceedings, the newspapers reported, the Pentecosts and the Robinsons stood to lose all their property.

A date was set for the arraignment—September 22 at nine-thirty.

Meantime, FBI agents turned over to the district attorney's office the items seized from the motel room in Daytona. Listed among them were items seldom found in most vacationers' rooms: pawn tickets in the amount of $150.00 in the name of Robert Allred in exchange for a carbine rifle and a gold chain; another pair for a lady's quartz Seiko watch and man's Bulova watch, for $36.00; a sales receipt from the Easy Pawn Shop for a Charter Arms Bulldog .44 Special, a powerful handgun of the Dirty Harry variety, purchased by Robert Allred for $260.00; a pawn ticket from Max's gun shop for $125.00. Driver's licenses bore two of their five aliases, and there were copies of birth certificates for Lisa Jo-Ann Richard, Robert Allen Allred, Judith Ann Metcalf, and Tammy Renee Haskins. The clothing bore labels of designers Yves St. Laurent, Jordache, Levi's; makeup products were from Clinique; there was an array of nail polishes and removers; a backgammon set; horoscope books: Sagittarius (hers), and Aquarius (his); a deck of Rook cards, a card game named Won Over; a jump rope; birth-control pills; hydrogen peroxide; two toothbrushes, one brown, one purple; eight instant color pictures of Kirk and Evans posed together and separately; a receipt from Tom's Gun and Coin Shop showing the purchase of a Northern Arms C-3100, price $89.25; two magazines: *Eagle Survival* and *Soldier of Fortune*; one bulletproof vest; and a book entitled *The Anarchist's Cookbook*, an underground how-to manual for terrorists, revolutionaries, and across-the-board outlaws, filled with tips ranging from creating your own passports to how to make a bomb.

Attorneys for both defendants filed petitions ranging from a request to dismiss some of the charges to demands for additional trial-preparation time and the suppression of evidence. Fifty-six witnesses were listed to be called by the state, including Janet Vest, Jim Bell, Bob Ritchie, and Cynthia D'Andrea. Oak Ridge police officers were furious that District Attorney General Ramsey had granted D'Andrea, who had committed a felony by sending them money, immunity from prosecution in return for her cooperation.

Throughout her many court appearances for preliminary motions Mary sat, her face immobile, her eyes downcast.

An anonymous tip was phoned in just before one of the proceedings. TBI agents received information that someone was planning to slip Kirk a gun in the courthouse. Two dozen police officers from five law enforcement agencies were stationed inside and outside the courthouse.

Kirk was escorted into the courtroom surrounded by guards carrying automatic shotguns. Outside in the hall one of the reporters worried, "If someone drops a bottle of Coke and it explodes, they're going to think it's a bomb going off." A female reporter was warned not to snap her purse shut too loudly or she might get herself shot.

The arraignment lasted fifteen minutes. Both defendants entered pleas of not guilty to the charges of armed robbery, aggravated kidnapping, and escape. Afterward, Judge Scott permitted Mary and Kirk to meet in a conference room with their attorneys present for an hour and fifteen minutes. The purpose of the meeting was to discuss their defenses. It was the first time they were able to be together since their capture. For a moment Mary rested her head against Kirk's shoulder. They stood off to one corner talking quietly while their attorneys talked among themselves.

Mary had been writing long letters to Kirk at the main prison in Nashville, mailing them inside legal envelopes in the hope that the guards wouldn't read them.

Prison mail is routinely inspected for contraband, supposedly in the inmate's presence, but as often as not this rule is violated. One of the prison staff was overheard to quip, "Kirk's gettin' all this mail from some attorney—I never knew an attorney to write six- and seven-page letters in longhand."

Kirk was being held on death row, two cells down from the electric chair. Maximum-security prisoners considered extreme escape risks were housed there along with those who were sentenced to be executed. James Earl Ray was also kept on death row, since his escape attempt from Brushy Mountain. Both men were considered targets, in that any black who could take credit for killing either of them would make a name for himself among the black prison population. Therefore, neither Kirk nor Ray was ever permitted out in population.

Kirk placed collect calls to Mary at home. Her father accepted one of the calls and took the opportunity to say, "I am a Christian man; I know the meaning of forgiveness." But after several more calls Bob Pentecost told him that never, under any circumstances, was he to try to contact his daughter again. From then on Mary would go to a friend's house to await his calls.

There was considerable speculation, especially among those who had known Mary at one time or another, about why she and Kirk had got no farther than Florida. If she was serious about not getting caught, why Daytona Beach, where half of Knoxville goes for vacation? If they had nine thousand dollars as the papers reported, couldn't that have got them out of the country? Someone else pointed out that they could have even gone up on top of one of the ridges around Knoxville and no one would have found them. Or New York, for that matter.

"Yes, but how would we have supported ourselves?" Kirk asked when those questions were put to him. "I don't even have a Social Security number. We live in a computerized society; a man without a history is immediately suspect. We were just waiting for enough money to go and *stay* gone."

When asked what he thought Mary's mental condition was at the time of the escape, Kirk smiled, his boyish grin setting his eyes atwinkle, and said, "Well, take a look at me—she'd have to be crazy, wouldn't you say?"

But when pressed, the eyes grew serious, the gaze direct. "We knew we were in love by the third time we saw each other. Maybe before."

In late October, Bob Ritchie made an off-the-record comment to a reporter. "We have a very, very sick girl on our hands." And on October 26 the *Knoxville Journal* ran a story, "Mental State to Be Evans' Defense Basis." Ritchie had already filed a motion stating that he would rely on his client's mental condition for the defense.

Insanity laws are not uniform throughout the country. In Tennessee, the three questions the jury must answer in determining insanity in terms of guilt or innocence are: Was the defendant suffering from a mental illness at the time of the commission of the crime? Did that illness prevent the defendant from knowing the wrongfulness of his/her act? Did the mental illness render the defendant incapable of conforming his/her conduct to the requirements of the law he/she is charged with violating? If the jury answers "yes" to the first question and "yes" to either the second or the third, it can return a verdict of not guilty by reason of insanity. Answering "no" to the first question or answering "no" to both the second and the third would not allow the jury to return such a verdict.

In October, Bob Ritchie sent Mary to see Dr. Jerry Embry, a Knoxville psychiatrist Ritchie had asked on six previous occasions to examine other clients charged with crimes. Over the next five months he would spend fifty-nine and a half hours with Mary.

On November 29, Mary was admitted to the forensic division of the Middle Tennessee Mental Health Institute in Nashville. She was sent there by order of the court for an evaluation of her ability to stand trial and for an assessment of her mental condition at the time she committed the crime.

During her stay at the health institute, Mary told members of the evaluation team that she'd become "obsessed" with the Kirk case, especially since the other lawyers in the firm seemed convinced that Kirk would be sentenced to die in the electric chair. She also told them that this was her first experience in a prison and she was "repulsed" at the way the prisoners were handled and led around and touched by the guards at Brushy. She was "panicked" as Kirk's trial approached and was sure her boss would "botch the case and Kirk would get the death penalty." The escape, she said, was planned about two weeks before, and was mostly for her rather than for Kirk.

The Staff Conference Report, written on December 20, went on to say, "It is apparent that Ms. Evans had struggled with a marked need to conform to parental wishes, specifically her father's, while at the same time experiencing alien feelings and wishes which she tried to keep concealed.

"She explained that the escape was not a Romeo and Juliet thing like the newspapers reported and 'the point was not sex. The point was I would not be me anymore.' "

But Kirk said Mary's letters to him worried him. "They're filling her full of drugs—they're brainwashing her, that's what they're doing, and I'm sitting down here helpless as a baby."

Tennessee law required that a person seeking to avail himself of a defense of insanity must undergo a thirty-day examination by three medical experts: a psychiatrist, a psychologist, and medical physician.

During the months of January and February, Mary kept almost daily appointments with Dr. Embry.

In February, Ritchie made an appointment for Mary to fly to Philadelphia, accompanied by her parents, to see the noted psychiatrist Robert Sadoff. Sadoff had testified in trials all over the country. Famous among them was the murder trial of Green Beret Captain Dr. Jeffrey MacDonald, accused of the murder of his wife and two children. Dr. Sadoff examined Captain MacDonald for the defense; in his findings he stated that MacDonald was not capable of having murdered his family.

Sadoff saw Mary on February 9 in his office for three hours. The next day he saw her alone for two hours and with her parents for one hour. On February 29 he saw her once more, again with her parents, for an hour.

Mary's trial date was set for March 27. Two hundred and fifty subpoenas were mailed out to prospective jurors, as opposed to the usual seventy-five; Attorney General Jim Ramsey filed a list of fifty-six potential witnesses, including Mary's own attorney, Bob Ritchie; her former boss, Jim Bell; John Lockridge; Janet Vest; psychologist Gary Salk; and Knoxville psychologist Kathleen Broughan, who treated Mary in 1981 after her suicide attempt. Also on the list were Kirk's parents, his former wife, Kirk's former mother-in-law, and Ricky Moorman, inmate at Brushy Mountain, and his brother Ron, who sent Mary the five hundred dollars.

On January 8, the defense scored its first victory. Judge Scott ruled that the taking of evidence by law enforcement officers from a motel room belonging to Mary Evans had violated her rights to privacy and was an unlawful seizure. Therefore those items would not be allowed as evidence. But items belonging to Kirk seized from the same motel room would be allowed as evidence because Kirk was a convict on the run and was not entitled to the same rights of privacy. Only the evidence taken from Mary at the time of arrest—her driver's license, and birth certificate cards with aliases—would be admitted in the trial.

The following day an outraged Attorney General Jim Ramsey made a statement to the press. He said that Judge

Scott's ruling might result in an acquittal and that he intended to appeal the ruling.

The disagreement between judge and attorney general was a continuation of a five-and-a-half-year battle between the two. Judge Scott had cited the Dartmouth-educated "hillbilly preppie" attorney general for contempt of court twenty times, for misconduct fifteen times, and had thrown him into jail twice.

Taking note of his record, "General" Ramsey (the honorific given to attorney generals in the South) wrote to the *Guinness Book of Records* in England to apply for entry. He proclaimed that in his first eighteen months in office he had been censured more than any prosecutor in the world. Guinness editors wrote back, "Alas, we have no such category."

A year later General Ramsey would treat the press to a full-page story with color photographs of him locked up in the Anderson County courthouse jail, where he was serving a ten-day sentence for contempt. The handsome six-foot-six prosecutor was wearing the prisoner's orange jumpsuit.

Buddy Scott and Jim Ramsey both grew up in Oak Ridge; Scott preceded Ramsey at Oak Ridge High School by seven years. Both were normal, rational men of unusually high intellect. Scott was respected as a thoughtful, serious man; Ramsey saw himself as a white knight put on this earth in East Tennessee to do battle with the evils of the good-ol'-boy network that he swears the judge is partial to.

Each court appearance for a motion hearing was like another segment in the season's live miniseries. The spectators would arrive early to get there before the TV crews. They liked to watch for the anchor men and women whose faces were as familiar to them as their own family's, and they'd get themselves all shined up in case the cameras happened to catch them in the background. Soon it was time to line up to have their purses and pockets inspected by armed guards who'd also run the electronic scanner up and down their bodies in search of concealed weapons.

Inside the courtroom they'd take their seats and watch for the press to file in, and strain to hear what it was they were saying to each other. Now and then they'd hear an unfamiliar accent and figure *The New York Times* was there too.

They had their favorites among the lawyers. Zane Daniel, Kirk's newly appointed attorney, was well known in the county. He'd tried some pretty big cases in that courthouse. Besides, he had the sound of country in his voice. He used to bring his lady friend, an actress on *Hee Haw*, to court sometimes and sit her in the front row so she could watch him try a case. Nobody would pay attention to much else when that TV star they watched every Saturday night was sitting right there. Zane had a good sense of humor too. He knew how to get a laugh out of a jury. "That Zane," one of his colleagues said after losing a court battle to him, "he's chuckled more people out of the penitentiary than any ten lawyers in East Tennessee you can name. Zane says 'no,' and the jury shakes their heads; he says 'yes,' and the jury nods."

Bob Ritchie they were not too sure about. He was a bit too smart, "one of them scholarly types," a spectator noted, a little too smooth for their tastes.

Scott and Ramsey each had their fans. Ramsey was a favorite with the old ladies, but they clucked their tongues and shook their heads over the "feud."

Still, it was the leading lady and her leading man they were waiting to see. As in any well-staged event, they were the last to arrive, except for the judge.

Enter Mary, led by one of Bob Ritchie's young associates. She was wearing a gray pinstripe suit, an ivory-colored silk shirt, taupe shoes, and a matching shoulder bag, all of which would be described in detail in the next morning paper.

She walked brusquely, shoulders slightly raised, head held high, eyes lowered, pointedly ignoring the stares of the audience. Her mouth curved downward in a disdainful expression. Even the spectators who did not like her were fascinated by her.

The courtroom grew quiet as Kirk, in his flaming orange, appeared, his weighted boot sounding hard on the floor, the clanking of the chains jarring the senses. His face colored with embarrassment at the racket he made as he walked, but he held his head high nevertheless. He too looked neither right nor left, but there was something a bit tragic about him. Maybe it was the way his eyes drifted to the face of the woman he clearly loved, who never, ever returned the look.

The women spectators in the courtroom were intrigued. They saw a certain vulnerability that aroused their sympathy. The men secretly admired him—for the power he must have over women. To them Kirk was a real, living outlaw who not only got away but took a rich fancy woman with him.

The press agreed that if Kirk stood up there in front of a jury, they'd probably be hard put to convict him of escape, but Mary was another story. They wondered how Ritchie was ever going to put that girl on the stand.

At seven o'clock on the evening of February 22, a secret meeting was held in Ramsey's office with members of the defense team. Less than a week later an announcement was made that an agreement had been reached between the defense and the state. Mary would change her plea from not guilty of the nine severe charges of armed robbery and kidnapping—punishable by twenty years to life in prison—to guilty of the lesser charge of aiding and abetting, a crime punishable by one to three years in the state penitentiary.

As part of the package, General Ramsey would recommend to the court that probation be granted her on the condition that Mary would undergo psychiatric treatment and make certain restitutions. Dr. Salk would be repaid for the damage done to his telephone and for the twenty-five dollars that was taken from him. In addition, she would make restitution to the Department of Corrections for the loss of three firearms. A bargain by anyone's standards.

Kirk's deal, however, could hardly be called a bargain. In return for changing his plea to guilty he would have to agree to take an additional thirty-five years for the armed robbery and kidnapping charges and five more years for escape.

His attorney, Zane Daniel, said that Kirk had instructed him to do whatever was best for Mary.

When Judge Scott learned of the agreement, he warned the defendants that the attorney general's recommendations were not binding upon the court.

The news of a plea bargain caused a firestorm in the community. Law enforcement officials were furious and frustrated that after months of investigation and countless man-hours tracking the pair down, the attorney general had thrown in the towel. Arzo Carson, director of the TBI, said, "I've given up on it. You sometimes wonder after all this work whether it's worth it." He couldn't even guess what the cost of the five-month search was.

Jon Shipley, who'd put as many hours into the investigation as anyone, made a short, angry statement to the press. "Mr. Ramsey did not see fit to involve me in any of the negotiations. I'm not saying I agree with it and I'm not saying I like it."

Prosecutors in Knoxville deplored the plea bargain. "Ramsey had a considerable public duty to try the case," said one of the federal attorneys. "It is a phenomenal human interest question. The public has a right to know. Did she really supply the tape, smuggle the gun, and set up the switch car? If she did actively and voluntarily help, then a layman would conclude she wasn't crazy. Ramsey should have provided her the opportunity to prove that, to throw herself up to public examination and explain *why* she did it. You don't stand silent unless you have something to hide.

"The enormity of what she's done can't be underestimated. Mary Evans has fundamentally repudiated the principles of our profession."

But Ramsey insisted, "There was no way to win. . . . it would have been irresponsible for us to go forward. What would people say if we'd spent two hundred fifty thousand dollars trying this case and lost with a John Hinckley verdict?" he asked.

He had received the written reports, and they had convinced him. Three psychiatrists, two of whom were engaged by the defense, and one psychologist had agreed that an insanity defense could be supported in Evans's trial. However, a state psychologist disagreed with those findings.

Citizens of Anderson County were calling for Ramsey's impeachment. Ramsey, undaunted—if a little sheepish— told reporters, "My own mother gave me hell. She said 'How could you let that girl go free just because her daddy works for the university?' "

One of Mary's law school classmates observed wryly, "Looks like that system she deplored for its hypocrisy and its deals might be the very one that's going to keep her ass out of jail."

The next morning the *Knoxville Journal* ran the following editorial:

Please Explain Evans' Situation

It may be possible, between now and the formal sentencing of Mary Pentecost Evans, for someone to make a convincing argument against her confinement as a penalty for assisting her former law client, convicted armed robber and killer Tim Kirk, in his escape from prison. Anything, we now guess, is possible.

If that comes across as a dare to find justice in the prosecutorial decision to take Evans' guilty plea to a single charge of aiding and abetting an escape in return for a recommendation for probation, that is because it is intended as a dare.

The defendant's license to practice law in Tennessee, which at the very least should have been surrendered as part of the bargain, was left intact under the terms spelled out in Anderson County Criminal Court.

Judge Buddy Scott has the last word on accepting the recommendations of District Attorney General Jim Ramsey. Ordinarily such plea-bargaining agreements are approved by the courts of Tennessee. But in Anderson County the open and constant contention between Scott and Ramsey leaves the odds unknown. It can be stated firmly that any notion of justice is better left to prayer whenever that judge and prosecutor are engaging one another in court. But that's another matter, and the citizens of Anderson County, who are abundantly aware of the feud and its detractions from the business of justice, seem to like it that way and keep re-electing the antagonists.

That doesn't seem to be an issue in this instance, although it could be suggested that Ramsey may have perceived Scott as enjoying the publicity attendant to the Evans-Kirk case and sought to remove the source of enjoyment from Scott's venue as quickly as possible, precluding the judge from presiding over a highly charged trial in front of the nation's press. Something like that is possible, if not probable, such is their relationship.

Justice is sometimes elusive in any jurisdiction. But in this instance it is altogether hidden from anyone taking note of the facts, the state's accusations and the allegations, however meager, of the defense.

Evans' attorneys said they might use her mental condition as a defense. She was examined by several psychiatrists and two psychologists. The prosecutor maintains that since all psychiatrists, including the state's, indicated they would testify she was mentally ill at the time of the escape, that he would be wasting his time if he took the case to trial, even though all said she was mentally competent to stand trial. The state's psychologist said she was not mentally ill at all.

Ramsey says the final hearing on the sentencing recommendation will include testimony from the experts that she should be submitted to a prolonged hospitalization for mental treatment. If that is the situation, forgive us this quizzical reaction: What is she doing walking around among us now?

That's not to suggest that Evans is a clear and present danger to society at large. This is a woman who, after throwing away her career by springing a convict who said he loved her, spent months on the run in an adventure whose high points seem to have been betting on dog racing, taking care of her fingernails, and avoiding pregnancy. If there is a mitigating circumstance to her now-admitted participation in a felony escape of a previously dangerous criminal, it is in that they were accused of no further felonies while on the lam.

But to suggest that she was so mentally ill that she could not be held responsible for her acts with Kirk—when they planned and executed in concert an escape from the system, disarming guards and taking the wallet of an Oak Ridge psychologist whom they had set up as a screen to get Kirk outside prison walls—is an insult unless it can be better explained. It is an insult to the public conscience, but it is particularly insulting to any woman serving a prison sentence because she went so wacky as to help a convict escape. Certainly such a woman was disturbed, too. She took leave of her senses to get a man out of prison and got herself in. Was she therefore so impaired that she should have been kept unaccountable? More to be pitied than censured?

The reason that we can allow mental competence to be a defense to criminal acts is that we do not allow professionals, at law or at psychiatry or psychology, to make the determination in borderline cases, indeed where there is any question whatever. We put that to our juries, to our peers. They decide. Neither the judge nor the prosecutor is granted that power on purpose.

Jim Ramsey has usurped it. He has bargained it away. He has done so in the interests of a fellow member of the bar who committed a felony and will not be prosecuted for it. And he is asking that the court agree that that is the way the public's need for justice is served.

That public is owed an explanation. Perhaps it can be explained. Anything, as we said, should be possible when free and open minds seek to see justice.

On the eve of her probation hearing, Mary Evans voluntarily surrendered her law license. According to the rules of the Tennessee Board of Professional Responsibility, Mary would be eligible in five years to ask to be licensed again.

On the morning of March 27, 1984, Ash Wednesday,

Judge Buddy Scott turned the page of the calendar that sat open on his desk. Under the date was the word for the day: *contrition*.

Press, TV media, and spectators appeared in force; security was tight. The atmosphere in the halls outside the courtroom was that of an opening night. Denied the satisfaction of a full-blown trial, the audience had accepted the sentencing hearing as next best.

Judge Scott called the crowded courtroom to order. The first order of business to be taken up by the court was the question of Kirk's sentencing.

The judge addressed Kirk.

"Realistically I don't know how one reaches someone like yourself as far as sentencing."

The state, in the person of Jan Hicks, Ramsey's assistant, had presented proof that Kirk had been convicted of three felonies within the past five years, thereby meeting the requirements that classified him as a habitual offender. Thus, his forty-year sentence should run consecutively to—not concurrently with—the sixty-five-year sentence he was already serving.

The judge asked Kirk to stand. Chains rattled as Kirk, his orange coveralls garish amid the lawyerly pinstripes, rose to his feet. He listened calmly, responding, "Yes, sir," as Judge Scott added forty years to the sentence he was already serving, giving him a possible parole date of 2048.

Mary, seated at the defense table, kept her eyes fixed straight ahead. She listened stone-faced as the judge said that those forty years would not include the sentence Kirk had yet to receive from the Morgan County judge.

Kirk was then remanded to the custody of the sheriff. He would remain in the sheriff's office throughout the day's hearings in the event Ritchie wanted to call him.

The court was recessed for ten minutes.

Members of the press wondered about Jim Ramsey, whose absence was puzzling. Strange that he would turn a hearing with this much notoriety over to his assistant. Jan Hicks's dress was bulging with her five-month pregnancy—her ninth child.

Across the aisle sat Mr. and Mrs. Pentecost with Mary's younger brother, Chris.

When court reconvened, Bob Ritchie called Department of Corrections official Gary Tullock to the stand. Tullock had conducted a six-hour interview with Mary for purposes of preparing a presentencing report for the court. He also interviewed Dr. Gary Salk, who told the probation officer that he did not think "a great deal would be served by her going to prison." He told the court that Salk said that he felt very much like an object at the time of the offense, that he was just kind of there like office furniture. And that if Mary Evans were granted probation, he would like her to contact him, to be around him, possibly around his family, even in his home, so that she could hopefully come to understand that he was a real person. She might come to some understanding of what could have occurred in that office that day—of the lives that would've been affected by her actions.

It was Tullock's recommendation that Mary give one thousand hours of community service if she received probation. He suggested as part of her duties she might work on the grounds of the zoo, cleaning out cages.

Bob Ritchie called Dr. Jerry Embry next. Embry had an ingenuous, almost apologetic manner. He seemed to know he had his work cut out for him.

His demeanor was explained by a theory of Knoxville attorney Judy McCarthy, who also taught part-time at the University of Tennessee Law School. "An insanity defense is the hardest to sell. It just doesn't fly here—and it's rarely used. The tradition in the South is if someone in your family goes crazy you lock them away in the attic. People around here are very suspicious of psychiatrists, which stems from a deeply ingrained belief that everyone is responsible for their own actions."

Another prominent attorney, who preferred not to be named because he sometimes had to hire them, said, "Psychiatric hired guns add nothing to the legal process."

Ritchie began by getting Embry to recite his qualifications for the court's benefit. Then he asked him, "Would you just simply—we don't have a jury here, and I think it best, sir, if you just simply tell His Honor the course of your examination and what your findings have been in regard to Mary Pentecost Evans."

"Your Honor, what I have found is that Mary Evans has been—has suffered from a serious mental illness known as schizophrenia for at least the last—oh, at least since 1975 and perhaps even before then. . . . Do you want me to go with pretty much the full story?"

Judge Scott leaned forward. "Let me tell you something, Doctor. . . . there are certain things in regard to your profession that cause this court some concern. I do not know how one retrospectively looks into the past to evaluate someone like Mary Evans." He asked the doctor, "Can you address that?"

Embry bravely launched into his testimony.

He said that for at least two years preceding the crime, Mary felt herself constantly tormented by alien forces that tried to make her weak and submissive. "She would hear voices in her head talking, laughing, whispering. When these episodes would happen, she would hide and curl up and face the wall in little sheltered spaces that she would find available where she was living. She would find it difficult to breathe. She would start screaming at the voices to stop. . . . In 1981, while a law student, there was an episode that helped convince her that these were something outside of herself. In that she had an experience of visual hallucinations. She'd gotten up in the night. Was sitting in a chair near her bed. Looked across the room and saw the things that she—she sometimes refers to them as the things. Sometimes demons, sometimes it. She really doesn't know what they are. In the form of little balls of color. Green and red, about three-quarters of an inch, kind of dancing around.

Reporters began to look at each other as if to make certain they hadn't imagined what they'd just heard.

"She became very frightened. She thought—this was the first time she had encountered them before they got in her head. She called somebody for help. Okay. That . . ."

"Who was that somebody, Doctor?" Judge Scott asked.

"She called John Lockridge, a friend of hers, and asked him to please come over. And he—I understand he did."

"Let me interrupt you, Doctor," the judge said.

"Okay."

"I have available here, in the limited library that I have, certain legal publications pertaining to a defense of insanity. What you have just told me is available for Mrs. Kirk to read in a law library. About voices inside . . ."

Ritchie corrected the judge. "Mrs. Evans, Your Honor."

"I mean Mrs. Evans. Excuse me. Thank you. They are available to her."

"Yes."

"And I have read those, and I could parrot what you have just stated to me if I were an individual appearing before you with something so vital as my freedom at stake. Now can you tell me what would prevent somebody of the intelligence of Mrs. Evans from reading those publications and any other publications that are available to you, and if you interview only that one source from telling you that they had had these hallucinations and that they have experienced these things? How could you yourself evaluate that as a professional?"

"Well, first of all, the description of hallucinations was only one part of the overall picture. For her to be able to fake the illness that I found would not only require knowledge of symptoms from having read, as you say, but also would require a good deal of knowledge of theory that is just very unlikely that she would have to explain everything that happened. Also, much of this erratic behavior, including other things that I haven't gotten to yet, occurred before she even started the Brushy Mountain case when there would be no motive to, as you point out. The other thing is that I rely on my twenty-two years in full-time practice in psychiatry—I even include my training and army time—to learn a little bit about how to see the genuineness of what somebody tells me. And after forty or fifty hours, I think it would be hard to fool me, frankly."

"Well, it may be, Doctor. But one of the problems . . ."

"But I understand your point."

"One of the problems I have, you say that you have testified I think in three previous cases. Most of the individuals that come here and are charged with a crime are usually economically depressed and are deprived of defense counsel. I have to appoint them one. And those individuals who come here really do not have the intelligence to read about certain matters involving psychiatry. Mrs. Evans has that, and she has available publications that I can show to you that would present a picture of hallucinations and lights, flashing lights, of individuals talking to them outside themselves, jabberers, or at least rambling and a source of talking, demons and things of this nature. And it concerns me that this would be available to her. And she brings that knowledge to an individual like yourself. Now do you know of any prior reports of these happenings? Prior to her—you examining her after the events occurred involving this crime? In other words, is this the first time that you know of that she has reported these events to anyone other than John Lockridge?"

"Well, as far as the hallucinatory experiences, that's possibly so. In terms of emotional disturbance, that's not the case. She had seen a psychiatrist and a psychologist before the Brushy case," Dr. Embry said.

"And there was an episode I believe where—it might

have been where she called John Lockridge, according to the probation report, that she attempted to take her life. Is that correct? At least there was some reflection upon that."

"Yes. In 1981."

"In 1981. And was that not the time that you have referred to that she called John Lockridge and was taken to . . ."

"No, she called—well, that was not the time I referred to."

"Oh."

"The time I referred to was the visual hallucinatory events."

"All right."

"Let me find my place again." Dr. Embry studied his notes. "Okay. These were some disturbances. She also experienced during these attacks visual imagery, inside her head but not daydreams, of dots which she thought were the things. Of various images such as flying carpets, tigers jumping through hoops, waterfalls, very frequently little blobs which she could best characterize as the little one-celled animals, which might be different colors. Might be blue, might be pink, might be blue with purple edges, and so forth."

Reporters were scribbling madly. "Tigers in the waterfalls?" one asked the reporter seated next to him. "No dummy, tigers jumping through hoops " "What color were those blobs?" another wanted to know. "Pink?"

"And this is an abnormal kind of phenomenon," Embry went on. "She had frequent shifts in mood. Considerable rage to deep depression to anxiety which might last a few weeks at a time or might—or perhaps for a shorter time—without apparent external exciting causes. She had poor behavioral control. She would have urges to do things. Break things that were—which she was fond of. Such as plants or little ceramic things that she had made. Sometime she would get an urge to break them, and she would.

On one occasion she had a little stuffed bear that she liked, and she took a knife and cut it open. Doesn't know why. Just had an urge to do it. And it was something she was quite fond of. On one occasion—and this was back when she was still married—prior to her divorce in, I believe in 1980, she had a little ceramic cat that she made to match her real cat. And she took it out and just smashed it. Along with other things. There were these episodes of behavioral control. During the two years prior to—well, particularly around a few months in early 1982. It probably started around Christmas 1981 but continued for a few months. Was an exceptionally bad period for her. In January, under the influence of one of those spells that had lasted for several hours, she took an overdose of Tranxene. Subsequently did report this to someone—perhaps Lockridge. I'm not sure. But anyway she was taken by him or some friend to Saint Mary's Hospital and from there was referred to Doctor Glenn Wright. She saw him a few times. Began to think that maybe she should ask for help, which she never had before for several reasons. And I'll explain those later. But at any rate she asked her father to go with her on one occasion so that Doctor Wright might explain to her father her illness and her need for help, and her father went. And Doctor Wright, as I understood, did. But then her father, as I understand it, discouraged her to continue with treatment and she dropped it. Later I think Doctor—I know John Lockridge for sure insisted that she see a psychologist. Made the appointment for her. I think paid for the first few visits to see to it that she would go because he was that concerned about her. He would find her doing strange things like sitting on the floor or sitting in the sink, curled up in fetal positions around. Also some of her impaired behavioral control—I forgot to mention. She would get up in the night and pack, and on one occasion drove to Atlanta and ate at McDonald's and drove back. But often would get out in her car and drive around. I think maybe she went to Nashville once. Anyway, part of what was going on during the year preceding Brushy was impinging on her consciousness, was something she had tried to deny for years. And that was knowledge and the awareness that she was mentally ill. The voices used to tell her, 'You mustn't tell anybody' about them or about anything much. 'People mustn't know that you're sick or they won't like you.' And she would try to argue with them and say, 'Well, John likes me, and he would stand by me.' And they'd laugh and say oh no he wouldn't. And they would frequently laugh. But that was the one thing that they would tell her. With Doctor Broughan she kept things superficial. She never reported the voices. She didn't report them to Doctor Wright, although she did have some concern about him helping her. I think she was a little fearful of some of the things he wanted to do that involved medication and having blood drawn and so forth. Because she's very sensitive to anything that has to do with control over her. But this impinging awareness of her illness was very threatening, and she began to feel more futile about herself. All the things that made most—seemed to bring contentment and happiness to most people, she had found hollow. They just didn't do it for her. Things like an education, her law career, marriage, friends, all the things that most of us find pleasure in, she just realized increasingly they just didn't do anything for her. And she was beginning to feel really bad about her future and her life. She started the Brushy case. . . ."

Judge Scott looked bewildered. "Let me interrupt for something."

"Yes, sir."

"Why was it that she was told not to tell about these things, these hallucinations, and yet she told you about it? What . . ."

"Well, she only told me about it after a lot of things had occurred. And she told me not only about that but a great deal about herself that she really hadn't ever told anybody. And here's another instance where she would have to know an awful lot of theory to be able to pull the whole thing off. All her life going back into early childhood. Third grade, second grade, through elementary school. All her life she employed the classic defensive mechanism of paranoia, with people who have psychotic personality cores. And that is distancing. Or that's jargon. And what it means is that you keep emotional distance from anybody else, from everyone else. You keep—you have to resist emotional involvement with anyone because of the—and it's not in the conscious knowledge that this is why you do it—but the fear is of the intrusion and the loss of your own sense of ego boundaries, and the regression being drawn into psychosis."

"All right. Had you at the time that you examined her asked her if she had had any courses at the University of Tennessee or any other place?

"Oh, I know that she had a psychology course at UT."

"Do you know to what extent . . . ?"

"I know for example, sir, along those lines that she had done some reading when she was thirteen and fourteen because she felt—her image of herself was that she was different from everybody, she was a freak. She went to the school library and got some books on mental health and tried to read and tried to diagnose herself."

"How do you know that?"

"She told me."

Ritchie seemed willing to let the judge continue to conduct the cross-examination.

"All right. She told you. Did she tell you that she only had one course and when she took it what was offered?"

"I don't know clearly the history on that," Embry admitted. "Well, throughout her childhood and as far back as she can remember, she was a loner. She might have a friend at a time, which was kept superficial. She might relate to certain people. For a while she particularly enjoyed sitting around with some of the kids from a nearby area of less social circumstances. More rebellious kids. They liked to sit and smoke and spit, and some kid taught her how to spit, and she enjoyed that and so forth. But it was partly the defined element. She never—she never fit in with her peer group. She never joined anything. She always felt there was something different about her. She has always been very personal and private. There were also times when she would get into quarrels with people. There were also other evidences of childhood disturbance, like prior to age thirteen—from about nine to thirteen—the kids played with Barbie dolls. She would treat her Barbie doll as if it were her child I suppose, but she would frequently find things that it had done wrong and that required punishment. And one time she held it up to a light bulb and burned a hole in it. Other times she would step on it and throw it and so forth."

Snickers were heard coming from the press section. Larry Daughtrey of *The Tennessean* muttered, "Well, she just lost me. Anyone who abuses her Barbie doll is no friend of mine."

Bob Pentecost's eyes squeezed shut for a second: his arm tightened around his wife's shoulder.

Embry continued, seemingly unaffected by the mood in the courtroom. He was describing her teenage years now, a date she had had with a young man whom she liked, except that for fourteen nights in a row after their date, she dreamed that she stabbed him repeatedly for no reason. Choosing incidents at random now, he jumped ahead to Mary's law career and how she'd grown bored with routine legal work.

"Doctor, that is no sign of insanity, I hope," the judge said.

"Probably not. Probably not," the doctor answered pleasantly. "At the same time she met Tim, she liked him. As time went on she—she also could identify with him. She brought into that job—I'll tell you what she brought in and then explain a little and elaborate a bit. But she brought into that job at Brushy some prior feeling that in a sense she was a criminal. She had some identification of herself as a criminal. And to elaborate a bit, a part of her illness was identity uncertainty."

"How do you differentiate that from a compassionate, Except for the grace of God there go I?"

"I think you're talking, yeah, a bit about empathy maybe. Empathy with—you know—'I can understand why that person did that' or his circumstances. But this was a little different. This was more like the feeling 'Well, maybe I should be a criminal. Maybe I'm a criminal.'

"She began to idealize certain things about him," Dr. Embry went on. "And what they were were her perceptions of characteristics about him in terms of his power. His ability to conform things. His absolute rebellion against any kind of submission. No matter what anybody did to him, he maintained his own integrity. He just didn't submit. This in face of the fact that he was in prison."

The judge interrupted. Before the doctor went into any further detail he wanted it made clear that Mary Evans had voluntarily submitted a plea of guilty, "and that she is accountable for criminal conduct. For escape. The defense of insanity is no longer available to her, and I am concerned about a condition that existed at that time only for the purpose of mitigation of the punishment that she would receive. Do I make myself clear in that regard?"

"Yes, sir," the doctor answered.

"It is not material at this point as to whether or not she could conform her conduct to the requirements of the law because that has already been foreclosed."

Bob Ritchie stood. "May I be heard in that regard, Your Honor? . . . If it please the court, the term 'culpability' as used in the mitigating factor—"

"I understand that, and that has to do with intent and the culpability of a—"

Ritchie, determined to make his point, raised his voice. "And whether or not she could conform her conduct to the requirements of the law as that would relate to culpability."

"No, Mr. Ritchie. No. No. Not to conform her conduct to the requirements of the law as that would relate to culpability. But just to what degree her intent would be impaired, as far as this court is concerned. Her intent to commit the crime. Do you understand?"

Embry stepped into the fray. "Perhaps I could just explain how I saw what happened, and then you can fit it in with the needs. I—"

The judge was rapidly losing patience. "Yes. Try to capsulize it though, Doctor, if you would. And I know that you are trying to do justice to your evaluation."

". . . as this relationship developed and there was this idealization of Tim, and as this regression took place, the psychosis enlarged."

"All right. Now I understand that, Doctor. I understand that she has identified with Kirk, and that she really is finding him an attractive personality."

"I'm going a step further. . . . the next thing really to develop was a merger phenomena [*sic*] with Tim, and in this case a psychotic merger. . . . She developed the belief that he could save her from her emotional—just from psychological disaster."

". . . that by adopting some of his traits that she could fight . . ."

"No—well—"

". . . these hallucinations and other demons . . . is that not true? Is that not what you said?" the judge asked.

"Actually what she developed was the belief that he could make her into a different person with characteristics such as he had . . . if she could learn all he knew that somehow he had the ability to transform her into a strong person. Which then made him really necessary to her psychological survival. As the trial began to get close, she felt increasingly desperate because they would be separated. She became even sicker. Her world was spinning.

And so she decided that she had to take some action. In her mind to help him, but in actuality to really save the relationship upon which her emotional survival was dependent. To save the unit. To save the merger. . . . In terms of the demons she did think if she became a strong person, they wouldn't want to be with her anymore. . . . I think she did care about Tim, . . . really idealized him in this screwy kind of way. But it was not like the love that one individual has for another."

"Would you say that while they were together, she probably told him that she loved him?"

"She very well might have." In describing the merger, he said, "She always thought of herself as having cycles of moods, and she thought as she worked at Brushy that many of the prisoners had these too. And with Tim she decided that his cycle must be the same as her cycle—this is psychotic so don't—it's going to be hard to understand but—that his cycle must be coinciding with her cycle because it appeared to her that he would act the way she felt without her telling him how she felt. Like she might go in angry, and the guards would take her to the interview room, and then they would be bringing him to the room and she would hear him being angry. Throwing a chair, screaming at somebody or making noise or indicating his anger. And her interpretation of that was he was acting out her feelings."

The doctor remembered something she had blurted out to him, something that he felt showed the need for distancing. He read from his notes, quoting Mary's words: "It seemed like to her that whatever it is—whatever this stuff is that people are made of, if you tell somebody things about yourself, you will lose all that stuff that you're made of."

"I know a person," the judge said, "who charged a doctor in this community with stealing their [sic] soul. I know that individual, and I know that they suffered from a condition. And it appears that what you are telling me is that that person felt that they really stole an inner part of him. But I do know that an individual who studies the traits of a person who is suffering from a mental disorder might also have available that information just as you are talking about it."

Embry tried again. He remembered another instance of delusional merging. "Like once her brother's head was cut, and her head hurt in the same place. She might see somebody with a cast on their leg. Her leg might buckle. Another time when her blood hurt. . . . Going back to age sixteen, she refused to go to church anymore because she was convinced that the preacher—the preacher was preaching to her."

Judge Scott nodded his head and smiled sheepishly. "Everyone has that to some degree, do they not?"

The courtroom burst into laughter, not just at the joke but at the excuse it gave them to release the laughter they'd been suppressing.

"The same thing with—like if she sees a movie on TV—if it's the right movie, not just any movie—or if somebody's talking on the TV, she may think that they're directed at her. I'm not positive of that. But I do know that she's seen movies and felt like that they were copied after her."

"And she has looked at record albums and felt like the eyes on the record albums looked at her." Judge Scott tried to keep the sarcasm out of his voice.

Embry didn't get it. "She has a particular record album that if she plays the record, she hides the album because it seems like—I mean it isn't that she believes that—it's that—the experience of feeling like those eyes are looking at her. It gives her the jeebies."

When asked later why he asked about the record album cover, Judge Scott answered, "Because that's what it said in the textbook. It was the next example." He was referring to the textbook on his desk that lay open, *Proof of Facts,* the section "Mental Disorder and Incapacity."

Was Bob Ritchie going to let Judge Scott conduct both the examination and the cross? Finally he stood, and with some deliberation approached his witness.

A reporter who'd covered several other of Ritchie's trials whispered, "Now we get to see what's in his bag of tricks."

"I hope Scott gets paid for standing in for Ramsey today," another journalist whispered back.

"What d'you bet he produces a demon?"

"My money's on a one-celled animal."

"Yeah, but what color?"

"Doctor Embry," Ritchie said, "let me ask you this, please. Do you sometimes tape sessions with your patients?"

"Yes."

"And under what circumstances, Doctor. do you do that?"

"Well, it isn't always the same circumstance, but occasionally if I feel like I need to retain what's said and I'm—the machine can do it better than I can do it with my hand."

"Did you tape some of the sessions with Mary Evans?"

"Yes, sir."

"And why did you do so in her case?"

"Well, I started out trying to take hand notes, and I realized rather quickly that I couldn't really keep up with her. If I were going to try to write down what I could, I wouldn't be able to do anything but act as a machine. I wouldn't be able to pay attention to her or—I just couldn't keep up with her. And so I asked her and you if I might use the tape recorder."

Ritchie, deep in thought, turned, took a few steps, then stopped and turned again, this time to his witness and asked, "When you did so, was there any expectation that anyone other than you would ever hear those tapes?"

"No."

"In fact was that a condition of her consent that you could tape those sessions? Was it a condition that no one else would hear those tapes?"

"Oh, yes. She was very concerned about it. She wanted—yes, she wanted them erased immediately."

"Did you talk to—obviously from what the court's already said, you were interviewed by Gary Tullock [the probation officer who'd testified earlier] in this matter. Right?"

"Oh. Yes. Yes, I was."

"And after your interview with Gary Tullock, did you seek permission to permit Mr. Tullock to listen to one of those tapes?"

"Well, as I recall I called you and suggested you listen to it and see what your reaction was because I couldn't get . . ."

The judge interrupted. "Doctor Embry, did you seek permission?"

"Not exactly. What I did—if I may go on—was that I felt like I had told Mr. Tullock what I wanted to tell him, but I wasn't sure I was able to do it in a convincing manner. I wasn't sure that he—you know—he raised the same question. Could I have been fooled by her. Could she have acted . . ."

"What did you say to him in that regard?" Ritchie asked.

"I told him that I could not have been fooled. But I felt the tape was convincing to me, and it might be convincing to him."

"And why that particular tape? What happened on that particular tape?"

"Well, primarily because it was the best example that I could readily come up with in terms of condensing a number of aspects in the shortest amount of time. Mary's quite elaborative, and she can—maybe if she starts talking about a movie, she might go on about it for ten or fifteen minutes before she gets back. And I tended to be fairly unstructured in my interviews with her. On this one I was a bit more structured and tried to kind of pursue certain things that I had in mind. And I thought it was probably the best illustration in what was the purpose . . ."

"Was there any effort to rehearse anything on that tape or indicate that any use would be made of that tape?" Ritchie asked. "Was there any thought of using that tape in any regard?"

"I don't believe it," a reporter muttered. "He's going to play us the God-damned tape."

Ritchie glanced sharply at the press section.

Dr. Embry went on. "Only in the sense that I actually started that session with a pencil. And as time—as the interview progressed, it soon became apparent that it was a session that had important material, and so I asked—I said well, let's plug up the tape recorder. It was sitting there on the floor in the case."

"All right, sir. And did you in fact then record it?"

"I did."

"Again, for your own purposes?"

"Exactly."

"Was there any idea that you'd ever play it to anybody?"

"No."

"All right, sir. Do you have that tape with you? A copy of that tape?"

Embry hesitated, looked inquiringly at Ritchie.

"It's behind you, Doctor," Ritchie said.

"If it please the court," Ritchie said, "I would mention as predicate or preliminary that there is one approximate five-second blackout where a fellow law student's name is mentioned, and that's the only blackout. But we would seek to offer this tape for the court to listen to at this time."

The judge looked skeptical: "Mr. Ritchie, to be quite honest with you, this court cannot evaluate Mrs. Evans the same as this doctor. If he could tell me what it is about this tape that I would expect to be listening to in order to convince me that there is a genuine mental condition, then I would be happy to listen to it. Otherwise I cannot draw conclusions from what she might be stating."

Ritchie argued vigorously, in his best courtroom voice. "Well, Your Honor, as a preliminary statement in that regard, let me suggest to the court that I have listened to the tape, as has Mr. Tullock listened to this tape. . . . the manner in which this session occurred I think demonstrates without a doubt that this was not a matter which was concocted. That it was sincere. And I think that the point of it and the reason for offering it into evidence and asking this court to listen to it is that although it says for example, as the doctor has already testified, that she had read some things. It shows the tone of her voice. It shows the desperation in her voice. It shows all of the indicia, may it please the court, of sincerity, and to demonstrate to this court, and the decision-making process that this court will go through that this is not something which is taken from reading books, if you will, to learn about the symptoms that would indicate a mental illness. I realize that this doctor of some twenty-two years has already indicated to the court that based on all of his experience as a psychiatrist he has not been fooled. Or that this is not made up or that no kind of a fraud is being attempted to be perpetrated on the court. But I simply suggest that the listening of this tape will tend to corroborate that. Now obviously there is some struggle, if you will, that I have had as counsel for Mary Evans in the playing of this because it further strips her of whatever privacy she has left by so doing. But I think it would be helpful to the court, and that's the reason that we offer it."

"I will hear part of the tape," Judge Scott said finally. "How long does it last, Mr. Ritchie?"

"Well, Your Honor, it's about forty minutes. I'm not sure this court has to listen to all of it. There are certain pertinent portions of it toward the end that deal with Mr. Kirk and how this fits in from what was said during that particular session. The first part of it, Mary is very calm, and I think that the court ought to hear that."

Before the tape was played, Embry explained that this session had been recorded a month earlier, in February, after months of therapy. There were other tapes that showed her far more upset. He also added that Mary would not only have to be an awfully good actress, she'd have to know a good bit of theory to fake symptoms of schizophrenia. "And that's in terms of the relationship that developed with Tim and how it served her purposes because that kind of thing is just not described in literature. . . ."

"Your Honor," Ritchie said, "it is recommended that Mary be allowed to sit in Your Honor's chambers or Winzle's [the court reporter's] chambers during the playing of this tape. We feel it might be too stressful for Mary during the time this is being played."

"It might be stressful, but here she is giving you an interview, and I do not quite understand why she cannot sit here and hear her own voice. What is it about this being stressful, Doctor? I do not understand it."

Embry answered, "Because she's listening to her own illness. Like looking in the mirror and seeing something that's terrifying to her."

"What would be the difference between listening to this and imagining about it in my office?"

"I don't think it's that critical," Embry admitted.

"All right. Let us hear it."

The tape recorder was switched on. Mary's voice was startling; it was so deep and husky that it might have been a man's voice. Her words tumbled out, rapid-fire:

> . . . that was—I don't know if that was those drugs or if they were in any way making me think weird stuff even more. I don't know. They

were probably supposed to not. I don't know really if Doctor Wright ever knew what they were supposed to.

Judge Scott asked the doctor, "Was she under medication at this time?

Embry shook his head. "Excited."

Mary's voice continued:

He never really told me that. Or if he did I didn't listen. But anyway I thought—I had developed this sort of theory that I had for a while that I thought that it must be something like that. Now I didn't just read in there "demons possessed people" so I started calling them that. I was already calling them that, and I had been calling them that for about a year. So I guess maybe I—I thought I should look up stuff about that. So I read all of these books. And there were all of these weird things, and there were all these supposed to be respectable-type scientists and people like that saying that there's really all these kinds of phenomena that nobody understands, and nobody knows how people can do certain things and why they do, and like those monks or whatever they are. Indian-type people that can get buried under the ground and stay alive and there is no air and that people have proven that that's really true, and that they can really do it. And then they can twist up into a ball that nobody could never get in really and get their legs all up around their noses and all that weird stuff that they can do. And walk on nails and glass. And so I started thinking, 'Well, if stuff like that's true,' and like the crap in South America. All the pyramids. I read all about the pyramids and the sundials and the things that looked like

junk from the air, and the airstrip that there is,
and that there was a time—

DR. EMBRY: There are some corrections. That's
              a long time ago.

MARY EVANS: . . . you know—that there couldn't
              have been any airplanes unless
              they came from outer space. And
              Chariots of the Gods. And that
              talks all about how there had to
              be aliens on earth and all that stuff
              that I was reading. And there was
              this thing in the mountains where
              people . . .

DR. EMBRY: Anyway, let's—let's—

MARY EVANS: Okay. Well, anyway, so I started
              thinking that stuff like that was
              really true that—you know—well,
              I mean that they said in those
              books, that that kind of stuff, it
              just couldn't be explained but
              that it really happened. And so
              I thought maybe that's what this
              is—you know. It's something like
              that. And then I didn't know what
              to do exactly. And then I started
              thinking—just over time I started
              thinking, "Well, that sort of stuff's
              probably not right"—you know.
              "I don't think that's what it is."
              Or either [*sic*] I just got disinter-
              ested in that subject.

DR. EMBRY: When you said—when you got in-
              terested in the subject and you said,
              "Maybe that's what this is," . . .

Judge Scott lifted his head. "Shut it off a second. She
talks awfully fast. Is that any indication of anything?"

"It's an indication of a lack of control or modulation of . . ."

"Is that what you were referring to? Modulation?"

"Yes. That's one example, yes."

"All right."

The tape resumed:

> MARY EVANS: . . . some kind of psychic phenomenon. That's how they put it in that book. There's all different kinds. I thought it might be—it was something like that because it wasn't like anything that I ever heard anybody talk about. See, you just don't go around to mental hospitals. . . .

Embry turned to the judge, "She's trying to explain to herself what these things are."

> MARY EVANS: . . . and ask people—you know—tell me about your—you know. Except one time when I was in law school I had this—well, I'll tell you about that in a minute. Before I got divorced. Do you want me to tell you about it first?
>
> DR. EMBRY: Yes. Go ahead.
>
> MARY EVANS: The only time I had ever heard about it was we one time went—okay. I took this seminar called Law and Mental Health and we had to go to Oak Ridge Mental Health Center every Thursday. . . .

Judge Scott interrupted. "All right. Now, she is relating several things. Is there a point in there where she is more regular?"

"Close, Your Honor. Right there."
Mary's voice continued:

. . . I think it was. Or every other Thursday.
Something like that. And talked to these—like
we would be in there, and there would only be
like three of us because they had small groups.
And then there would be this psychiatrist who
was coteaching it—or either [sic] he was a psychologist. I forget which he was right now. But
anyway, they would bring in one patient at a
time and they would talk. And we were supposed to ask them questions and things . . . if we
wanted to. And I thought it was ridiculous. I
thought it was horrible because it was like "why
should they have to do that." I mean they volun-
teered to do it, but I knew that they probably
gave them incentive. Like they would give them
extra breakfast or—I don't know what. You know
how they do people—you know—to get them to
do stuff like that. Why would they want to do
that? But anyway I didn't even like the idea
that—but this one girl came in there once and
said—who the doctor told us that—she would—
they would tell their history before they came
in—and they said that she had schizophrenia,
and she has hallucinations and la, la, la, la, la.
And she doesn't mind talking about it, so you can
ask her about it. And so there was this one girl in
our group named [blank in tape]—right when
the girl got in there she started talking a little bit
about herself and stuff, and she had had all these
hallucinations about doing real horrible stuff. And
she had a little baby which she finally gave to a
foster home because she was afraid she was going
to do something to it because she had had hallucinations about it—you know—being cut in half

and all these different things. And she could
really see it. And I kept noticing the people were
asking her stuff like, see, "Is it really there or is
it the thoughts in your mind or can you really see
it or what?" and she couldn't say. She said, "All I
know is I can see it. I don't know if you could see
it. I don't know if anybody"—you know—and I
said—I just said, "I gotta go,"—you know—and
that psychiatrist said, "Well, wait just a minute.
You can't just leave." And I said, "I gotta go"
—you know—and so I just left the room. And I
didn't hear the rest of whatever it was she said,
but that was the only time I ever heard anybody
talk about stuff like that. And that's the only time
I ever have since.

DR. EMBRY: Why did you have to go?

MARY EVANS: I just didn't want to hear it.

DR. EMBRY: Why?

MARY EVANS: Because. I didn't want to hear it.

DR. EMBRY: I know, Mary. It made you think
maybe you had the same thing she
had?

MARY EVANS: Oh, yeah. And she was—she
was . . .

DR. EMBRY: She was sick.

MARY EVANS: . . . there. She was in a mental
hospital. [Emotional. Crying.]

DR. EMBRY: Okay. But you could relate to what
she was saying because of these spells
and things that you had had. Now
when did you first start having those?

MARY EVANS: I guess—[crying]—they weren't always like they are now when they
happened. They—they weren't so
bad. Sometimes—I guess they
started sometime when I was married, but they were a lot milder

then. I got married when I was nineteen so that was probably when I was about twenty I guess. [Calmer] Like it wasn't right after I got married, but I—I guess when I was about twenty maybe. Twenty-one. I don't know. But they were sort of different then. They were —mostly then is when I could hear stuff. I couldn't really see stuff so vividly like I do now.

DR. EMBRY: What could you hear?

MARY EVANS: That—things saying stuff. They would be saying things real fast, and I would always try to [emotional and crying] listen to them, but I couldn't get it because it was so fast. I could just remember certain things. But see I would be talking too at the same time they were talking. So I couldn't quite get it. And I always thought if I could figure it out—one time I had this idea that I was—[composed]—one time I had this idea that I would—I had this little bitty tape recorder that I used for work, and it was—I—it was mine. They had bought it for me. So I kept it. And during that time I wasn't working—I think I had it too—but this might've been while I was working. At one time I thought, "I should record it and see what"— you know—what I said and what happened because I couldn't remember very good. But then—

see once it—you can't just go
calmly over and turn on the tape
recorder when you get like that.
You know. It wouldn't work because then you would have to
keep it on all the time. And then
whenever it would happen I just
wouldn't think of it. I wouldn't
never do it. And so I never did it.
It's all—it's like there's a bunch of
them talking at once, and then
there's me talking, and there's me
screaming. So I can't tell what
they're saying except I would—I
know what I say. I always say,
"No, not again." [Crying] Always.
And then I'd say stuff like, "Oh
God" and stuff like that. I'd start
to say over and over real fast and
repeat it a bunch for a long time.

The machine was switched off. Bob Pentecost's hand,
which had been resting across his wife's shoulders, was
now holding on tightly. His granitelike face looked about
to crumble. Kaye Pentecost blinked back tears.

Judge Scott sat thoughtfully a moment. Then he turned
to Dr. Embry. "Let me ask you something. . . . Doctor
Embry, is it your opinion because the emotion was being
displayed at the same time as the symptoms that were
being related to you, that you felt that this patient was
sincere as opposed to someone who would be fabricating
their condition?"

"That is a consideration."

"What other consideration was there?"

"You mean to challenge the possibility of faking?"

"Yes. You tell me that—I asked if it was the emotion
and actually the symptoms that she related to you at the

time she was demonstrating these emotions, was that the basis for your actually coming to the conclusion . . ."

"To believe her?"

". . . that she was not fabricating them."

"That's one basis."

"Well, what are the others?"

"Well, the other basis is that—that there is a consistency in that it fits theory. The theory that it is beyond possibility that Mary's feigning it or knowing it."

"All right. I do not need to hear any more of the tape."

Ritchie interjected, "There is—very well, Your Honor. There are portions of this tape which relate specifically to Mr. Kirk later on in that obviously. And we would offer the tape into evidence."

"Well, what I am concerned about now, Mr. Ritchie, is what this doctor has to say about her present condition and what treatment pertains to that person. With his concluding remarks about her condition at the time of the crime. What he has to say about the treatment of this individual."

"Very well, Your Honor. We would ask that this be marked as an exhibit.

"Doctor Embry," Ritchie asked, "what is your prognosis for Mary's condition at the present time?"

"It would depend greatly on what the disposition is."

"In what way?"

"Well, her prognosis without adequate expert treatment is quite grim. It will be very poor. If she—if adequate treatment is available, and she has access to it, then the prognosis improves. The prognosis for her becoming stronger, healthier definitely improves. The prognosis for a full cure even with treatment is not so good."

"Doctor, have you had occasion to hospitalize her in the past?"

"I did hospitalize her in October."

"And what was the reason for that hospitalization?"

"She was out of control. Very depressed and suicidal."

"Any way she could've faked that in your opinion, Doctor Embry? From what you saw?"

"Well, not from what I saw."

"What kind of treatment would you suggest to this court if the court saw fit to place her on probation . . . ?" Ritchie asked.

The judge leaned forward. "Well, now, Doctor, she's not getting treatment other than an outpatient now, is she?"

"No. That's correct."

"But why do you feel that hospitalization as opposed to what she is getting now is necessary, if you do?"

"Why would I prefer hospitalization?"

"Yes, sir."

"Well, it's a more intensive treatment approach. Right now, leading up to this hearing and getting all of this settled it's been a matter of getting through it and providing enough support to Mary that she can survive to this time. If she gets involved in adequate intensive treatment, it's going to be more stressful and traumatic for her, . . . the risk of suicide would go up . . . and I think the hospital would be necessary. The other . . ."

"Let me interrupt you here," Judge Scott said, "because I am very much concerned. Here we have a sentencing hearing today. Mary Evans has been out on bond for a period of time, and you have hospitalized her."

"For two weeks."

"For two weeks. And what you are saying to me now is that you recommend she be hospitalized again? Is that correct?"

"I would recommend that she be hospitalized, probably for long-term treatment."

"Let me tell you what bothers me. It concerns me that she has been out on bond and is not in the hospital at this time, and yet the very day that we are to decide what to do with her and what fate, you tell me that she should be hospitalized."

"Well, Your Honor. I'd recomm—"

"Doctor, let me ask you something. Was there a possibility that a person suffering from the condition that you have described that Mrs. Evans suffers from—is there a possibility that that individual would feel better about paying their debt to society? Or better about themselves?"

The doctor shook his head. "Uh-uh."

"You talk about self-image."

"Yeah. I don't think that Mary—I'm not—I don't know that I've ever asked her. I'm not sure that she feels she owes society anything or that see's really done anything that wrong."

"Have you asked her that?"

"I've asked her that, and she's elaborated. I've never asked it just the way you asked it, but I—"

"All right. If you have asked her that . . . can you tell me why you are not sure?"

"Well, I know that she doesn't consider what she did as wrong in the way that I imagine you do. She's—"

The judge looked stunned. *"Even today?"*

"Even today. I think she saw it as a very desperate attempt to maintain sanity, and that that wouldn't be wrong really. And she doesn't understand. She's amazed by all of the interest. She—to her it's never really seemed like it should've been such a big deal."

Ritchie leapt to his feet. "May it please the court, for the purpose of protecting the record . . ."

"Certainly you can protect the record. But again I want to remind you, and I want the doctor to understand that she has surrendered her defense of insanity, and the question is not accountability."

"We understand that."

"All right."

"We're offering it only on the issue of culpability and the mitigating factors. . . ."

"All right. Now, you have read the ethical considerations that you have as an attorney?"

"Certainly, Your Honor."

"And those that address themselves to the attorney general's office and those that I feel that address themselves to me?"

"Certainly, Your Honor."

"Now you two came here with a plea agreement."

"We're not trying to undo that, Your Honor."

"Well, let me finish, Mr. Ritchie."

"I'm sorry."

"You came here with a plea agreement. With the knowledge that you and the attorney general have, and I do not have the benefit of that knowledge . . . I just want to make sure that you understand where this court finds itself in the way of decision making here. And that is I am not deciding whether or not she is culpable. She was culpable . . . but the degree of culpability is all that we are talking about. Now if you have any further questions pertaining strictly to that issue . . ."

Ritchie addressed his witness. "Doctor, do you have an opinion, sir, based upon a reasonable degree of medical certainty as to whether or not on March thirty-first, 1983, Mary P. Evans was suffering from a mental disease or defect?"

"Yes."

"And what is that opinion?"

"That she was."

"And what mental disease or defect was she suffering from?"

"Schizophrenia."

"Doctor, do you have an opinion based upon a reasonable degree of medical certainty as to whether or not the illness that you have described rendered Mary P. Evans on March thirty-first, 1983, of—rendered her substantially incapable of conforming her conduct to the requirements of the law?"

"It is my opinion that she was substantially incapable of conforming her conduct to the requirements of the law."

"Thank you, Doctor."

Judge Scott announced a thirty-minute recess.

It was noon, and the small pizza shop across the street from the courthouse was suddenly a swarm of reporters.

Who would save Mary, they wondered to one another as they ate. They didn't think Embry had. The consensus on the tape was, "Scott didn't buy it." No one could save Mary, they said, but Mary.

In the sheriff's office, Kirk was waiting anxiously for news. Zane Daniel brought the tape in so he could listen to it. Kirk was furious. "*Damn* that," he said. "What's Ritchie doin', making that stuff public?" He knew that for Mary there could be no greater humiliation.

In a recent telephone conversation she'd said, "I have no control over anything now." And she had implored him once more not to pay any attention to what was said in court.

Chapter Twelve

After lunch Ritchie asked Dr. Robert Sadoff to take the stand. Sadoff, a man well into his fifties, was a weightier witness and spoke with more confidence. He rattled off his impressive credentials to the court, listing his professorship at the University of Pennsylvania where he headed the Forensic Psychiatric Clinic as well as its training program in law and psychiatry, the several books he'd written, and the many awards he'd received over the years.

Ritchie let that sink in a minute. Then he led the doctor into a lengthy and very articulate report of his findings. He'd spent a total of nine hours in sessions with Mary. He'd also ordered a battery of psychological and neuropsychological tests performed on her at a nearby Philadelphia clinic. His conclusion was almost the same as Embry's. Indeed he had consulted at length with Embry by telephone after his initial visit with Mary.

He rephrased—more skillfully—the Barbie doll, teddy bear, and ceramic cat incidents, and he added one or two more violent outbursts.

"At one time when she was living with her husband Tom she said she had a dream about him and could not differentiate the dream from a reality. So she hit him in bed when she awoke because she thought it had happened

227

in reality, but it was all a dream. She also told me she took a knife to her husband on more than one occasion . . . once when she wanted to be alone. She did not describe this in the same bizarre pathology that she described seeing the bubbles, red and green balls that were her first hallucination. But she described it in terms of the demons or those things out there. . . . When those things get into her head, she does not want to be bothered by anyone. It's my feeling this was the reason she jumped out of the car when she was with John Lockridge and his friends and why she did some other bizarre things. . . . Once when she saw these balls, she called John to come over. He couldn't see them. And—well, by the time he got there she said they weren't out there anymore. They were in her mind. And once they get into her mind, she doesn't want to be bothered with anybody and so she sent him home. And she went to hide in her—she has a cubbyhole under the sink or in the kitchen which is surrounded by three sides. So she can feel protected but not totally closed in. With respect to her husband, he had been bothering her. And she got very angry with him and went to the kitchen and grabbed a knife and went after him. She recalls chasing him in a parking lot. It was February, it was cold, and they didn't have anything on except light clothes and she did not feel very cold. She said had she caught him, she is sure she would have cut him."

Judge Scott asked, "You are saying that she went into the kitchen, got a knife, and chased him out of the house into the parking lot?"

"Yes. Yes, sir. And because he was bothering her because she wanted to be alone. She did not catch him, but she said to me that had she caught him she would have stabbed him or cut him. I also asked her what she would have done had he taken a knife to her. She said, 'I would not have run because that's weakness. I would've stood there and tried to get the knife away even if I'd got cut. Because it would not have killed me, but you cannot run because that's weakness.' I think that's a very important concept for her in the whole idea of Mary's illness. And that is that she has to be strong, in control, and do this her way. That is, she has to get well on her own. And that's one of the reasons she did not tell Doctor Wright, Doctor Broughan, or others about these symptoms that she was having."

Judge Scott addressed the witness. "Well, let me ask you the same question I asked the other doctor. If she would not tell them, how come she told you?"

"She told me because she had already told Doctor Embry, and she knew that I was examining her and wanted to find out everything about her. . . . I'm a forensic psychiatrist, and I'm aware that patients that I see try to con me, and they try to lie to me. They put their best foot forward and I know that, and I want to find out if they're conning. My opinion, Your Honor, if Mary Evans were trying to con me, she'd have done a much better job. She didn't do a good job of it, if she were trying. That's why I don't think she was trying. She took one symptom—if she took it—out of the law books that you read and that she could've read. There are so many other ones that are much more unusual, bizarre, and crazy that she could've told me about if she were trying to convince me that she were nuts. . . . And she didn't tell me the kinds of things that I hear from people who do try to con me. Because they hear from other inmates. They hear from other people, 'Tell the doctor A, B, C. That you're hearing voices. Tell the doctor that you're seeing crazy things. Tell the doctor this and he'll find you insane.' Usually they go overboard. They do too much. She did not do that. If she was trying to con me, she did an excellent job because she was subtle about it."

"Well. let me tell you the problem," Judge Scott said. "I do not know how . . . a test can be given that would reflect upon my mental condition. I mean if today I am competent to stand trial, how can you people give a test today that would reflect upon my ability at the time of the commission of the crime?"

"Well, Your Honor, it's not easy. . . . I think that with this case I have, as you asked Doctor Embry, a reasonable degree of medical certainty. Psychiatric certainty."

"Well, your lawyer probably knows what that means."

The doctor laughed. "I'm not a lawyer. I can't even claim to be one, but I . . ."

"Well, you teach the law and psychiatry and forensic services."

"Yes, sir. I've gone to law school. Yes. But I believe that her diagnosis is very clearly paranoid schizophrenia on axis one of the DSM 3. The diagnostic and statistical manual number 3. That her axis one diagnosis, without question in my mind, is paranoid schizophrenia. Axis two are these personality problems which I call borderline for her. . . . That her highest level of functioning was only fair. But she worked as a lawyer. But even as a lawyer she told me she did some bizarre things, one of which she said was she was investigating a case up in Appalachia. And in a dangerous situation with another attorney with her—a male—she drove chasing a man who was a witness who was trying to get away from her into a dangerous area of the mountains. Somebody on the porch had a gun, loaded, and she rushed by him into the house without being invited and said, 'I'm going to see him. I don't care if you have a gun.' And she later said, to me, 'That was really crazy. I could've been killed.' She said at the time she had no concept, no awareness of the danger that she was facing. The guy with her did. He didn't want to go. He thought she was crazy. She told me. Now I didn't verify that. But it's another instance of her judgment and her ability to function maybe not so effectively as we think. Then we get to the—we get to the issue of her relationship with Tim Kirk and Brushy Mountain. Why did she do something like this? Why would anybody do something like this? It's strange. It's bizarre. It's unusual. People have speculated that she was in love with him. I don't think she's capable of love. I don't think she's able to know what a mature relationship with another human being is like, because of her feeling of emptiness inside and the way she relates. She needed Tim Kirk in a way to save her own life. The alternative to that, in my opinion, was suicide. She had tried it at least twice. I think she is actively suicidal now."

"She tried suicide twice?" the judge asked.

"Yes. Once she actually took fifty Tranxene. [Here the doctor was mistaken. The hospital records show that Mary took fifteen Tranxene.] I have the date of January 1982. I also have a note that she had some Mellaril, ten of them, that she was going to take, but John Lockridge had come over and she did not take them, but she was planning to take them to kill herself. She has been variably suicidal throughout her illness. And my concern is that Mary Evans is actively suicidal now. . . . The desperation that she felt on the night before this happened. Having her bags packed, sitting in front of her, waiting to go to London, Kentucky, to take the job as public defender the next day. She had the option. She could've gone. Saved herself. Saved her career. Done everything. But she told me. She said, 'I had no choice. I had no option. I had to go through with this to save my life. To save my soul.' She said, 'Because I was mentally ill, and Tim Kirk offered the only salvation for me. He would teach me how to be in control. How to cure myself.' Is the way she told me. Nobody else could do it. Nobody she'd ever met had that magic that Tim Kirk had that she had to latch onto in a psychotic way. Why is it psychotic? She sees Tim Kirk as being in control. He's locked up for a number of years. He does what everybody tells him to do in the prison, but she doesn't see that. What she sees, the way she perceives it, is if he wants quiet, he gets quiet. If he wanted to go down and kill two people he could do it. Nobody stopped

him. He has the power to get what he wants. He can even
have his own privacy in a crowded penitentiary. That's not
true. That's delusional. That's the way she perceived it.
I've been in penitentiaries. I've worked there for years.
I've seen people in there. It's not quiet, and it's certainly
not private. And he certainly has no control in the penitentiary. He is controlled. That's ironic. She saw it that
way. Crazy as it may sound. She depended upon him for
her last attempt at saving herself. The alternative was
suicide. Not going to Kentucky. That's just an escape
temporarily. That had no meaning for her. Being a lawyer
had no meaning for her. Dressed up, she said. 'Look, I
have an image. I'm a lawyer. I dress up. I look the part. I
play the role. But it doesn't mean anything. I'm not throwing away a career. I never had a career. It's not for me. I
don't know who I am or where I am or what I'm going to
do. The only thing I knew,' she tells me, 'at that point was
I had to go with Tim because I had to save myself.' I think
she lost sight of the larger picture. Of other people being
in danger, other people being tied up, other people doing
other things. And if you know her psychosis and you get
into it as I tried to do and understand, the craziness of her
thought processes—that icy Mary Evans—is a very, very
psychotic individual who requires intensive supervised treatment. I don't like her sick on the street. I'd like her in a
hospital because I'm afraid she's going to kill herself."

Once again Judge Scott found himself conducting the
cross-examination. "Let me tell you something. I had
attorneys come with me—or to me—with a plea agreement. Mary Evans sat in that same chair and looked up at
me just like you are here. She said she understood what
she was doing."

"Yes, sir."

"And she voluntarily entered a plea of guilty."

"Yes, sir."

"Of aiding and abetting an escape."

"Yes, sir."

". . . from the penitentiary."

"I think she did understand. She intellectually knew exactly what she was going to do. She's an extremely bright woman. She knew what she was doing. She aided and abetted. But she didn't do it in order to spring him. She did it in order to help herself, and that was the focus of what she had. How do I know? Because once they got out, disillusionment. He wasn't the magic person she thought he was. He was human like all the rest of us. He could make mistakes. She wanted to get away from him. She wanted to leave. There was no reason for her to stay anymore, but she was stuck and she saw it through."

"She was stuck and she saw—?"

"She said she saw it through with him. Afterwards, I'm talking about."

"Doctor, how can Mary sit there and look so normal and to some extent function as an attorney and previously as a student, and be as crazy as you indicate she is?"

"She doesn't look normal to me frankly. I'm sorry, but she doesn't."

Mary lowered her eyes. Her hair fell around her face like a veil.

"She looks very disturbed," the doctor continued, "and she looks very sad and without much affect or feeling tone. Very bland."

Bob Ritchie asked the doctor what his recommendation was for treatment.

Dr. Sadoff told the court that what Mary needed was prolonged treatment in a private hospital such as the Menninger Foundation in Topeka, Kansas.

"And I know some of the doctors there . . . and I know two of the Menninger—boys, I was going to say, but they're I think older than I am. Walter and Roy. Who are both excellent therapists . . ."

The judge wasn't impressed. "Well now, how, Doctor, would that be any different from yourself treating her?"

Ritchie asked Sadoff what he thought would happen to Mary if she were sent to prison. "She would deteriorate, ultimately kill herself or put herself in a position where someone else would kill her."

He added, "When she realizes that she has nothing, I think suicide will be an alternative. When she realizes there are no Tim Kirks around, there's no magic where she can learn how to be strong and in control."

After Dr. Sadoff was excused, Ritchie presented in evidence a stack of letters written by friends and former associates of Mary's and many more from her parents' church congregation, all imploring the court to grant Mary probation.

Judge Scott said that he had two doctors who had been subpoenaed from the Middle Tennessee Mental Health Institute. "Is Doctor Watson here?"

A short, bespectacled man in the front row behind the prosecutor's table stood. "Yes, Your Honor."

"Doctor Watson, would you come up, please? The court has a couple of questions."

Dr. Watson explained that he was one of three doctors who had examined Mary over the thirty-day period she was under observation at the hospital at the state's request. He stated that the doctors there were in agreement that Mary was mentally competent to stand trial, but they did not agree on the support for the insanity defense.

When the judge asked him in what way he differed from Dr. Embry's evaluation, Dr. Watson said that he did not find Mary to be psychotic or to be suffering from paranoid schizophrenia. In his opinion she had a personality disorder which he did not classify as a mental illness or defect supportive of an insanity defense.

That brought Ritchie to his feet. "I have not called Doctor Watson and the prosecutor has not called Doctor Watson. . . ."

A verbal duel between the court and the defense ensued, followed by a lengthy and thorough cross-examination by Ritchie. Try as he might, he was not able to weaken the doctor's testimony.

Judge Scott addressed the defense. "I am very much concerned, Mr. Ritchie, that I have heard so much testimony about the mental condition of this individual, and the position that it places me in as far as the original plea that you have. I am very much concerned that in reading this probation report and hearing from these witnesses, that even though your client is criminally responsible for her acts, in reading the probation report it appears that she does not really have a repentant spirit or even understand that what she has done is wrong. Your testimony . . ."

"May I address that, Your Honor?"

"Yes. And you know it is—this is an area that really concerns me, frankly, Mr. Ritchie. I have got to make a decision in this case, and I have not even heard from the individual. And you say it is because of her condition that you do not want her to testify in this case. And yet as a judge I need to have information. Do you see all this security around this courtroom?"

"Yes, Your Honor."

"It is not because I am concerned that she is going to shoot anybody or hurt anybody. I am afraid somebody may in fact come in here, that she herself participated . . . along with Mr. Kirk, in having certain activities to assist her in helping him escape, that might come here and do some harm."

"To her, Your Honor?"

"Well, I do not know. I just do not know. I have read this report, and here we have Mrs. Evans who states that 'William Kirk got a gun at the penitentiary,' and you know as a judge that concerns me. And I know he had one at one time because he was convicted of that."

"There were at least five guns up there at the time he had these two, Your Honor."

"Yes. And if she has a repentant spirit, I would like to

know about that. And I cannot help but feel like—that she and Kirk discussed that. I mean after all, there is some evidence that she cared about him, that she lived with him, that she left the state of Tennessee with him, that she did not return and they stayed together. There is evidence that at that time that she left this area that they left in an automobile that was supplied by someone. I have the report, and it appears to me that she does not want to tell even where she went in North Carolina."

"Your Honor, I wish I had . . ."

"And those are the things that concern me, Mr. Ritchie."

"I wish I had addressed that when Doctor Sadoff was on the stand."

"Well, I do not want to hear it from you. I want to hear it from—you know—I am concerned about those things. I am concerned that . . ."

"I understand."

". . . we have eight thousand people in the penitentiaries of this state. They have mothers and fathers, brothers and sisters, girlfriends and boyfriends that are looking here at what we do here in this courtroom."

"I understand that, Your Honor."

"And I am concerned that Mrs. Evans in this case failed to relate one item of evidence of the individuals that assisted and helped in William Kirk and his leaving the state of Tennessee. I am concerned that she did not tell the complete truth about what occurred in the statement that she gave our probation officer, Gary Tullock."

"Which aspect, Your Honor? I'm not sure."

"Well, there is a showing here in the report, Mr. Ritchie, that she pointed a gun at Doctor Salk. I see it in her statement that she had it in the waistband. And I also see in this statement of the probation report that the gun came from the penitentiary. She placed it in her briefcase and left the penitentiary with that in her briefcase and supplied it to Mr. Kirk at the doctor's office. You know, I am concerned about who is getting the guns into the penitentiary. I mean I can only think that anybody that is logical, as Mrs. Evans is, would not only discuss Kirk's past that she could relate to so well, but also discuss those individuals who supplied this gun and how it was done. And I am concerned . . ."

"Well, Your Honor . . ."

"Let me finish. I am concerned that when she said that she supplied the getaway vehicle, that she supplied the clothes, part of the money, gave him access to that gun. I am concerned that when she said that she drove that getaway vehicle that they went to a place in Anderson County—and I am from Anderson County, and I could not have found it unless I had some help—and she said that Kirk directed her to that, and I would bet he could not find it today. I am concerned that when they left there, they left in another vehicle. But she says she does not know the individuals' names. I am concerned that they went to North Carolina, and she says she does not know where in North Carolina. I am concerned about those aspects of it, to that report because I have got to pass judgment on an individual who may or may not be a threat to society. I have got to make sure that there is in fact some consideration for the detrimental effect that this would have upon those other individuals who entertain getting individuals out of the penitentiary. And I cannot help but think myself that individuals who are there for the longest period of time, who have in fact committed the more serious crimes, are the individuals who have more to gain by getting out than someone else. That is what I am concerned about, Mr. Ritchie. And you have denied me really the source of information so that I can pass judgment by denying me the right to ask Mrs. Evans this. She is accountable and if she is not accountable, then perhaps I ought to take this matter under advisement and let you talk with your client and be here tomorrow so that I can consider the options that I have in this case. I know it is a late hour, but I want to do justice."

"I know you do, Your Honor."

"And I cannot do it based upon what I have heard here. I do not know what I am dealing with. I have heard a very strong case from the evidence that you have presented, and I have called upon a doctor who agrees, and I am sure that all of the state psychiatrists and psychologists agree that she has a mental defect. And I know that I do not make these laws, and I did not make the testimony. I do not make the defense of insanity. I have to deal with them. But there is one thing that I can do, and that is to be as fair as I can in this situation. I cannot do it unless I can talk with her."

"We would appreciate . . ."

"You consider that."

"Very well, Your Honor."

"Now, Mr. Kirk is going back tonight, gentlemen."

"We have no need for him."

"So be here at eleven o'clock tomorrow. I have not seen what I have gotten in the mail today, and I want to make sure that we have sufficient security and that these people can arrange this tomorrow."

"Very well, Your Honor."

"But I want to hear from her. And I want to hear from her in those areas. Because I frankly do not feel that there is a repentant spirit. And from what your specialists said, she still doesn't feel this was wrong."

"Your Honor, may I just address that one point?"

"Yes."

"And then we will save for tomorrow the rest of it. What I was told by Doctor Embry—and I think Doctor Sadoff testified to it too—is it's not that she did not have a repentant spirit. That's not the case. And I can testify—I mean I can state to the court as an officer of the court. I'll be sworn if you want me to."

"Well, let me put it this way," the judge said. "She

did not think it was wrong and she does not today, and that was very clear in my mind."

"No."

"She felt like that these things—she does not understand why . . . people are so upset with her. . . . I have not heard from her. . . ."

"I understand, Your Honor."

". . . other than [to] see her here with her downcast eyes, looking as they say a rather blah personality today. Or bland personality. I do not know. But I need that source of information that you have had all these many months. And you have denied me that. And that is part of my decision making. I cannot help that. I cannot do justice in this case. And even if Mrs. Evans feels so much about herself that she feels that she cannot talk about these things. Then I have got to judge it without it. You see what I am saying?"

"Yes, sir."

". . . I have not seen a reluctance to talk to any of the psychiatrists. And yet she is reluctant to talk with me. And I want to hear some of that."

"I will confer with my client, Your Honor."

"All right. We will take this up then at eleven o'clock tomorrow."

In his chambers Judge Scott once again looked at the textbook open on his desk. Later he confided to a visitor the thoughts that crossed his mind as he reread those pages. "If I were an attorney, and I wanted to fabricate a condition like the one that's being presented to me, this is what I'd turn to to do my research." Page 45 described the symptoms of schizophrenia; page 49, visions and voices; page 52, voices, demons, and bodily sensations; page 53, anxiety about "spells," and fear of mental illness. Looking further he found the balls of lights and colored balls. Downright strange, isn't it, how her symptoms go right down dead center?"

He picked up the pack of letters that Ritchie had given him and scanned them briefly. They all seemed to follow the same format, beginning with an introduction, giving an explanation of how and when and under what circumstances they knew Mary, and finally leading to statements about her fine, but mentally unstable, character. All of them ended with an ardent appeal to the judge's wisdom or Christian sense of forgiveness in the hope that he would grant her probation.

The one from her former husband was truly moving in its sincerity. Seven pages long and written by hand, it began, "Hello Judge Scott, How are you?" He read it through:

Judge James B. Scott
Anderson County Courthouse
Clinton, Tennessee 37716

Hello Judge Scott,
How are you? My name is Tom Evans, Jr., and I am responding on behalf of Mary P. Evans, my ex-wife, in regard to her application for probation. I don't really know how common it is for divorced people to speak out in favor of one another in a situation like this, but I'm very glad to have the opportunity to give Mary any help. We have remained friends, and kept in touch, since our divorce in 1980.

Mary and I first met when we were students at U.T.K. I had graduated high school from Webb School of Knoxville, and was beginning my third year at U.T. I originally majored in Business Adm; but changed my major to Recreation Adm. in Education and graduated in 1977. I met Mary while I was still in the Business college. I was very unhappy with school, and Mary was very instrumental in helping me to decide to pursue something that I thought I could really enjoy. This was probably a first indication of a sign of idealism in Mary that I liked and could understand. We both felt that a career choice should be something one can really enjoy and get some personal satisfaction from. For that reason, after graduation and for several years, I worked at a variety of jobs. Since a student at U.T., I've had experience ranging from restaurant management to recreational programming; from sales to constructive manual skills (home building). Needless to say, my searching was definitely a thorn in our young marriage and I take the blame for a lot of the pressures on us at the time. We were never really financially stable, add that to her being in school and the results with us were trouble. We were divorced and soon afterwards Mary graduated Law school. I moved, worked mostly in restaurant and recreation settings, but I am now in southern Florida working for a building contractor. I feel my various experiences will always support me, and I'm optimistic about my future.

My future is not the focus here, of course, but it is Mary's future that all of her family and her friends are so worried about.

It may seem strange that I'd want to help my ex-wife, but our breakup was not bitter and antagonistic, but was more a matter of basic incompatibility and, thus, we've remained friends. I think we were first attracted to each other because of our very different personalities, the old "opposites attract" theory. That is not the only explanation for my attraction to Mary, as she has many qualities which intrigue and confuse people. I think that uncertainty, the mysteriousness about her, was one of the first attractions for me. She always seemed to have a little something smoldering just beneath the surface; a sort of pent-up energy that she seemed to try to control, but wasn't too successful. Mary fell into that tough, totally independent mold that many feminists tried to assert during the liberated 1970s, except that she had always had that naturally and unintentionally. Since I first met her when she was eighteen she has spoken her mind intelligently but quite adamantly, and sometimes damning the consequences. People sometimes admired her for this, but many times people were also offended or shocked. Normally it concerned something fairly petty, like an honest opinion about politics, movies, or even the party we were attending. Social gatherings were definitely not her strong point, and descriptions of her in the press as being "cold and aloof" probably were given by people who knew her in just such a brief encounter. People who know her privately know her as a giving, sincere, and fun person, and as a loyal friend to them. Even close friends might sparingly use "aloof" in a description of Mary, but I think not in a negative way. She was often reserved, but probably because she was very introspective about a subject or already had set opinions about the subject. It bothers me that she would be thought of as "cold and aloof." We can always be apathetic and disinterested at one time or another (we all are) but I consider it pretty cruel to call someone "cold" when you don't really know them. At times Mary was anything but cold; that is, her interest and her devotion to something or someone could get pretty heated up. Whether it was her new ceramic hobby, her classical piano ability, or her idealism of the Law, Mary always went into it with both feet and high hopes. A good example of her sincerity and idealism was when she worked in a Legal clinic one quarter in Law school. She always believed strongly in the fundamentals behind our legal system, and we talked often of [how] the people who really needed help from the Law were hurt the most. Mary has always had a weak spot for the underdog, the supposed "lower class," and she got real satisfaction from helping those people in the clinic, and was really rewarded by the appreciation those that she helped showed her. She may have never been able to regain that feeling of "giving" to her neighbor because it seems like it wasn't long afterwards that she became more and more disillusioned with the prospects in her law career. She always did well in school, and later as a clerk in a firm, but she appeared to have lost some of her fire, or belief, in the Law. Our troubled family life (my career indecision) had a lot of effect on her, but there was also a certain questioning of her goals that she had never shown before. One time, shortly before we divorced and before she graduated, I even remember her saying one day that she wished she could just lead a normal life and work at a department store or something. It was almost like she had realized that Law wasn't the "end-all" but that it was too late for her to just drop it and try something else.

In my personal opinion, I feel that her involvement with Kirk was born out of that growing dissatisfaction she had for the Law combined with the pressures of defending in a capital offense case and the personal problems she was having with the man she was dating. All of that could add up to mental strain for anyone, particularly someone like Mary who I had learned had a pretty delicate temperament. The escape with

Kirk could have been just that for Mary—escapism.
The dictionary defines escapism as "the avoid-
ance of reality." I think that could be a fair
assessment of what she was going through; she
subconsciously wanted out of her life's situation
and she allowed herself to be taken by a con-
man, disregarding the consequences.

Again, this is a personal opinion since I don't
know what her real reasons were. I do know,
though, that her interest was not criminal in
nature. I realize since she is a lawyer that she
should understand what is criminal and what is
not, and she would in a normal state of mind.
But I also think that the word "intent" is important here because it was not her intent to harm
anyone, their reputation, their property, but was
instead her intent to release herself from her
own pressures.

I know how serious the consequences to her
actions can be; I would hate to see Mary, a first
offender and a high caliber person, put behind
bars because she had what amounts to a mental
breakdown. I hope that I've been able to somewhat paint a picture for you, Judge Scott, of the
basic personality of Mary that caused her recent
actions, and I hope you will see fit to grant her
probation. Incarceration would only damage her
further, psychologically, and would serve no justice to our society as a whole.

Thank you for honestly considering her
friends' pleas for her probation.

> Sincerely,
> Tom Evans, Jr.

Later Tom Evans explained that Mary had contacted
him in Florida to tell him that she and her attorney
needed personal and professional "character letters." Bob

Ritchie had followed up by calling Tom with the basic outline of what they needed.

The following morning's *Tennessean* carried a front-page story written by Larry Daughtrey. It was typical of the press's sentiment:

> Mary Evans: a confused schizophrenic who abused her Barbie doll as a child and now has demons and "alien forces" dancing in her head? Or Mary Evans: a cold, calculating lawyer who sprung [*sic*] her lover-client from a maximum security cell for a five-month spree and now has few regrets about it?
>
> The mystery remained murky yesterday in an Anderson County courtroom seeping with drama. Today, the judge wants the truth from the one person who hasn't talked: Mary Evans.

Court was reconvened the next morning at nine-thirty. Judge Scott asked the defense if he had any announcements to be made to the court.

Ritchie stood and addressed the court. "If it please the Court, last night I talked with both Doctor Sadoff and with Doctor Embry at quite some length. Doctor Sadoff and Doctor Embry advised me, Your Honor, that it would be very detrimental medically for Mary Pentecost Evans to take the stand. Based upon their advice and based upon the entire record of these matters, about which we will address ourselves, I assume very soon, we have no alternative but to decline the court's invitation for Mary to make a statement or otherwise testify in this matter. We rely upon the provisions of the statute which indicates that it is the defendant's choice. We realize the difficulties with which that presents the defendant, but from the standpoint of her medical health we must respectfully decline to do so. . . . There's no question that if Mary's fate were to be decided by the press, her fate would already be sealed."

Ritchie then presented his argument on the question of probation. He began by telling the court what a long seven months, filled with anxiety and frustration, it had been for him. "Perhaps it's not even relevant for me to attempt to describe the burden I feel at this moment standing before the court. . . .

". . . It should be obvious to everyone that's involved in this case, at this point, that certain elements of the media have made a blatant effort to sensationalize these proceedings and to create an atmosphere in which even a semblance of justice would be almost impossible to achieve without great risk to the participants of this case."

He continued by retelling Mary's history representing Kirk, and the burden that fell on her shoulders. "Couple these pressures, Your Honor, with the knowledge of the likelihood that some escape attempt was likely at the trial of the case, at great risk to many innocent parties that might be involved. . . ."

When Ritchie had finished, Judge Scott said, "Let me tell you the problem I have, Mr. Ritchie, and you can address it for the record. . . . Mary Evans is equipped today with a competent mind. She is here. According to the experts—and everyone agrees with that—she is competent. And you tell me at this point that because of her mental condition that this court cannot have the benefit of her testimony."

"I think the—"

"Let me say this. I should not have to solicit that from Mrs. Evans. She is asking for the privilege of probation, Mr. Ritchie. A privilege that in a case such as this, that society expects this court to discharge its responsibility in making sure that those individuals are proper candidates for probation. . . . And when you yourself have entered into an agreement with this state stating that Mary Evans is competent to stand trial, and she has voluntarily and knowingly pled guilty to this crime. Now that is the problem, Mr. Ritchie. And it is a problem that this court finds is really almost insurmountable on your part. Regardless of how long you argue, I still feel that I have to discharge my function as a judge.

". . . those things that she said [to Mr. Tullock] in my opinion show a loyalty to those individuals who assisted her and Tim Kirk to escape the penitentiary. . . . It is still there in my mind. I believe she skirted those issues. I do not believe that she cooperated with authorities."

Ritchie took the offensive. ". . . If I am hearing the court correctly . . . what the court is doing—and I say so quite respectfully—is putting the defendant in a situation wherein the court is acting in the role of a police officer in the investigation of a case in order to determine the identity of other persons to prosecute—or have prosecuted—arising out of this matter. . . . I do not know whether or not Mary Evans knows the identity of any other person who might be culpable as far as these matters are concerned. . . . But I would suggest to the court, most respectfully, that in the event she did know, it would not recommend her for probation that she would place someone else in that chair to sit where she is sitting in order to save her own skin. It would be abominable and immoral. And I would not recommend it. . . ."

"Mr. Ritchie, this court is not asking for anything that is unreasonable in my opinion. . . . If you say the mitigating factors are that she had such a condition of mind that she was almost in a position of not being able to control it—and that is what you are saying to me—then perhaps you should not have pled your client guilty. But she is guilty. And with that in mind and with the fact that she, at this time, is found to be competent to stand trial, I charge her with more responsibility than I do the average citizen, even though she has submitted on disbarment. She is not disbarred today."

"I understand that, Your Honor."

"Well, you have told me that I am acting as a policeman, and I do not feel that I am, Mr. Ritchie. And if I am it is only for the purpose of finding out what I am dealing with and in seeing what type of loyalty that this lady has. Now I do not make the facts. I harbor no ill will against Mary Evans. But the acts themselves need to be addressed, and I do not know of any other way to address them except to tell you that I am concerned about that portion of society that not only sympathizes with those individuals who are in a penitentiary that might also lead to further activities involving escape, and to that degree I believe that I would be remiss in the discharge of my duties as a judge unless I addressed an attorney about that and asked them about that so that I could have confidence that here is a repentant spirit. A spirit that shows sufficient remorse and, as I say, contrition to come here and ask this court to forgive to the extent that I suspend the sentence. Not forgive her for a crime, but at least to forgive her to the extent—but I do not get that, Mr. Ritchie.

"She participated in obtaining and seeing to it that Mr. Kirk had access to a weapon. It was an active participation in this crime. She drove the getaway vehicle. It belonged to her. I do not believe her story about Kirk directing her to an isolated part of this county for the vehicle to be left and picked up by someone else. I do not believe her when she stated to me in this probation report that she does not know who picked them up. I believe she knows not only who picked them up, but where she went in North Carolina, and what she did there. I think she read newspapers, and I think she and Kirk were very much aware, not only of their presence but of who was with them and what they did at that time. I am sure that during the time that she was in escape that she had reservations about it, but she also reported that it was the happiest time of her life—according to her friend, when she called. She stated that she had thought about calling home and calling her father, catching a cab or catching a plane and going home. She helped finance the whole operation. She helped plot the mental evaluation. Procured the tape to tape these victims. Supplied the gun. Supplied the clothes to Mr. Kirk. These are active acts. This is not an act of someone just being passively involved. And she continued to live with this man in Florida. And she continued to stay away from those individuals that you say now that she has hurt. And she is accountable for this crime. I cannot help but judge her on the basis of her coming here and pleading guilty to these things. During the time that she was on escape she didn't surrender herself. She was captured. And after her capture, she did not cooperate with authorities.

"I must consider the deterrent effect on other individuals, other people that she knows that exist and may even be here in this courtroom today that assisted them. I don't know. I don't know where they are. So, with that in mind, Mr. Ritchie, I am ready to pass judgment on your client. Have her stand."

A hush fell over the courtroom. Bob Pentecost closed his eyes as his daughter stood. Even those who, over the months, had had little or no sympathy for the unyielding—and somehow unlovable—young woman now held their breath as the awesome moment was upon her.

"Mary Evans, it is the judgment of this court that you shall receive a three-year penitentiary sentence for the crime of aiding and abetting a jail escape."

With those words, on cue as if rehearsed, two uniformed policewomen stepped forward and stood on either side of her.

"It is also the judgment of this court that you should not be placed on a suspended sentence, and your probation is denied. Your bond will be revoked. Mr. Ritchie, in this case, because I have now pronounced judgment and because of the testimony that you have presented to me, I do believe your client to be a valid suicidal personality.

She will be placed in the custody of the sheriff. She will go to classification first."

That was the single instance in which she showed emotion. Brushy Mountain had recently been converted to a classification center for both men and women. Mary huddled excitedly with Ritchie, who turned to the judge and pleaded that she be sent anywhere else. "Taking Mary back to Brushy Mountain Prison would be increasing multifold the stresses. The attitude of people at Brushy toward Mary is one of extreme hostility." He asked that she be sent instead to Anderson County jail.

The judge refused to allow it. "It is no place for Mrs. Evans to be." He pointed out that it did not have adequate facilities to care for persons with suicidal tendencies. "If I were you," Judge Scott told Ritchie, "I'd be concerned about that. I am concerned about your client."

A compromise was reached. She would be taken to Knox County jail while awaiting two appeal motions to be heard in the criminal court of appeals in Knoxville—one to appeal the probation, the other to allow Mary to remain on bond until the appeal for probation was heard.

The reason he revoked the bond, Judge Scott explained, was "so she can adjust as quickly as possible to this situation. I have the greatest confidence that my decision to send her to the penitentiary is to protect her from herself."

One of the two policewomen started to take Mary by the arm. Mary's head snapped in reflex as she pulled her arm away. Then she walked briskly ahead of them through the courtroom.

As she passed the press section she lifted her chin and, looking at them dead on, smiled—not a real smile, but a contemptuous flicker.

On March 30, 1984, the eve of the day one year before when first she'd set her course, Mary boarded the prison transportation van bound for Nashville, to the State Penitentiary for Women.

A camera crew for one of the local TV stations caught her as she was taken from the Knox County jail. The story ran on that evening's news.

Kirk watched it on the TV in his cell. He'd been tormenting himself for days knowing that this moment would come and that he'd have to sit helplessly by when it did. He was leaning forward to snap it off, when suddenly he sat up and stared at the screen. For the first time since their capture, he was seeing her smile. She was chewing gum and talking in a relaxed and easy way to the guard. He looked closer. "God damn," he said aloud, and looked again to make certain. He couldn't help smiling. She was going off to prison wearing his blue jeans.

Epilogue

The men's and women's prisons situated on the outskirts of Nashville, to the northwest, are separated by ten miles and a river.

The moment he heard Mary's probation had been denied, Kirk wrote to his old friend Dale Graves, who was serving a life sentence for the murder of Kirk's former associate Red Nix. Dale had been incarcerated in the women's prison for fourteen years. Kirk began his letter with an apology: "Dale, I know as well as anybody that in these places we've all got our own time to do, but if you could just keep an eye out for Mary. . . ."

Dale promptly wrote back that she was arranging to have Mary room with her, and to "rest easy, my friend, Mary will be looked after."

As it turned out, Mary had little need for anyone's protection. Sometime during her first week in prison, a black girl whose brother was one of the Brushy inmates Kirk had shot confronted Mary in the dining hall. The personality merger that the defense's psychiatrists claimed was Mary's ruination now served her well. According to reports, Mary lashed out at the girl. "You got a problem with me, bitch? 'Cause if you do, I'm ready to settle it with you right now."

The girl backed down and Mary won herself some respect.

That same week across the river, seventeen rounds of ammunition were found in Kirk's cell. The disciplinary board took action, and Kirk was kept in isolation for thirty days.

He and Mary were more careful about their communications now; instead of writing letters, they spoke them into a cassette. The first five minutes or so were taken up by music in case they were checked by the staff. Kirk told her how proud he was that she'd preserved her integrity in that courtroom. It took real courage, he said, to choose prison over testifying against those friends who'd helped them. He swore she was the finest person he'd ever known in his whole life.

Mary admitted to him how hard she was finding it to do time. How awful it was to shower in open stalls without a curtain, to ask a guard, "May I speak?" before talking to another inmate. And the strip searches! She asked him how a prisoner could ever get used to that constant humiliation. "What they really want," she said, "is to break you. They have control over your body and they want to control your mind, but they won't get mine."

Mary was assigned to manual labor in the prison warehouse, lifting fifty-pound boxes all day until her back hurt. Later she was reassigned to work in the commissary with Dale.

Toward the end of May, Mary broke her long silence, called *The Tennessean,* and offered them an interview. In that interview she was described as "almost elegant with her long blond hair swept back in a braid as she pointed to a newspaper clipping with long, shiny fingernails."

She said she had decided to talk because she was angry—"furious"—over the extensive press coverage of her story, angry with the "weary, wearying" life behind bars and "mad" at people who assumed they knew what she wanted "when there's no possible way they could know."

"This says I was denied one of the two paralegal positions in the prison," she said. "The fact is, there is only one paralegal position here and I have never asked for it!"

The Tennessean went on to say that despite claims that she was suicidal, Mary said little had been done in the way of keeping tabs on her medical stability since she entered prison. Had she wanted to take her life there was ample opportunity for her to do so.

She told of the continuing efforts by the media to court her. The TV program *60 Minutes* had sent her a music box with a note attached, begging for her story. "It shows you how stupid some people must be, even at *60 Minutes*. You can't send a music box to someone in prison! They won't let you have it."

She said that the week before she'd got a letter from a man in Malaysia offering his hand in marriage; and another from a man in the West Indies who wanted to "come and take you away from all this." But perhaps her most telling comment was one she made only in passing: "I fully expected to be here."

Kirk's appeal was heard before the state supreme court on the trial in absentia and was denied despite an impassioned plea made by Professor Neil Cohen. "I'm proud of Tennessee and much about our judicial system; I'm not proud of this historic first."

In October, Mary met with the parole board. Her earliest possible date for release was four months away, in February 1985.

It was a polite and subdued Mary Evans who answered the five-member board. She wore a suit of muted brown tones and knee-high leather boots. Her hair was pulled off her face in a French braid.

She told them it was Kirk who had supplied her with

the gun used during the escape. "At the time I had gotten the impression that justice is something that is hard to find in the court. . . . there's no doubt that it was a serious mistake," she said, swinging her foot nervously.

She also said that she'd had no contact with Tim Kirk, except once about the case, and that she didn't plan to have any in the future.

After a cliff-hanging 3–2 vote, the parole board recommended that she be put on work release until her February 4 parole date.

The next cassette Kirk received in the mail was in answer to one he'd sent her asking if she really meant all those things she'd said to the board. Mary blasted him. "How can you be so thick-skulled? You of all people—why should I even have to explain this to you? I can't *do* time. I just can't." Her voice on the tape softened. "I still think about how . . . a couple of weeks more and we'd still be out there."

On Sunday, February 3, ten months and twenty-four days after she was sent to prison, she was released on parole. Her father stood quietly outside the gates, waiting, while her mother stayed in the car. Mary came out wearing a wide-brimmed hat, the front rolled back, her long hair flowing. She and her father smiled at each other and hugged; then they got into the car.

Kirk waited for the appointed time when Mary would go to her friend Lisa's house to get his phone call. "Everything's going to be all right now," she said to him, emphatically. "Understand? *All right*."

Kirk explained to a visitor, "she's been doing research, she's going to work on my cases behind the scenes now, to find a way to get me out legally. Mary and I both know, no matter what, we're going to be together again."

In early May a guard, strolling past Kirk's cell, stopped a minute to chat. He asked if Kirk had heard the latest news about his girlfriend.

Kirk kept his face impassive and asked which news he was referring to.

"She's moving to Florida," he said.

"Yeah," Kirk said, as though he already knew, "it's the best thing. Give her some privacy from the damned press."

But whatever it was Kirk saw in the guard's expression made him want to see a newspaper right away. He wasn't able to get one until later that day. The story stated that Mary had obtained permission from the parole board to move to Florida, where she would continue to report to a parole officer. Reason given: to marry.

The next day's account produced the name of the groom-to-be, William Stuart Evans, first cousin to Mary's former husband, Tom Evans, Jr.

Guards and inmates alike kept their distance. This was the kind of man trouble that demanded respect. Kirk was left to deal with his feelings the way he preferred, alone and in silence.

But a reporter from *The Tennessean* went out to the prison seeking a statement. Consistent with Kirk's stare-'em-down policy, he agreed to be interviewed.

"Tennessee State Penitentiary inmate Timothy Kirk wished his former lover Mary Evans all the luck in the world yesterday regarding her recent marriage and said he is happy for her. 'I'm glad that she is getting her life back together,' Kirk said."

Privately Kirk remarked "that William" was undoubtedly better suited than "this William" was.

At the bottom of the story that recapped the events surrounding the notorious couple was a brief paragraph that read like an afterthought: Kirk said he asked the warden at the main prison last May 10 for permission to marry Mary Paris, who he said lives in Nashville."

Mary's decision to move to Florida had been made some months back, in March. She had called her former husband, Tom, to tell him she was considering the possibility of such a move and asked whether he would help her. He said he'd be glad to help her find an apartment and a job—he'd be her buddy, he said.

For the past two years Tom and his cousin Bill had been sharing an apartment in Pompano Beach. He and Bill had been best friends ever since Bill's divorce.

When Mary called to say she was in Miami, Tom immediately invited her to come have dinner with him and Bill, whom she'd met when they were first married.

Tom was leaving a day or two later to go to Knoxville. When he returned ten days later, Mary and Bill told Tom they were getting married.

Obligingly, Tom packed up and moved to Knoxville, leaving the apartment to the newlyweds.

They were married on May 24 at the Palm Beach County courthouse.

In a sudden turn too far-fetched for fiction, William Timothy Kirk married Mary Paris on August 10, 1985. The ceremony was held in the exercise yard of the maximum-security unit. It was explained that the thirty-one-year-old brunette had been visiting Kirk on and off for the past two years.

TRUTH IS ALL TOO OFTEN STRANGER THAN FICTION

These investigations into the world of true crimes prove just that point.

Unveiling Claudia:
A True Story Of Serial Murder

by Daniel Keyes
author of *Flowers for Algernon*
and
The Minds of Billy Milligan

On an icy winter night, Mickey McCann, owner of
"Mickey's Eldorado Club," the go-go girl who lived
with him, and McCann's elderly mother, clad only
in her nightgown, were found shot to death in
McCann's luxurious home—the biggest murder case
in the history of Columbus, Ohio. One month later,
a beautiful woman approached two off-duty police
officers in an all-night Western Pancake House.
What she told them got her arrested and charged
with murder. Yet Claudia Elaine Yasko had never
fired a gun in her life. This is the story of how the
killers were brought to justice, and of how Claudia
came to be embroiled in a life of sex, drugs, money
and religion that brought her close to death herself.

Unveiling Claudia:
A True Story Of Serial Murder
a Bantam hardcover book

Look for it wherever Bantam books are sold, or
use this handy coupon for ordering:

Special Offer
Buy a Bantam Book
for only 50¢.

Now you can have an up-to-date listing of Bantam's
hundreds of titles plus take advantage of our unique
and exciting bonus book offer. A special offer which
gives you the opportunity to purchase a Bantam
book for only 50¢. Here's how!

By ordering any five books at the regular price per
order, you can also choose any other single book
listed (up to a $4.95 value) for just 50¢. Some restric-
tions do apply, but for further details why not send
for Bantam's listing of titles today!

Just send us your name and address and we will
send you a catalog!